Paul and the Therapy of Desire

Paul and the Therapy of Desire

Epithymia, God's Grace,
and Love in the Spirit

NÉLIDA NAVEROS CÓRDOVA

CASCADE Books • Eugene, Oregon

PAUL AND THE THERAPY OF DESIRE
Epithymia, God's Grace, and Love in the Spirit

Copyright © 2025 Nélida Naveros Córdova. All rights reserved. Except for brief quotations in critical publications or reviews, no part of this book may be reproduced in any manner without prior written permission from the publisher. Write: Permissions, Wipf and Stock Publishers, 199 W. 8th Ave., Suite 3, Eugene, OR 97401.

Cascade Books
An Imprint of Wipf and Stock Publishers
199 W. 8th Ave., Suite 3
Eugene, OR 97401

www.wipfandstock.com

PAPERBACK ISBN: 979-8-3852-3030-3
HARDCOVER ISBN: 979-8-3852-3031-0
EBOOK ISBN: 979-8-3852-3032-7

Cataloguing-in-Publication data:

Names: Naveros Córdova, Nélida.

Title: Paul and the therapy of desire: *epithymia*, God's grace, and love in the Spirit / by Nélida Naveros Córdova

Description: Eugene, OR: Cascade Books, 2025 | Includes bibliographical references and index.

Identifiers: ISBN 979-8-3852-3030-3 (paperback) | ISBN 979-8-3852-3031-0 (hardcover) | ISBN 979-8-3852-3032-7 (ebook)

Subjects: LCSH: Bible.—Epistles of Paul—Criticism, interpretation, etc. | Ethics in the Bible. | Ethics, Ancient. | Philosophy, Ancient. | Emotions (Philosophy)—History.

Classification: BS2655.E8 N384 2025 (paperback) | BS2655.E8 (ebook)

10/28/25

Unless otherwise noted, Scripture quotations are from the New Revised Standard Version Bible, copyright © 1989 National Council of the Churches of Christ in the United States of America. Used by permission. All rights reserved worldwide.

Scripture quotations marked NETS are from A New English Translation of the Septuagint, ©2007 by the International Organization for Septuagint and Cognate Studies, Inc. Used by permission of Oxford University Press. All rights reserved.

Emphasis added to Scripture quotations.

In memory of Sister Leticia Plasencia,
who genuinely inspired love in Christ to those she encountered

Contents

Acknowledgments | ix

Abbreviations | xi

Introduction | 1

1 Paul's Background: The Understanding of "Desire" (*Epithymia*) in Greek Philosophical and Hellenistic Jewish Traditions | 15

2 Paul's Reevaluation of Jewish Monotheism: Desire's Connection with Idolatry and Sexual Vices | 52

3 Paul's Reevaluation of the Mosaic Law: The Problem of Desire and Sinful Passions | 91

4 The Grace of God in Love and the Spirit: The "Foundation" of the Remedy of Desire | 114

5 Conclusion | 149

Appendix A: Shocking Examples of Sexual Desire and Immorality in Paul's Jewish Tradition | 155

Appendix B: Paul's Biblical Background on Desire and Sexual Immorality | 160

Appendix C: Jewish Figures Facing Sexual Desire in Paul's Jewish Tradition | 164

Bibliography | 167

Index | 179

Acknowledgments

I WROTE THIS BOOK inspired by my students' intellectual curiosity. Their good desire for knowledge was instrumental in the shaping of this book. As a teacher, I serve my students and contribute to their academic formation, and as a religious woman, I consider myself an instrument in God's hand. I am grateful to God for giving me the intellectual ability to generate meaningful interpretation in regard to the Bible. My Doktorvater, Thomas H. Tobin, SJ, provided me with the essential tools, which are reflected in my very first book: *To Live in the Spirit: Paul and the Spirit of God*. His influence on my scholarly approach to the study of the New Testament has strongly marked my interest in the Greco-Roman literature and Hellenistic Judaism, especially Philo of Alexandria. To my benefit, both traditions have become a distinctive mark of my scholarly works and in my career as a New Testament scholar. When I was a PhD student at Loyola University Chicago, my Doktorvater taught me a great deal about the study of the New Testament within the larger Greco-Roman world and instilled in me a profound appreciation and respect for the New Testament. My mentor, Gregory E. Sterling, dean of Yale Divinity School, continues to encourage me to strive for excellence in research. To both, not only erudite scholars, but also amazing human beings, I would like to express my deepest gratitude.

I wish to thank William Loader, an emeritus professor at Murdoch University, Australia, for his willingness to read my manuscript before I submitted it to Wipf and Stock Publishers and for his kindness in offering me valuable comments and suggestions to improve the quality of my book. I am deeply grateful for my friend Billie Pringle, who patiently proofread early drafts of the manuscript. I wish to thank my religious community because their love and prayers have been fundamental in the process of

ACKNOWLEDGMENTS

writing this book. I would like to thank my siblings and relatives for their unconditional love. They have been there with me in my journey throughout my scholarly career. Last, but not the least, my sincere thanks to the editorial board of Wipf and Stock for accepting my manuscript to be published in such a prestigious publisher and for their impeccable work in the process of publishing my book.

Abbreviations

ANCIENT ABBREVIATIONS

Andronicus
    Pass.   *The Passions*
Aristob.   Aristobulus
Aristotle
    Econ.   *Economics*
    Eth. nic.   *Nicomachean Ethics*
    Eth. eud.   *Eudemian Ethics*
    Metaph.   *Metaphysics*
    Phys.   *Physics*
    Pol.   *Politics*
    Rhet.   *Rhetoric*
    Virt. vit.   *Virtues and Vices*
Apoc. Mos.   Apocalypse of Moses
Aphtonius
    Prog.   *Progymnasmata*
Cicero
    Tusc.   *Tusculanae disputationes*

Dio Chrysostom
- *Diss.* — *Dissertations*

Dionysius of Halicarnassus
- *Ant. rom.* — *Antiquitates Romanae*

DL — Diogenes Laertius
- *Lives* — *Lives of Eminent Philosophers*

Epictetus
- *Diss.* — *Discourses of Epictetus*
- *Diatr.* — *Diatribai (Dissertationes)*

Eusebius
- *Praep. ev.* — *Preparation for the Gospel*

Galen
- *Hip. et Plat.* — *Hippocrates and Plato*

Homer
- *Il.* — *Iliad*
- *Od.* — *Odyssey*

Jos. Asen. — Joseph and Aseneth

Josephus
- *A.J.* — *Jewish Antiquities*
- *B.J.* — *Jewish War*
- *C. Ap.* — *Against Apion*
- *Vita* — *The Life*

Jub. — Jubilees

Juvenal
- *Sat.* — *Satires*

Let. Aris. — Letter of Aristeas

Longinus
- *Subl.* — *On the Sublime*

LXX — Septuagint, the Greek Jewish Scripture

ABBREVIATIONS

Musonius Rufus
- *Fr.* — *Fragments*

Ovid
- *Metam.* — *Metamorphoses*

Philo of Alexandria
- *Abr.* — On the Life of Abraham
- *Agr.* — On Agriculture
- *Anim.* — Whether Animals Have Reason
- *Cher.* — On the Cherubim
- *Conf.* — On the Confusion of Tongues
- *Congr.* — On the Preliminary Studies
- *Contempl.* — On the Contemplative Life
- *Decal.* — On the Decalogue
- *Deus* — That God Is Unchangeable
- *Det.* — That the Worse Attacks the Better
- *Fug.* — On Flight and Finding
- *Gig.* — On Giants
- *Her.* — Who Is the Heir?
- *Hypoth.* — Hypothetica
- *Ios.* — On the Life of Joseph
- *Leg.* — Allegorical Interpretation
- *Migr.* — On the Migration of Abraham
- *Mos.* — On the Life of Moses
- *Mut.* — On the Change of Names
- *Opif.* — On the Creation of the World
- *Plant.* — On Planting
- *Post.* — On the Posterity of Cain
- *Praem.* — On Rewards and Punishments
- *Prob.* — That Every Good Person Is Free
- *Prov.* — On Providence

ABBREVIATIONS

	QE	*Questions and Answers on Exodus*
	QG	*Questions and Answers on Genesis*
	Sacr.	*On the Sacrifices of Abel and Cain*
	Somn.	*On Dreams*
	Spec.	*On the Special Laws*
	Virt.	*On the Virtues*

Plato

	Charm.	*Charmides*
	Crat.	*Cratylus*
	Gorg.	*Gorgias*
	Lach.	*Laches*
	Leg.	*Laws*
	Lys.	*Lysis*
	Min.	*Minos*
	Phaed.	*Phaedo*
	Phaedr.	*Phaedrus*
	Phileb.	*Philebus*
	Prot.	*Protagoras*
	Resp.	*Republic*
	Soph.	*Sophist*
	Symp.	*Symposium*
	Theaet.	*Theaetetus*
	Tim.	*Timaeus*

Plutarch

	Alex. fort.	*De Alexandri magni fortuna aut virtute*
	Am. prol.	*De amore prolis*
	Amat.	*Amatorius*
	Conj. praec.	*Conjugalia Praecepta*
	Lyc.	*Lycurgus*
	Mor.	*Moralia*

ABBREVIATIONS

    Stoic. rep.   *De Stoicorum repugnantiis*

    Virt. mor.   *De virtute morali*

Polybius

    His.   *Histories*

Posidonius

    fr.   fragment

Ps.-Phoc.   Pseudo-Phocylides

Pseudo-Philo

    LAB   *Liber Antiquitatum Biblicarum*

Pseudo-Plato

    Def.   *Definitions*

Quintilian

    Inst.   *Institution oratoria*

Seneca

    Ben.   *On Benefits*

    Ep.   *Epistles*

    Ira   *On Anger*

    Med.   *Medea*

Sextus Empiricus

    Math.   Against the Mathematicians

Sib. Or.   Sibylline Oracles

Stobaeus

    Anth.   *Anthology*

    Ecl.   *Eclogues*

The Testament of the Twelve Patriarchs

    T. Benj   Testament of Benjamin

    T. Dan   Testament of Dan

    T. Iss   Testament of Issachar

    T. Jos   Testament of Joseph

    T. Jud   Testament of Judah

	T. Lev	Testament of Levi
	T. Reu	Testament of Reuben
	T. Sim	Testament of Simeon
Theon		Aelius Theon
	Prog.	Progymnasmata
Tg. Onq.		Targum Ongelos
Xenophon		
	Mem.	Memorabilia

CONTEMPORARY ABBREVIATIONS

AB	Anchor Bible
AThR	*Anglican Theological Review*
BBR	*Bulletin for Biblical Research*
BECNT	Baker Exegetical Commentary on the New Testament
BETL	Bibliotheca Ephemeridum Theologicarum Lovaniensium
BHT	Beiträge zur historischen Theologie
BibInt	*Biblical Interpretation*
Bib	*Biblica*
BJS	Brown Judaic Studies
BR	*Biblical Research*
BSac	*Bibliotheca Sacra*
BZNW	Beihefte zur Zeitschrift für die neutestamentliche Wissenschaft
CBQ	*Catholic Biblical Quarterly*
CRINT	Compendia Rerum Iudaicarum ad Novum Testamentum
CurTM	*Currents in Theology and Mission*
CTQ	*Concordia Theological Quarterly*
ECL	Early Christianity and Its Literature
Enc	*Encounter*

FRLANT	Forschungen zur Religion und Literatur des Alten und Neuen Testaments
HTR	*Harvard Theological Review*
HTS	Harvard Theological Studies
LTQ	*Lexington Theological Quarterly*
JAAR	*Journal of the American Academy of Religion*
JBL	*Journal of Biblical Literature*
JETS	*Journal of the Evangelical Theological Society*
JLT	*Journal of Literature and Theology*
JSJ	*Journal for the Study of Judaism in the Persian, Hellenistic, and Roman Periods*
JSNT	*Journal for the Study of the New Testament*
JTI	*Journal of Theological Interpretation*
KD	*Kerygma und Dogma*
LCL	Loeb Classical Library
LNTS	The Library of New Testament Studies
LSJ	Liddell, Henry George, Robert Scott, Henry Stuart Jones. *A Greek-English Lexicon.* 9th ed. with revised supplement. Oxford: Clarendon, 1996
LTQ	*Lexington Theological Quarterly*
Neot	*Neotestamentica*
NICNT	New International Commentary on the New Testament
NovT	*Novum Testamentum*
NovTSup	Supplements to Novum Testamentum
NTOA	Novum Testamentum et Orbis Antiquus
NTS	*New Testament Studies*
OTP	*Old Testament Pseudepigrapha.* Edited by James H. Charlesworth. 2 vols. New York: Doubleday, 1983, 1985
PhA	Philosophia Antiqua
RJ	*Rhetorica Journal*

RelS	*Religious Studies*
ResQ	*Restoration Quarterly*
SBLDS	Society of Biblical Literature Dissertation Series
Scr	*Scriptura*
SCS	Septuagint and Cognate Studies
SHR	Studies in the History of Religions (supplements to *Numen*)
SNTSMS	Society for New Testament Studies Monograph Series
SP	Sacra Pagina
SPhiloA	Studia Philonica Annual
SPhiloM	Studia Philonica Monograph Series
ST	*Studia Theologica*
SVF	*Stoicorum Veterum Fragmenta.* Hans Friedrich August von Arnim. 4 vols. Leipzig: Teubne, 1903–24
TB	Theologische Bücherei: Neudrucke und Berichte aus dem 20. Jahrhundert
TDNT	*Theological Dictionary of the New Testament.* Edited by Gerhard Kittel and Gerhard Friedrich. Translated by Geoffrey W. Bromiley. 10 vols. Grand Rapids: Eerdmans, 1964–76
ThS	*Theology and Sexuality*
TS	*Theological Studies*
TSAJ	Texte und Studien zum antiken Judentum
TynBul	*Tyndale Bulletin*
UNT	Untersuchungen zum Neuen Testament
WMANT	Wissenschaftliche Monographien zum Alten und Neuen Testament
WUNT	Wissenschaftliche Untersuchungen zum Neuen
WW	*Word and World*
ZNW	*Zeitschrift für die neutestamentliche Wissenschaft und die Kunde der älteren Kirche*

Introduction

IN THE LAST CENTURY, renowned biblical scholars have devoted much of their time to the study of Paul's ethical teaching. One of the valuable approaches has been the study of Paul's ethics within his Jewish and Greek traditions. In a previous work, I studied the concept of *pneuma* (spirit) and its role in Paul's ethical discourse within the larger umbrella of Hellenistic Jewish and Greek philosophical traditions.[1] In this book, I follow the same approach but this time to study the passion of "desire" (*epithymia*) and its connection with sexual vices, and the remedy to avoid *epithymia* and its negative sequels within the philosophical and Hellenistic Jewish traditions of interpretations. The crucial questions that this study explores are: How does Paul treat the passion of *epithymia* in the context of the Greco-Roman context and what solution does he offer to overcome it? In my attempt to respond to these important questions, I explore Paul's seven genuine letters—1 Thessalonians, Galatians, 1 and 2 Corinthians, Philippians, Philemon, and Romans—written between ca. 45 CE and ca. 56 CE.[2]

Before we embark on the study of this exciting yet challenging topic, I want to be clear and say that in Paul's back-and-forth communication with the early believers through missives, the concept of *epithymia* (desire) is not central in Paul's ethics as is the Greek word *pneuma* (spirit). In comparison

---

1. Naveros Córdova, *Live in the Spirit*. There are other important studies devoted to the role of the Spirit in Paul's ethics; for example, Rabens provides a detailed analysis of *pneuma* in Paul's genuine letters and an overview of contemporary scholarship (pp. 2–24). One of the important highlights of Rabens's study is the robust appendix of 140 years of research on *pneuma* and ethics in Paul (pp. 253–306). Rabens, *Holy Spirit and Ethics*. See also Horn, *Angeld des Geistes*; and "Wandel im Geist."

2. The other letters attributed to Paul will be noted in footnotes insofar as I judge necessary.

to other Hellenistic Jewish literature, e.g., Philo of Alexandria and 4 Maccabees, which are treated in this book, Paul's seven genuine letters evince a modest use of *epithymia* and *epithymeō*. Despite its modest usage, however, Paul's treatment of the concept offers a fresh light on our understanding of Paul's ethical teaching and his place within the Hellenistic Jewish and Greek philosophical traditions of interpretations.

As a bad passion, the noun *epithymia* and verbal form *epithymeō* appear thirteen times,[3] and *epithymia* in a neutral or positive way is mentioned only twice.[4] In one occasion, that is Rom 1:27, Paul employs the term *orexis* (strong desire, lust, longing, or appetite), a word akin to and a synonym of *epithymia*. Although Paul gives sexual exhortation, especially in 1 Cor 5–7 and Rom 1, his main purpose is neither to provide a systematic set of sexual ethics (1 Cor 5–7) nor to expose the believers' sexual sinful condition (Rom 1). Likewise, it is important to note that Paul does not have in view a twenty-first-century audience. What I can say is that from his writings we can bring to the fore the connection that Paul makes between the passion of desire and sexual vices. In dialogue with central Pauline themes, such as monotheism, the Mosaic law, and the love commandment, or the law of Christ/the law of the Spirit, we shall not only envision Paul's view of *epithymia* but also how he tries to solve the problem of this deadly passion and its negative sequels within the larger context of the Greco-Roman world and his Christocentric monotheism.

In a broader view, renowned studies have focused on Paul's view of sexuality and gender in close connection to the Greco-Roman context. For example, Dale B. Martin, in his book *The Corinthian Body*, has offered a critical analysis of the different constructions of the human body in 1 Corinthians. Martin argues that some believers came to view the human body as threatened by polluting agents such as prostitution, sexual desires, and eating meat sacrificed to idols. Martin's analysis led him to suggest that Paul is somehow influenced by the notion of hierarchy in the construction

---

3. The noun appears in 1 Thess 4:5 and Rom 13:14 (*epithymias*); 1 Cor 10:6 (*epithymētas*); Gal 5:16 and Rom 7:8 (*epithymian*); Gal 5:24 (*epithymiais*); Rom 1:24 and 6:12 (*epithymiais*); 7:7a (*epithymian*); the verbal form in Gal 5:17 (*epithymei*); 1 Cor 10:6 (*epithymesan*); Rom 7:7b and 13:9 (*epithymeseis*).

4. 1 Thess 2:17 (*epithymia*) and Phil 1:23 (*epithymian*). Aune writes that Paul can use the term *epithymia* to describe the admirable desire for companionship with others in 1 Thess 2:17 and union with Christ in Phil 1:23. However, when Paul uses *epithymia* without a specific object (e.g., Rom 7:7–8) or without particular reference to "evil things" (e.g., 1 Cor 10:6), the concept suggests "transgression of God's law." Aune, "Passions in Pauline Epistles," 236n56; see also "Mastery of Passions."

of sexuality in Roman context (active/male and passive/female). Therefore, Paul's statements about the "weak" (lower-status group) and the "strong" (higher-status group) derive from these Roman hierarchical structures.[5] Although Martin mentions "sexual desires" as one of the "polluting agents" at Corinth, he does not develop further the connection between the passion of desire and sexual vices. Another valuable study is Cynthia Long Westfall's *Paul and Gender: Reclaiming the Apostle's Vision for Men and Women in Christ*. Westfall explores gender stereotypes in Paul using controversial sexual texts (e.g., Rom 12:2; 1 Cor 7:1–5; 11:2–16; 16:13; Gal 3:28) within the larger Greco-Roman cultural context. Even though she devotes a section to sexual immorality in her analysis of Rom 1:26–27 and 1 Cor 6:12–19,[6] she does not treat sexual desire in gender stereotypes.

There are important scholars who have explored Paul's use of the tenth commandment, "You shall not covet" (*ouk epithymēseis*), in Rom 7. Emma Wasserman, in her book *The Death of the Soul in Romans 7: Sin, Death, and the Law in Light of Hellenistic Moral Psychology*, interprets Paul's argument in Rom 7 in light of the philosophical tradition of Plato. Wasserman, who identifies Platonic ideas and notions in Paul's rhetorical structure of Rom 7, claims that the language, style, and argument of the text have Platonic influence.[7] Similarly, J. A. Ziesler, in his essay "The Role of the Tenth Commandment in Romans 7," interprets the tenth commandment, "you shall not covet," in Rom 7 within the Jewish tradition. He has proposed the view that the tenth commandment in Rom 7:7b–12 refers to desire in all its aspects (see Exod 20:17 and Deut 5:21).[8] For Ziesler, this commandment is

---

5. Martin, *Corinthian Body*, 32–39, 69.

6. Westfall, *Paul and Gender*, x. Westfall expands her study to an analysis of non-Pauline letters, e.g., 1 Tim 2:11–14; Eph 5:25–33; Col 2:9–10. The value of her methodology (modern linguistics) is that it allowed her to approach Paul's controversial topics of gender with sensitivity and made it easier to navigate the passages within the context of Paul's corpus.

7. Wasserman, *Death of the Soul*, 51–116. Wasserman analyzes Rom 7:7–25 within the context of Rom 5–8 and argues that Rom 6–7 must be interpreted in relation to Rom 1 and within the context of self-mastery, freedom, and slavery ("Death of the Soul"). Wasserman follows in part Stowers's interpretation in *Rereading of Romans*, 251–53. For a similar view, see Lichtenberger, *Ich Adams*, 13–105; Bornkamm, *Studien zum Neuen Testament*, 178–96. On Philo's Middle Platonic moral psychology, see Dillon, *Middle Platonists*, 174–78; Runia, *Philo of Alexandria*, 297–352.

8. Ziesler, "Tenth Commandment." For other views, see Bultmann, *Existence and Faith*, 173–85; Lyonnet, "Tu ne convoiteras pas"; Kreitzer, "Stevenson's Stranger Case"; Gundry, "Moral Frustration."

key for understanding Paul's argument in 7:7–25.⁹ In his analysis of other Pauline texts, Ziesler has argued that Paul uses *epithymia* and *epithymeō* neutrally or positively (1 Thess 2:17; Phil 1:23) and for negative things in general (e.g., Rom 6:12; 13:14; 1 Cor 10:6; Gal 5:16, 24). According to Ziesler, there is no absolute use of *epithymia* and cognates in reference to sexual immorality only.¹⁰

A new approach is taken by Andrew Bowden in his essay "A Semantic Investigation of Desire in 4 Maccabees and Its Bearing on Romans 7:7." Using the concept of "desire" (*epithymia*) in 4 Maccabees as Paul's background, Bowden argues that the two Hellenistic Jewish authors show similarities in their use of desire on a semantic level in three ways: (1) both authors discuss *epithymia* under the schemata of mastery; (2) both authors link *epithymia* with similar lexemes; and (3) both authors discuss desire within the themes of law, freedom, and slavery. The parallels found in the writings of Paul and 4 Maccabees led Bowden to conclude that Paul "situated his discussion within the linguistic frame of his day."¹¹ Recently, Bowden has explored Paul's use of the lexemes *epithymeō* (to desire), *epithymētēs* (one who desires), and *epithymia* (desire) in light of semantic observations within the context of Roman imperial literature and Second Temple Jewish texts.¹² Using Paul's seven genuine letters, Bowden provides a detailed analysis of specific texts where the term *epithymia* and cognates appear to show how Paul makes similar use of these lexemes to those frequently used in various philosophical schools and/or religions of the Roman imperial

---

9. The same view is later held by Janzen, "Sin and Deception."

10. Ziesler, "Tenth Commandment," 46.

11. Bowden, "Semantic Investigation," 423–24.

12. See Bowden, *Desire*. After Räisänen's study, "ΕΠΙΘΥΜΙΑ und ΕΠΙΘΥΜΕΙΝ," in which he offers a brief analysis of *epithymia* and *epithyein* in the Pauline texts where the terms appear, Bowden's work is, in my view, the first detailed study on Paul's use of desire in his seven genuine letters, to which I am much indebted. In Bowden's ch. 1 (pp. 5–44), he provides a robust bibliography related to the lexemes *epithymeō*, *epithymētēs*, and *epithymia* in Paul's seven genuine letters, including Friedrich Büchsel, "ἐπιθυμία, ἐπιθυμέω," *TDNT* 3:168, 170; Wilpert, "Begierde"; Stowers, *Rereading of Romans*; and Wasserman, "Death of the Soul." In his study, Bowden applies the semantic theory of Lyons's pioneering study on semantics, lexicographers of the New Testament, including Louw and Nida, Danker, Peláez, and Leer (pp. 45–90), to the semantic relations in Roman imperial texts (Dio Chrysostom, Epictetus, Lucian of Samosata's text *Tyrannicide*, the Cynic epistles, and Second Temple Jewish texts, such as the Septuagint [LXX], 4 Maccabees, Num 11, and Philo; pp. 235–312). Then, he explores Paul's use of these lexemes in light of these semantic observations (pp. 347–512).

period.¹³ The significance of his study is that Bowden further clarifies the way Paul, like his Roman imperial contemporaries, relates these lexemes (*epithymeō, epithymētēs*, and *epithymia*) with sexual immorality,¹⁴ with the law,¹⁵ with positive objects,¹⁶ and with the metaphors of enslavement and freedom from enslavement in Galatians and Romans.¹⁷ Influenced by Roman imperial texts, Paul does not always relate *epithymeō* and cognates to objects related to sex or illicit sex, even when this lexeme appears together with the term *pathē* (passions).¹⁸

While these studies have further enlightened our understanding of Paul's view on sexuality and gender (Martin and Westfall), the tenth commandment (Wasserman, Ziesler, and Bowden), and desire's connection with sexual immorality in light of Roman imperial texts (Bowden), certainly "desire" (*epithymia*) as a bad passion and its negative sequels have not been adequately explored using explicit Pauline texts where the term *epithymia* and cognates appear within Paul's Greek philosophical (Platonism and Stoicism) and Hellenistic Jewish (Philo and 4 Maccabees) traditions. In addition, these modern authors have only elucidated Paul's use of *epithymia*, but they have not explored his solution to the problem of desire. Therefore, to enrich our understanding of Paul's treatment of the problem of desire and its remedy within the larger Greco-Roman world, this study goes beyond Bowden's work by arguing that Paul suggests a higher doctrine and solution to the problem of *epithymia* founded in the grace of God, the Spirit of God/Christ, and the love commandment or law of Christ (Gal 6:2).

I believe that this is an innovative approach that shall enrich our understanding of the passion of *epithymia* and its connection with sexual vices in Paul's thought, and how he intends to provide a solution to avoid desire and its bad effects in the ethical lives of believers. I offer a study of "desire" (*epithymia*), a common term in the Greek philosophical and Hellenistic Jewish traditions. As I have shown in a recent article, "'The Worst of the Passions': Desire in Philo of Alexandria," in the Platonic and

---

13. Bowden, *Desire*, 4.
14. Rom 1:24a; 13:14; Gal 5:16, 17; 1 Cor 10:6; 1 Thess 4:3.
15. Rom 7:7; 13:9; Gal 5:16, 24.
16. Phil 1:23; 1 Thess 2:17b.
17. Rom 6:12; 7:8; 13:9; Gal 5:16.
18. Bowden restates his claim in his conclusion. See *Desire*, 515–26. Throughout his book, Bowden opts to use the term "emotion(s)" as the meaning of *pathē*, and not passion(s). In this study, I use the latter.

Stoic philosophical traditions *epithymia* is a "passion" (*pathos*) of the soul strongly connected with sexual immorality, passions, lusts, appetites, and pleasures. Paul, who traveled throughout Asia Minor during his missionary career, was not only familiar with the basic understanding of Greek rhetoric (e.g., the *progymnasmata*),[19] but certainly his knowledge about basic Greek philosophical notions and concepts is reflected in his letters.[20] Nevertheless, as mentioned above, unlike Greek thinkers, Paul does not give a profound analysis of the passion of "desire" (*epithymia*) in his ethical teaching. Influenced by Greek philosophical and Hellenistic Jewish interpretations of *epithymia* and *epithymeō*, he speaks of desire as a bad passion in close connection with sexual vices and "excessive" (*pleonazousa*) passions and desires, as we shall see below.[21] From Paul's treatment of the passion of desire, especially in 1 Thessalonians, Galatians, 1 Corinthians, and Romans, we can deduce his ethical message about sexual desire and vices and excessive or irrational passions and desires.

19. Several scholars have shown Paul's familiarity with the basic knowledge of Greek rhetoric and his application in his letters. See Naveros Córdova, "1 Corinthians 10:1–4"; Selby, *Not with Wisdom*. For arguments that Paul knew and employed basic Greek rhetoric, see Parsons and Martin, *Ancient Rhetoric*, 276–79; Webb, "*Progymnasmata* as Practice"; Kennedy, *Classical Rhetoric*, 143–48.

20. Scholars have identified specific texts where Paul reflects philosophical knowledge in his letters (Rom 7; 1 Cor 5:1; 15:33; 2 Cor 4:18; Phil 4:2, 11–12). Paul's style of argument, the diatribe, for example, has a Hellenistic background (e.g., 1 Cor 4:6–15; 9:1–18; 5:29–49; Rom 1:18—2:11; 8:31–39; 11:1–24; 1 Cor 6:12-20; 12:12—13:13; 2 Cor 11:16-33; Rom 2:17–24; 7:7–15). As Witherington and Myers suggest, it is plausible that Paul, who was both a Roman citizen and a Pharisee, had a prominent place among the elite in the Greco-Roman and Jewish society. Witherington and Myers, *New Testament Rhetoric*, 86. See also Sanders, "Paul Between Judaism," 79. However, the question of how he obtained philosophical knowledge is obscure. For various studies, see Engberg-Pedersen's selected essays between 1994 and 2023 in *Paul and Philosophy*; Aune, "Passions in Pauline Epistles"; Bultmann, *Stil der Paulinischen Predigt*; Stowers, *Diatribe*; Stowers, "Pauline Christianity"; Schmeller, *Paulus und die "Diatribe."*

21. I refute Bowden's claim that Paul does not use *epithymia* and lexemes for sexual immorality only. Throughout this book, I show how in Paul *epithymia* is generally used in connection to sexual vices and passions, or vices that lead to sexual vices common in the Greek world.

INTRODUCTION

A BRIEF OVERVIEW OF THE SIGNIFICANCE OF PAUL'S PROPHETIC CALL

I would say, around three years after Jesus' death, resurrection, and ascension (ca. 32 CE), the risen Christ appeared to the relatively young Paul (1 Cor 15:1–11; Gal 1:15–16), and according to the book of Acts, it happened on the way to Damascus (Acts 9:1–19; 22:3–21; 26:2–18). But how old was Paul (Saul) when the risen Christ revealed himself to him? If we place his birth between 8 and 2 BCE, as most scholars do,[22] he might have been either in his early or late thirties but surely not in his forties. What we know from his own letters (especially Galatians) and the book of Acts is that at the time when he was zealously defending Judaism (the traditions of his fathers) and its teaching[23] and violently persecuting "the church of God" (Acts 8:1–3; 9:1–2; 1 Cor 15:9; Gal 1:13–14; Phil 3:6), Paul experienced the most dramatic event of his life. According to his own biographical account in Gal 1:11—2:2, that event is described as a miraculous experience, a revelation that "would change his life forever."[24] Although his life changed dramatically forever, Paul never saw himself other than a Jew (Rom 9:3–4; 11:1; 1 Cor 10:1; Gal 2:15a)! He was divinely called by the risen Christ to be an apostle to the gentiles and was appointed to preach Jesus and his gospel to gentiles (Gal 1:12; 2:1–14). In light of the call of Jer 1:4–10 and Isa 49:1, 5–6, this divine experience is called Paul's "prophetic call."

---

22. What little evidence we have about Paul's life comes from his own letters and the book of Acts of the Apostles. In the Phlm 9 (ca. 61–63 CE), Paul describes himself as an "old man" (*presbutēs*). From this account, we can deduce that Paul was born in ca. 8 CE. He died sometime in the mid- to late 60s, perhaps ca. 68 CE. Murphy-O'Connor placed his birth in 6 CE and his death in the 60s CE. Murphy-O'Connor, *Paul*, 8. Dunn placed Paul's birth ca. 2 BCE–1 BCE, and his death early in the 60s CE. Dunn, *Beginning from Jerusalem*, 2:512; see also Schnelle, *Apostle Paul*, 47. For a reconstruction of the chronology of Paul's life, see Schnelle, *Apostle Paul*, 48–56; Haacker, "Paul's Life."

23. There is no explicit evidence from Paul's own letters about what exactly he was defending so zealously about Judaism. Based on his Jewish and Pharisaic background, we can deduce and suggest that Paul was primarily defending Jewish monotheism, the belief in the Jewish God and Lord. Certainly, for Paul, as a strict Pharisee, the claim by early believers that Jesus is the Messiah and Lord was the greatest threat to Judaism and to "the traditions of his fathers" (Gal 1:14). Their faith in Jesus (Gal 1:23b; 2:20b) and their gatherings to praise Jesus, singing hymns, telling stories about Jesus, and celebrating the Lord's Supper (or table fellowship, e.g., 1 Cor 11:23–27) were likewise strongly disapproved by Paul. Paul the Pharisee defended what he later as an apostle radically rejected (including the practice of the Mosaic law [Gal 2:19a]) during his missionary career.

24. Tobin, *Spirituality of Paul*, 23, 47.

Paul's Pharisaic way of life and his personal convictions about the practice of the Mosaic law (and the Decalogue) began to be seriously reevaluated. As a result, the Mosaic law, which had defined his character and governed his Jewish way of life (halakah), came to an end (against Mark D. Nanos and Paula Fredricksen),[25] and his life as a zealous Pharisee, a persecutor, a "defender" especially of Jewish monotheism and the practice and interpretation of the law (Acts 3:5–6; 1 Cor 15:9; Gal 1:13), took a 180-degree turn. Because of such a dramatic experience of the risen Christ, most people speak of the "conversion of Paul," a turning point not only in his Jewish-Christian career but also in the significance of the impact on the history of a religion, Christianity. Soon after his "prophetic call," Paul began his missionary career in gentile territories (mainly in Macedonia Achaia and Asia Minor) preaching the gospel (of Christ), which was revealed to him directly, as Paul himself says, from the risen Christ and without human intervention (Gal 1:11–12).

PAUL'S JEWISH IDENTITY IN CONTEXT

Following his "prophetic call," Paul's entire life and his Jewish knowledge are turned upside down. His experience of *seeing* Jesus, the risen Christ, on the road to Damascus divinely infused in his heart (Gal 1:11–12) and mind the gospel "of Christ" (Gal 2:1–10), which he was commissioned to preach, and he did faithfully (Acts 28:30–31; Rom 15:15–16; Gal 1:18–19) and defended to the end of his life. The fundamental convictions toward the prescriptions of the law previously held unquestioned become his most arguable topics of discussion, which ultimately shaped his new Jewish-Christian identity as a believer, pastor, teacher, minister, and missionary apostle to gentiles. Clearly, Paul's new experience of Christ radically and unexpectedly transformed his way of thinking about some central topics of Judaism: monotheism, the ethical commandments of the Mosaic law, righteousness, the righteousness of God and the faithfulness of God, and the means to attain salvation.

It is unconceivable for us to fathom the extent of Paul's radical transformation, from being a zealous persecutor of the church of God,[26] a Jewish "defender," a Pharisee and punctilious observer of the Jewish laws and Jewish

---

25. See Fredriksen, *Paul*, 94–130, especially 130; Nanos, *Mystery of Romans*, 5, 16, 22–23.

26. Gal 1:13; 1 Cor 15:9; 8:3; Acts 9:1–2; 22:4–5; 26:9–11.

monotheism, to becoming a pioneer in boldly questioning the status and ethical role of the Mosaic law and the validity of his Pharisaic persecutions (Acts 6). When we try to see Paul's identity through the lens of the Greek philosophical and Hellenistic Jewish traditions, we can say with certainty that he was a Hellenistic Jew who grew up in the hellenized city of Tarsus and studied Jewish Scripture in Greek (LXX) and, as most New Testament (NT) authors claimed, had the basic knowledge of Greek rhetoric and the preliminary exercises of prose and composition known as the *progymnasmata*.[27] In recent decades, however, much has been devoted to the study of Paul's Jewish "identity" after his prophetic call. The big question is, Who was Paul? A good number of prominent Pauline scholars have supported the view that Paul was and remained "purely" Jewish, and his apostolic career was entirely consistent with the Judaism of his time.[28] Others have emphasized Paul's diaspora Jewish identity before and after his becoming a Hellenistic Jewish believer.[29] Recently, an interesting new approach has been offered by Brant Pitre, Michael P. Barber, and John A. Kincaid in their book, *Paul, a New Covenantal Jew: Rethinking Pauline Theology*. Based on Paul's own identification in 2 Cor 3:6 ("Our qualification comes from God, who has indeed qualified us as ministers of a new covenant")[30] in connection with the prophetic words of Jeremiah in 31:31–34, these erudite scholars propose the argument that Paul is a "New Covenant Jew."[31] Their approach intends to maintain both continuity (covenant or Paul's faithfulness to his Jewish tradition) and discontinuity (new, or Paul's reevaluation

---

27. Naveros Córdova, "1 Corinthians 10:1–4." Paul's knowledge of classical Greek literature is also questionable. Harrington argues that it is plausible that Paul was trained in Greek rhetoric; in fact, he rightly notes that the city of Tarsus had various types of rhetorical schools and preserved the fame of being a *metropolis* in the region with its enlightened and knowledgeable public. Harrington, "Paul," 1034. On this topic, see Witherington and Myers, *New Testament Rhetoric*, 82–165.

28. This is the view of Fredriksen, *Paul*; Harrington, "Paul." For the view of Jewish but not halakah, see Sanders, *Paul and Palestinian Judaism*; Sanders, *Paul, the Law*, 111–14. For the view of a faithful Jewish thinker who did not take non-Jewish ideas, see Wright, *Faithfulness of God*, 1407–8, 1410. For the view of Jewish in line with Jewish Torah observance, see Nanos, *Mystery of Romans*, 8, 15; Frey, "Paul's Jewish Identity."

29. Good examples are Hengel, "Pre-Christian Paul"; Barclay, *Jews in the Mediterranean*, 88–97. For various arguments about Paul's Jewish identity, see N. Elliott, "Question of Politics."

30. All translations from Paul's letters are taken from the NRSV with some alterations.

31. Pitre et al., *New Covenantal Jew*, 4–5.

of that tradition). Identifying Paul as a new covenant Jew fits well when considering Paul's theology as eschatological and apocalyptic.[32]

However, while I agree in part with these scholars—in that Paul's identity after his prophetic call maintains to some degree continuity as well as discontinuity with his Jewish tradition—I argue that Paul's Jewishness has been deeply transformed by the Christ-event and the gospel (which was revealed to him by Jesus Christ himself) he preached to gentiles. Through his experience of the resurrected Christ, he comes to view himself, no longer as a "defender" of Jewish monotheism and the Mosaic law but as a "Hellenistic Jewish believer," an apostle holding the same credentials as Peter, James, and John, the so-called "three pillars" of the nascent church in Jerusalem.[33] As Paul, the new Hellenistic Jewish believer, moves westward to gentile territories preaching his gospel to both Jewish and gentile believers, he becomes the leading apostle—a "Hellenistic-Jewish-Christian apostle"—one who, inspired by his encounter with the risen Christ, would transform the whole understanding of his Jewish monotheism and the practice of the ethical commandments of the Mosaic law. It is important to note that he does not become a "rejecter" of Judaism; indeed, he becomes a Hellenistic Jewish *believer*, an apostle within the Jewish umbrella, and that is how he is identified throughout this book. I suggest that Paul is a good representative of early Christianity; he is one avenue to enlighten our understanding of the external and internal ethical challenges and struggles he and his mixed audience continuously faced in the complex pagan religious and cultural contexts of the first century CE.

THE PASSION OF "DESIRE" (*EPITHYMIA*) IN PAUL'S OEUVRE

There are fourteen explicit occasions when the term "desire" and cognates are used as a negative passion: *epithymia* nine times,[34] *epithymeō* four

---

32. Wright, *Paul and Recent Interpreters*, 64–86, presents the heated debates stimulated by Sanders's book, *Paul and Palestinian Judaism*. Wright shows the arguments of renowned Pauline scholars (Sanders, Käsemann, De Boer, Moore, Schoeps, Schweitzer, Davies, and Martyn, just to mention some) on Paul's approach to both Judaism and the apocalyptic view. In particular, Wright highlights the strengths and problems of Martyn's apocalyptic worldview.

33. Gal 1:1; 2:9; 1 Cor 9:1–2; 15:3–10; Rom 1:1.

34. 1 Thess 4:5 (*epithymias*); Gal 5:16 (*epithymian*), 24 (*epithymiais*); 1 Cor 10:6 (*epithymētas*); Rom 1:24 (*epithymiais*); 6:12 (*epithymiais*); 7:7a (*epithymian*), 8

times,³⁵ and *orexis* once.³⁶ Twice *epithymia* is mentioned positively. The first occurrence is in 1 Thess 2:17 in the context of when Paul is giving his second thanksgiving, encouraging believers in Thessalonica to be faithful and stand firm in times of persecutions and afflictions (2:13—3:13). Paul reminds the Thessalonian believers that they have received God's words through him and his coworkers Silvanus and Timothy and expresses his "great desire" (*pollē epithymia*) to see and be with them. This genuine and a kind of fatherly desire, as Aristotle would say, openly shows Paul's love and mutual friendship with his brothers and sisters in the community at Thessalonica. David Charles Aune, who has studied "passions" (*pathē*) in Paul through the lens of Greek philosophy, points out that Paul uses the term *epithymia* to describe the admirable desires for companionship with others.³⁷ His good desire, or longing to be with them, compelled Paul and his coworkers to make the decision to visit the Thessalonian believers. Although Paul feels spiritually united with them, the intensity of his desire to be physically present with them highlights Paul's personal sentiments toward the believers of the community he founded in a pagan city. Speaking in "brotherly love" (*philadelphia*), a virtue that was taught to them by God himself (4:9; see also Rom 12:10), Paul describes the physical and geographical barriers as the cause of "temporarily being bereft, that is, 'orphaned.' This orphaned condition has led to an intense longing or desire to be reunited with the community."³⁸ But for reasons unknown to us, Paul, Silvanus, and Timothy could not bring to fruition their genuine desire to be with them. Paul himself tried more than once to visit them, but those attempts had always failed.³⁹ His disappointment with the unfulfilled desire

---

(*epithymian*); 13:14 (*epithymias*). The Greek term *epithymētēs* (one who desires) in 1 Cor 10:6 is the only use in the NT.

35. Gal 5:17 (*epithymei*); 1 Cor 10:6b (*epithymesan*); Rom 7:7b (*epithymeseis*); 13:9 (*epithymeseis*). See also Col 3:5 (*epithymian*); Eph 2:3 (*epithymiais*).

36. Rom 1:27 (*orexei*). The word *orexis* is a *hapax legomenon* in the entire NT. In the Greek and Hellenistic Jewish traditions, the concept was used in both a good and bad sense, as well of natural and lawful and even of proper cravings, e.g., the appetites for food (Wis 16:2–3; Philo, *Migr.* 155–163; *Spec.* 4.126–131; Plato, *Def.* 414B; Plutarch, *Mor.* 635C), corrupt and unlawful desires (Sir 18:30; 23:6; Aristotle, *Rhet.* 1.10.1368b6–7). Bible Hub, "3715. orexis." See also Danker and Krug, *Concise Greek-English Lexicon*, 142.

37. Aune, "Passions in Pauline Epistles," 236; see also "Mastery of Passions."

38. Bergant and Karris, *Collegeville Bible Commentary*, 1156.

39. What exactly the situation was that Paul attributed to Satan's activity is unknown to us, though it may refer to some problem that has arisen in Thessalonica (3:5). See Bergant and Karris, *Collegeville Bible Commentary*, 1156.

is expressed negatively by Paul when he states, "Satan hindered us" (1 Thess 2:18). Most scholars interpret what Paul might have referred to with this statement as Paul failed to visit them because Satan had literally prevented it. Paul expresses his anguish and disappointment in the context of his Jewish tradition; Satan, who is a hostile force personified in late Jewish theology, is the obstacle to Paul's realization of his desire to go to visit them.[40]

The second positive occurrence of "desire" (*epithymia*) is found in Paul's Letter to the Philippians, the so-called "letter of friendship."[41] In this letter, Paul explicitly demonstrates his deep love for Christ; in Aune's words, his desire for union with Christ.[42] Within the context when Paul is giving news and instructions to the community he founded in Philippi (Phil 1:12—3:1a), a friendly Paul shares with the believers his personal situation (Phil 1:12–26). He calls them "beloved" (*agapētoi* [2:12; 4:1]) and tells them he is in prison for the sake of the gospel (Phil 1:13–14).[43] The Philippians are his true brothers and sisters in Christ; so, Paul has the confidence to share with them his internal struggles as he writes, "I am hard pressed between the two: my desire [*epithymian*] is to depart and be with Christ, for that is far better" (Phil 1:23).[44] Paul's longing and desire (*epithymian*) to depart from life and "be with Christ" are clearly in view. I argue against Fredrickson, who interprets *epithymian* in this text as Paul's "erotic desire" to die of love for Christ.[45] Rather, the language reveals the apostle's deep

---

40. Brown et al., *New Jerome Biblical Commentary*, 776.

41. For helpful essays on this topic, see Fitzgerald, *Friendship*.

42. Aune, "Passions in Pauline Epistles," 236.

43. Paul might have been in prison between the years 55 and 56 CE (or perhaps 53 CE). Both the Letters to the Philippians and to Philemon might have been written from an Ephesian captivity (see Phil 1:13; 4:22; 2 Cor 1:8–11; Acts 19:23–41).

44. A similar idea is expressed in 2 Cor 5:8. Häusser, *Brief des Paulus*, 87–103. Throughout his letters, Paul also uses the Greek term *epipothia* to express his desire or longing to see his fellow believers, especially Philippians, e.g., Phil 1:8 (*epipothō*); 2:26 (*epipothōn*); 4:1 (*epipothētoi*); Rom 1:11 (*epipothō*); 15:23 (*epipothian*); 1 Thess 3:6 (*epipothountes*). Paul likewise employs the word *deomai* to express his deep personal need to see the face of the Thessalonian believers in 1 Thess 3:10 (*deomenoi*). Fredrickson has explored the longing language (*epipotheō*) in Philippians. He argues that the Letter to the Philippians is about "Paul's longing for the church and for Christ, and Christ's longing for mortals." Fredrickson, *Eros and the Christ*, 3. For a detailed summary of Fredrickson's study, see Bowden, *Desire*, 30–40. For discussion about longing (*epipotheō*) and other passions in Paul's letters, see Malherbe, *Paul and Popular Philosophers*.

45. Fredrickson, *Eros and the Christ*, 132–33. Fredrickson briefly discusses this text within the context of marriage imagery combined with athletic imagery of Phil 3:7–14. As Bowden has noted (*Desire*, 39), it is surprising that Fredrickson does not devote a chapter to analyze Phil 1:23 as he does with other Philippian texts.

sense of loneliness; he is emotionally sincere, and why not say that at that moment when writing this letter (from prison) he is experiencing a profound feeling of sadness and loss of interest, which led him to question whether he should continue in his mission as an apostle to the gentiles. Paul's words in Phil 1:21 ("for me to live is Christ and to die is gain") not only express his honest love for Christ, but his personal view about death is positively emphasized. At first, Paul envisions a better situation, that is, not to continue in the flesh and die. But his love for Christ and the reciprocal love and friendship between the Philippian believers and Paul strengthen him, for now, to continue living, as he writes, "To remain in the flesh is more necessary for the sake of you. And having been persuaded by this, I know that I will remain and will continue with all of you for your progress and joy in faith" (Phil 1:24–25). In this honest confession, his genuine love for his brothers and sisters at Philippi and his strong feelings toward them are exposed openly.

THE TASK IN THIS STUDY

Throughout this book, key Pauline texts where the term "desire" (*epithymia*) and the verbal cognates appear are examined: Rom 1:18–32; 6:12–23; 7:7–25; 13:9–14; 1 Cor 5:6–13; 6:9–11; Gal 5:16–24; 1 Thess 4:1–12. These texts are explored in connection to Paul's approaches to the various challenges he faces in the early Christian communities: how amid divisions among believers—Jewish and gentile—Paul addresses the problem of desire and its connection with sexual vices; and how, in light of the Christ-event, he offers a solution to the problem of desire that would foster not only a holy life but also unity. In chapter 1, I explore the term *epithymia*, its connection with sexual vices, and the remedy to avoid this passion in Paul's Greco-Roman context. The literature selected for this study is Plato and the Stoics from the Greek philosophical tradition and Philo of Alexandria and 4 Maccabees from the Hellenistic Jewish tradition. Chapter 2 deals with Paul's reevaluation of Jewish monotheism in light of the Christ-event.[46] Using the Greek philosophical and Hellenistic Jewish traditions as Paul's background, I describe Paul's negative understanding of *epithymia* and *epithymeō* and their connection to idolatry and vices that lead to sexual immorality and vices. In this chapter, the focus is on Paul's Christocentric monotheism and

---

46. With the term "Christ-event," I refer to Jesus' suffering, passion, death, resurrection, and ascension. The evangelist Luke refers to it in his Gospel as Jesus' *exodus* (Luke 9:31).

idolatry and its close association with sinful passions, excessive desires, and sexual vices. In chapter 3, Paul's new understanding of the Mosaic law is explored in light of the Christ-event. As Paul proves to his Jewish-Christian audience that the practice of "the commandment" is not the remedy of desire, three important themes are treated: (1) Paul's identification of the problem of the passion of desire; (2) the dangers of desire as a sinful passion beyond measure; and (3) the faithfulness of God and his righteousness in opposition to sinful passions. In chapter 4, I explore Paul's contribution to the solution of the problem of "desire" (*epithymia*) founded in the grace of God coming to fruition in the love commandment, the centrality of Christ, and the Spirit. The themes of God as a rewarding Father, the outpouring of God's two blessings (belief and the Holy Spirit), and the faithfulness of God and his righteousness in the grace of God are central for the renewal of the community of believers in Paul's approach to overcome the passion of desire and sexual vices, and, thus, to eliminate excessive/irrational desires and passions. The effectiveness of love in the Spirit, as reflected in the "fruit(s)" of love/of the Spirit, is further shown using explicit examples from Paul's Jewish tradition: the ethical commandments of the law, the law of circumcision, eating food sacrificed to idols, and the food laws. In chapter 5, I summarize our findings, and I highlight Paul's Christocentric approach in his doctrine to avoid *epithymia* and its sequels, where he offers the believers a new ethical message founded in the grace of God, the Spirit of God/Christ, and the love commandment or law of Christ.

1

Paul's Background
The Understanding of "Desire" (*Epithymia*) in Greek Philosophical and Hellenistic Jewish Traditions

BEFORE WE EMBARK ON the analysis of Paul's view and treatment of desire and its connection with sexual vices in his seven genuine letters, it is apropos to first place Paul and his mixed audience (Jewish and gentile believers) within the larger Greco-Roman world. This creative method would give the basic picture of Paul's background about the understanding of "desire" (*epithymia*) in the Greek philosophical and Hellenistic Jewish traditions. It shall also give a broader picture of where Paul's thought on desire derives from and its association with sexual vices. Paul was a Hellenistic, first-century Jew from Tarsus, the capital of the ancient province of Cilicia (today located on the eastern Mediterranean coast of Turkey), and one of the most hellenized *poleis* in Asia Minor. His thought and ways of approaching and appropriating Greek concepts were influenced, directly or indirectly, by the cultural diversity and philosophical avenues he encountered in Tarsus as a young man[1] and later as a Hellenistic Jewish believer, an apostle to the gentiles.

---

1. Harrington argues that the city of Tarsus had various types of rhetorical schools and preserved the fame of being a *metropolis* in the region with its enlightened and knowledgeable public. Harrington, "Paul." Paul traveled to Jerusalem, where he was probably trained as a Pharisee, perhaps under the feet of Rabbi Gamaliel (Acts 22:3). However, we do not have a solid argument that shows the time Paul lived in Tarsus before

Like his gentile audience, Paul was exposed to popular philosophies and ideas from speakers in markets and public competitions.[2] Thus, it is important to explore Paul's larger Greco-Roman context in order to enrich our knowledge about the ways he understands and deals with sexual (pagan) vices closely connected with the passion of "desire" (*epithymia*) in his ethical arguments. When Paul joined the early community of believers (ca. 32 CE), surely he neither had a "blank" mind, nor had he forgotten the knowledge of "everything" he had at once in his encounter with the risen Christ as his letters evince. Instead, like most of his Hellenistic Jewish contemporaries, Paul was familiar with the current interpretations of "passions" (*pathē*) in Greek philosophy, and "desire" (*epithymia*) was not the exception. Thus, his dealing with the problem of desire and passions and sexual vices reflects the influence of Greek knowledge, philosophy, and culture. He was, I would say, "a lover of wisdom" (*philosophos*) in his own way.[3]

In the Greek philosophical tradition of interpretations, "desire" (*epithymia*) originally had a neutral meaning and was commonly connected with natural and "good emotions" (*eupatheiai*). For example, in Plato's dialogues *epithymia* is not always a bad passion; what is bad is the feeling of desire without restraint.[4] However, it is with the Stoic philosophers that desire becomes evil and one of the four "passions" (*pathē*) of the soul.[5] John M. Rist points out that in the Stoic tradition the four passions (desire [*epithymia*], pleasure [*ēdonē*], grief [*lupē*], and fear [*phobos*]) are always viewed

---

he moved to Jerusalem. Some scholars argue that he moved during his teen years and others when he was in his early twenties. It is, however, probable that Paul was already in Jerusalem by his mid- or late twenties. Harrington, "Paul," 1034. For various arguments, see Unnik, *Tarsus or Jerusalem*; Schnelle, *Apostle Paul*, 68–69; Haacker, "Paul's Life"; Murphy-O'Connor, *Paul*, 46.

2. Keener, *Mind of the Spirit*, xviii; Fairweather, *Jesus and Greeks*, 387–88.

3. In a study about Paul's use of the Stoic concept of *pneuma* (spirit) in his ethical discourse, I argue that Paul is an eclectic Middle Platonist who used philosophical ideas and notions and even altered some of these philosophical ideas and language about *pneuma* to frame his own ethical discourse around the Spirit of God. See Naveros Córdova, *Live in the Spirit*, 152–55.

4. In Aristotle's ethics *epithymia* plays no essential role; like other passions, e.g., *orgē*, *phobos*, *chara*, and *philia*, desire is one of the passions of the soul (*Eth. nic.* 2.4.1105b21). Büchsel, *TDNT* 3:168, 170. All translations of Aristotle's works are from *Complete Works* (Barnes).

5. *SVF* 2:378, 3:377–490; DL, *Lives* 7.110–7.118; Cicero, *Tusc.* 3–4; Galen, *Hip. et Plat.* 4–5; Aristotle, *Eth. nic.* 2.4.1105b19–28; *Rhet.* 2.1.1378a20.

contrary and disobedient to "reason" (*logos*).⁶ The complexity of the nature of desire as a bad passion and the remedy to either eradicate or moderate it led Greek philosophers to engage in continuous debates, especially among the Stoics.⁷ While Platonists and Stoics agree in that desire is one of the four passions of the soul and the worst of the four, they disagree in two key points: (1) the definition of desire (*what* the proper definition of desire should be), and (2) the remedy or solution to eliminate or moderate desire (*what* can solve the problem of desire), thus its sequels such as irrational desire, irrational impulse, immoderate passion, and immoderate desire.

In Hellenistic Jewish tradition, the authors often follow the Greek philosophical interpretation of "desire" (*epithymia*). In their ethical discourses, desire is presented as one of the four passions of the soul and a deadly passion. Good representatives treated in this book are Philo of Alexandria and 4 Maccabees. I believe that Philo's interpretation of desire is an important addition to enlighten Paul's own understanding of desire and the dangers of this evil passion.⁸ Similarly, I consider the analysis of 4 Maccabees (from the LXX) helpful, for the text was written roughly around the first century BCE and the first century CE. Both authors are influenced by Greek philosophical thought (Philo in greater detail); their understandings of the failure to practice the ethical commandments of the Mosaic law (and Decalogue) are presented within the parameters of passions and vices connected with the philosophical interpretations of Plato, the Stoics, and Middle Platonists. As a matter of fact, for these Hellenistic Jewish authors, "desire" (*epithymia*), too, can become a sinful passion and associated with sexual vices, other passions, gluttony, and bodily pleasures.⁹ In this chapter, then, we shall get a good sense of the close association between desire and sexual vices in the traditions of Plato, the Stoics, Philo of Alexandria, and 4 Maccabees.

---

6. Rist, *Stoics*, 241, 243. Stobaeus, *Ecl.* 2.88; *SVF* 3:378.

7. See Naveros Córdova, "Worst of the Passions," 50–51. For important primary Stoic sources, see Long and Sedley, *Hellenistic Philosophers*.

8. For a short biography of Philo of Alexandria, see Naveros Córdova, *Philo of Alexandria*, x–xiv; Royse, "Works of Philo."

9. For a detailed analysis of the attitudes toward sexuality and its connection with sexual desire in ancient Jewish literature within the larger Greco-Roman context, see Loader, *Pseudepigrapha on Sexuality*; also *New Testament on Sexuality*. In both works, Loader provides an extensive analysis of selected texts from major Hellenistic Jewish literature dealing with sexuality, sexual desire in marriage, and sexual wrongdoings or misdirected sexual desire.

PLATO: DESIRE AND ITS EVIL "BUDDIES"

The larger Greco-Roman world in which Paul and his mixed audience lived displays a complexity of ideas and concepts, which constantly changed from tradition to tradition and from time to time. "Desire" (*epithymia*) is one of these terms.[10] The writings of Greek philosophers reflect the ongoing debates regarding the correct definition and nature of *epithymia*. The original definition of the term goes back to the Platonic tradition. The verbal form *epithymeō* (to desire) is derived from the words *epi* (upon) and *thumos* (breath, eagerness, or desire). It is worth noting that in ancient Greek literature, the word *thumos* originally denoted a violence of air, spirit, water, the ground, animals, or men. For example, in Homer (ninth or eighth century BCE), *thumos* refers to the vital force of animals and human beings (*Il.* 13.654).[11] Eventually, its various meanings developed and took on the sense of desire, impulse, spirit, anger, sensibility, disposition, mind, thought, and consideration.[12] In the Greek tradition, both the noun *epithymia* and the verb *epithymeō* are not found in Homer, but they appear later in the pre-Socratic literature; the words denote the direct impulse toward food, sexual satisfaction, and also desire in general. However, there is nothing objectionable or even suspicious about them in the ethical sphere.[13] So, *epithymeō* has simply the meaning of "desire something strongly."[14]

When analyzing the works of Plato (ca. 429–347 BCE),[15] we find both the neutral and negative meanings of desire.[16] As in the pre-Socratic tradition, in Plato *epithymia* and verbal cognates (deriving from the verbal form of *epithymeō*) appear as a *vox media* or neutral word and often in reference

---

10. Another good example is "piety" (*eusebeia*), a Greek term that went through a transition in Greek literature and the ethical systems of Plato, Aristotle, and the Stoics. For a detailed analysis, see Naveros Córdova, *Ethical Discourse*.

11. Philo, who follows the Platonic tradition, often makes use of the word *thumos* according to which the term is one of the three parts of the soul with *logos* and *epithymia* (*Spec.* 4.92; see also *Leg.* 3.116–118). He advises the control of *thumos* in *Ios.* 73, 222, and Josephus often uses it for anger (*A.J.* 20.108; *B.J.* 2.135, 5.489; *Vita* 143, 393).

12. Büchsel, *TDNT* 3:167.

13. Büchsel, *TDNT* 3:168.

14. Léon-Dufour, *Dictionary of New Testament*, 164.

15. All translations of Plato's works are from *Collected Dialogues* (Hamilton and Cairns).

16. Plato makes a distinction between rational and irrational desires; similarly, Aristotle writes, "Appetite is contrary to decision, but appetite is not contrary to appetite" (*Eth. nic.* 1111b15). See Irwin, *Plato's Ethics*, 206.

to the natural and direct impulses toward food, knowledge, sexual satisfaction, and any desire in general. As Hendrik Lorenz has noted, not all the uses of desire have the pejorative meaning of covetousness and lust.[17] For example, in the *Laws* Plato, similar to Aristotle,[18] affirms that the three desires for food, drink, and sex are basic in human nature; for human beings, everything is dependent on them (*Leg.* 782D–E).[19]

For the purpose of this study, we focus on the negative use of desire only, especially in association with sexual vices as well as other aspects associated with passions, desires, and pleasures of the body. The Athenian philosopher often lists desire together with the other primary passions of the soul (grief, pleasure, and fear).[20] According to the Platonic definition of *epithymia*, this passion becomes dangerous to the human soul only when it goes beyond the rational boundaries.[21] That is, there is a limit when desire becomes a bad desire. What is inherently evil is not desire itself but the *excessive* quantity of desire, also called irrational impulse or immoderate desire. Therefore, it is this inappropriate desire that is linked with evil passions, sexual desires, and pleasures of the body.[22] Significantly, in the Platonic tradition, desire takes a distinctive moral meaning connected with "excessive impulse" (*pleonazousa hormē*) and "irrational desire" (*alogos epithymia*).[23] This important connection is especially found in Plato's *Republic, Laws, Phaedrus, Gorgias, Philebus,* and *Charmides.*

---

17. Lorenz, *Brute Within*, 18–34.

18. In Aristotle's tradition, desires for bodily pleasures (e.g., food, sex, sleep) arise in the normal course of having a body. See Annas, "Aristotle on Pleasure," 286. Aristotle writes, "And perhaps they actually pursue not the pleasure they think they pursue nor that which they would say they pursue, but the same pleasure; for all things have by nature something divine in them" (*Eth. nic.* 7.13.1153b30–32).

19. See also Plato, *Gorg.* 496D, 517B–D; *Resp.* 328D, 436A–438A, 475C, 559A–B; *Phileb.* 34E–35B; *Lys.* 221D–E. Irwin, *Plato's Ethics*, 342.

20. Plato, *Lach.* 191E; *Crat.* 419B–E; *Symp.* 207E; *Resp.* 429C, 430A–B; *Theaet.* 156B; *Leg.* 631E–632A, 732E–733A, 934A.

21. Pseudo-Plato, *Def.* 411E, 415D.

22. Plato, *Leg.* 802C, 854A; *Charm.* 167E; *Phaedr.* 237D–238E; *Resp.* 328D, 439D, 485D–E, 558D; *Phileb.* 34C.

23. Plato, *Gorg.* 493B, 587E; *Crat.* 419D; *Phaedr.* 238E; *Resp.* 359C, 561A, 573A–576E, 587B–E.

Excessive Desire and the Dangers of Food and Drink

In ancient Greek philosophy there was the notion that if everyone desires the good, everyone can also desire evil (and vice versa), and the desire of evil things is equivalent to a state of unhappiness (evil desire = unhappiness). In other words, desiring good things means happiness (or virtue), and desiring bad things means unhappiness (or vices). In *Meno*, Plato's Socrates discusses the nature of evil; in it, Socrates speaks of the human capacity of "desiring evil things," warns his friend Meno to avoid such desires, and exhorts him to always desire the good in order to experience true happiness (*Min.* 77D–E). According to Socrates, "Virtue is identical to happiness";[24] it is in human nature, the good desire to be happy, to feel genuine happiness. Later in the dialogue Socrates claims, "Nobody desires what is evil" because no one desires unhappiness (*Min.* 78A). His statement assumes the notion that human beings have power to choose the good and thus control evil desires (vices). Within this Platonic context, *epithymia* as a bad passion comes to constitute a powerful entity in human nature. As a matter of fact, in his definition of evil desire in the *Republic* Plato states, "Desire is a passion and power in the soul" (*Resp.* 430B).[25]

Moreover, in *Philebus*, a dialogue between Protarchus and Socrates, the evil nature of *epithymia* is described along with the understanding of "pleasure" (*hēdonē*),[26] a passion akin to desire. In their discussion about whether wisdom or pleasure is the greater good, Socrates explains his interpretation of desire by giving examples related to two important and natural desirous urges of the body: thirst and hunger. He explains that when a person is thirsty, his or her thirst is a desire to a certain extent, for the person has a strong desire to drink (e.g., water). Socrates goes on to say that when a person becomes empty (or lacks something), he or she desires the opposite of what he or she is experiencing at that moment; that is, when being empty, the individual longs to be filled with what is desired. The point Socrates intends to make is this: a person who desires, strongly desires something lacking, e.g., water. If one experiences what she or he desires, it is because he or she is thirsty. If "thirsty" is an equivalent to "emptying," whereas what he or she desires is "replenishment," what then is that something in the makeup of a thirsty person who apprehends replenishment? It cannot be

---

24. Irwin, *From Socrates to Reformation*, 65.
25. See also Plato, *Soph.* 228B.
26. Plato, *Phileb.* 34C–35D.

the body because the body is being emptied. Therefore, it is the human soul that apprehends the replenishment, and it does it through the faculty of memory. Inasmuch as it has proved that memory is what leads people towards the objects of desire, it is to the human body that both impulse and desire belong. Plato's Socrates makes the argument that all desires are of the human body, not of the soul.

In Plato's philosophical tradition, the definition of *epithymia* goes consistently in line with desire to eat and desire to drink. Plato believes that human beings are born inherently with excessive desires for food and drink and sexual activity or appetite.[27] The happy person is truly the one who not only has the power to satisfy his or her passions and desires but can lead them to growth and to the uttermost goodness. What is dangerous for the human body, according to Socrates, is the *excessive* quantity of abundant and delicious food and drink; therefore, ethically speaking, the excessive quantity of food and drink certainly harms the individual. Plato's Socrates asserts that if a person wishes to live constantly trying to satisfy his or her bodily appetites—eating and drinking as much as the person wishes when hungry or thirsty—he or she lives a kind of a "diseased life" (*Gorg.* 505A).

In Plato, we find two essential considerations a true philosopher must distinguish: (1) desires for the corporeal and unceasing pursuit always imprison the human soul; (2) self-control and integrity are acquired through habit and practice and thus cultivate virtues toward goodness (*Phaedr.* 81D–83E). Regarding the first consideration, we can say that whereas the person surrenders to excessive desire for food and drink, the individual distances himself or herself from goodness (virtues).[28] In other words, as the person practices gluttony, selfishness, and drunkenness, he or she lives a life of vices, and the body becomes trapped in or enslaved to cravings, including excessive desire for "lust" or "lasciviousness" (*lagneia*), a vice generally associated with the vices of licentiousness, shamefulness, and lack of self-control.[29] In the ancient Greco-Roman world, sexual relations

---

27. Gaca, "Pentateuch or Plato," 128.

28. Socrates defined virtue as the "knowledge of the good." Irwin, *From Socrates to Reformation*, 14.

29. Musonius, *Fr.* 12.12–16, 29–34, 46–48. Reno, "Pornographic Desire," 173; Lutz, "Musonius Rufus," 84–88. In Cynicism, a philosophical tradition heavily influenced by Socratic ethics and which greatly influenced Stoicism, especially Zeno of Citium and Chrysippus, we find the connection of gluttony with both lust and pleasures of the body, as well as the association of vices (especially vices related to sexual pleasures) with the lack of knowledge. Interestingly, this is particularly observed in the writings of Demetrius the

are often accompanied with the enjoyment of abundant food and wine and the pleasure of songs and dances.[30] Regarding the second consideration we can say that a true philosopher, whose primary task is the development of his own character, knows that the cultivation of the virtues of self-control, courage, and integrity leads to the highest goodness. Even though no soul is pure when it leaves the corruptible body, the attainment of the good opens the possibility to reach the divine. For Plato, the true philosopher knows that abstaining from all bodily desires, pleasures, griefs, and fears through the practice of "self-control" (*enkrateia*) is key to freeing himself completely from the bondage of the body.[31]

Gluttony: The Doorway to Love of Pleasure and Excessive Sexual Desire

One of the greatest dangers of indulging oneself with the pleasures of food and drink is gluttony, a vice closely associated with excessive sexual desire and immorality in the Platonic tradition. In Plato, "gluttony" (*gastrimargia*) is as an excessive desire and pleasure without reason (*Phaedr.* 238A; *Symp.* 187C–E). Food is an intrinsic human necessity for survival. However, love of food or the pleasure of food empowers the passion of "desire" (*epithymia*) in the individual, which in turn becomes tyrannical and rules over judgment and other desires. This kind of pleasure is associated with the vice of gluttony, and the person engaged in it is called a glutton. "Excessive" (*pleonazousa*) eating and drinking is contrary to "reason" (*logos*) and a sin opposed to the generic virtue of "temperance" (*sōphrosunē*) or "self-control" (*enkrateia*) because it is an immoderate indulgence in the delights of food and drink.[32] If an individual eats and drinks only moderately and

---

Cynic, who is a contemporary of Paul. See Seneca, *Ben.* 7.2.2–7.2.3, 7.9.3–7.9.5, 7.10.6; Seneca, *Ep.* 91.19; DL, *Lives* 6.5.85–6.5.89. The connection between Paul and Cynicism, particularly Demetrius the Cynic, is an important one but beyond the scope of this study.

30. Ludwig, *Eros and Polis*, 61.

31. Diogenes Laertius defines "self-control" (*enkrateia*) as "a disposition never overcome in that which concerns right reason, or a habit which no pleasures can get the better of" (DL, *Lives* 7.93 [*SVF* 3:265]).

32. It is important to note that Plato does not give much importance to *enkrateia*/*sōphrosunē* in his dialogues, e.g., *Charmides*, where Plato refuses the very notion of *enkrateia*. Plato's negative view of *enkrateia* is observed in the *Phaedo* where Socrates deals with the common conception of *sōphrosunē*. In *Phaed.* 68C, Socrates discusses his conception of *sōphrosunē*, that is, moderation of desires. Here Socrates makes fun of those

minds the necessary limits of sexual activity, the proliferation of other immoderate (sexual) desires would not occur, and the Athenian society would be at peace.[33]

In ancient classical Greek the term *erōs* (here translated as "love") had a range of meanings, such as caring, longing, sexual pleasures, sexual desire, sexual arousal, passionate love, even romantic love.[34] Plato regards *erōs* "as the type of sexual desire that expresses attraction to a particular person."[35] The term *erōs* is also connected with sexual desire and often takes the form of passionate and intense desire, rather than calm and mild desire. It is demanding, irrational, even obsessive. In the *Symposium*, one of Plato's two greatest dialogues, where the topic of discussion is "love" (*erōs*) in all its degrees and forms (human and divine), *erōs* is described as desire for good and for happiness (*Symp.* 204E) and as the desire to give birth in beauty (*Symp.* 206B7).[36] In the *Symposium* Socrates explains that when someone feels a want, this person is wanting something that is not yet at hand, and the object of his or her love and desire is whatever is not and whatever he or she has not gotten. Aristophanes's encomium of *erōs* is the most memorable speech and his views about male homosexual *erōs*, where he praises pederasty, represents his legitimation of male-male sexual desire and relations in the political sphere (*Symp.* 191E–192A).[37] In the same way, for Plato's Socrates, love is always the love of something, and that something is what

who conceive *sōphrosunē* as a kind of trade that consists in abstaining from certain pleasures in the hope of enjoying greater pleasure (*Phaed.* 68E–69A). Indeed, Socrates qualifies *sōphrosunē* as a form of "intemperance" (*akolasia*). Thus, *enkrateia* is not among the virtues defined by Socrates (see also Xenophon, *Mem.* 3.9; 4.6). Some scholars argue that Plato in the *Gorgias* and the *Republic* becomes reconciled with *enkrateia*; for example, in *Gorg.* 491D and in *Resp.* 430E, *enkrateia* is sometimes used in the sense of *sōphrosunē*. That is the reason why it is hard to distinguish between *enkrateia* and *sōphrosunē* with regard to the moderation of food and drink and sexual desires. For discussion on the development of *enkrateia* in Plato, see Dorion, "Plato and *Enkrateia*."

33. Gaca, "Pentateuch or Plato," 129.

34. For details on the various meanings of *erōs*, see Ludwig, *Eros and Polis*, 7–14.

35. Irwin, *Plato's Ethics*, 303.

36. For the various understandings of *erōs* in Plato's dialogues, see Irwin, *Plato's Ethics*, 303–6.

37. For discussion, see Ludwig, *Eros and Polis*, 27–39. In 1 Cor 13, Paul praises "love" (*agapē*) as the queen of all virtues, above faith and hope. Paul's treatment of love reflects the love commandment that Jesus gives to his disciples in John: "Love one another as I have loved you"; if we love one another God dwells in us (e.g., 13:1, 34–35; 14:15; 15:9–17; 17:23–24); and the Synoptic Gospels: "You shall love your neighbor as yourself" is the "greatest commandment" (e.g., Mark 12:31; Matt 7:12; Luke 6:31).

the person lacks (*Symp.* 200E).³⁸ Though, what is dangerous is when the "love" (*erōs*) for something becomes uncontrollable or beyond human control and becomes "irrational" (*alogos*) or "excessive" (*pleonazousa*) desire. At this point, human reason has lost to this irrational wanting. This is problematic because this wanting is the doorway to excessive sexual desire, described also in terms of irrational desire, harmful desire, unsatisfied desire, and erotic desire. For Plato, this excessive/irrational desire is like a power crashing and entering the human soul (*Crat.* 419D; *Phaedr.* 238E). Plato's Socrates further explains what excessive sexual desire is: excessive desire is when desires of the body reside in foolish people, who are not governed by the "mind" (*nous*), and in the uncontrolled and unretentive part of the body, which is the part below the belly where the sexual organ is located.

In the *Phaedrus*, Socrates assigns *erōs* to the irrational part of the body because "it is an expression of madness, and madness seems to belong to the non-rational part or the appetitive part (*Phaedr.* 238b7–c4)."³⁹ In his discussion of "love" (*erōs*) against Phaedrus, who claims that making love is a good physical desire, Socrates states, "To fall in love starts a man on the path upward to where love is satisfied in the perfect beauty of the truth."⁴⁰ Socrates argues that love is some sort of desire; he explains his statement in terms of two principles given by the Creator to humans: love and acquired judgment. The first, love or *erōs*, is a principle that human beings follow and is an innate desire for physical pleasure; the second principle, acquired judgment, aims at what is best (*Phaedr.* 237E). The internal guides of both principles are sometimes in accord with each other, but other times they are at variance. Plato's Socrates then speaks of the human struggle between these two principles: sometimes one gains mastery of the body but other times the other way around; this happens when judgment guides the individual rationally toward what is the best (second principle). The individual acquires not only mastery but also temperance. When the individual is controlled by *erōs* (first principle), the passion of "desire" (*epithymia*) drags the individual irrationally toward excessive sexual pleasures (and immorality), and it (desire) comes to rule within the human soul.

38. For a good discussion on love and its relationship with desire, see Tan, "Denial of *Eros.*"

39. Irwin, *Plato's Ethics*, 304. Plato explains his argument for the tripartition of the soul—reason, spirit, and appetite—in *Resp.* 4.

40. Plato, *Collected Dialogues*, 475. It is impossible for us to grasp what exactly "beauty" meant to the Greeks. It was a mighty power exercising a profound influence upon their daily lives.

According to Lysias, the lover, who is consumed by *erōs*, acts against his judgment out of purely selfish interests, namely, the gratification of his sexual desire.[41] The appropriate name that Socrates gives to this kind of irrational or excessive sexual pleasure is wantonness (*Phaedr.* 238E–239A). This sexual vice (*erōs*) requires a virtue that is opposite to sexual desire, that is, self-control or moderation.[42] In *Phaedrus*, Lysias urges his listener(s) to attempt to escape from "the bestial quality of sexual desire."[43] A similar exhortation we shall find in Paul's ethical exhortation against "sexual immorality" (*porneia*) and "idolatry" (*eidōlolatria*), the source of sexual vices.[44] Furthermore, in his speech, Lysias "condemns *erōs* as a form of madness harmful to the beloved (the one who is loved), and as a source of indignity to the lover (the one who loves), who suffers while he is in love and regrets its loss once the spell of love wears off and his sanity is restored."[45] Socrates describes metaphorically the uncontrollable part of the body—the part below the belly—as a leaky jar because it can never be filled (*Gorg.* 493B). So the philosopher must advise his pupils that one must discipline and moderate his uncontrollable sexual appetites and pleasures (*Gorg.* 507E); otherwise, desire will overpower the human "mind" (*nous*), and desire will become covetousness or excessive desire (*Resp.* 359C). A similar idea is also found in Plato's *Republic*. Sexual appetites are connected to lawlessness and pleasures, and *epithymia* is identified closely with a ruling passion, yearning unsatisfied in frenzy (*Resp.* 573A–576E). In the *Republic*, the individual's desire becomes "tyrannical" in the full sense of the word,[46] and *erōs* likewise becomes tyrannical, erotic, and maniacal. At this

---

41. Tan, "Denial of *Eros*," 205.

42. "Moderation," according to Stobaeus, is the science of what should be chosen and avoided and of things that are neither, and deals with man's impulses (*Ecl.* 2.7.5b [*SVF* 3:264]). See Gourinat, "*Akrasia* and *Enkrateia*," 220. For Socrates, "virtue secures pleasure or peace of mind"; practical reason is the means to secure adaptation or control of desires. Irwin, *From Socrates to Reformation*, 66.

43. Tan, "Denial of *Eros*," 208–9.

44. See ch. 3. In the present study, as a matter of consistency, the term *porneia* is translated as "sexual immorality" (e.g., fornication, prostitution, adultery, and the like). In this regard, I follow Wright Knust and Bowden, who relate *porneia* and cognates to sexual immorality in general. For a summary of Wright Knust's study, see Bowden, *Desire*, 23–29.

45. Tan, "Denial of *Eros*," 209.

46. For a good analysis of Plato's tyrannical desire, see Svebakken, *Philo of Alexandria's Exposition*.

point, human affection is felt powerfully;[47] the human soul has truly been indwelled and overpowered by "passionate and tyrannical desire" (*erōtikai te kai turannikai epithymiai* [*Resp.* 587B]).

Excessive Sexual Desire Versus the Mind and Reason

In the Platonic tradition, excessive desire enters the human soul (*Crat.* 419D-E); puts the soul in danger and, against "reason" (*logos*), becomes angry (*Resp.* 439E-440B); and together with pleasure becomes harmful to the human soul (*Resp.* 561A). Lysias's speech tries to overcome the violent and irrational nature of sexual desire, not in reason but in the realm of social convention. This is done in terms of the social benefits of association with those who are not in love. Particularly, Lysias seeks to maximize social benefits through the practice of public discretion that conceals from public view the erotic nature of a man's sexual relationship with a young boy (*Symp.* 181C3-4).[48] In the ancient Greco-Roman world, male-male sexual relation was viewed as an expression of "manliness" and considered a "political virtue."[49] However, Lysias's strategy does not result in the extension of desire. The person who is dominated by excessive desire becomes enslaved to sexual pleasures and aims at getting the greatest pleasure an individual can get (*Phaedr.* 238E).

In the Platonic tradition, the passion of desire is associated with sexual immorality in several forms. In the *Timaeus*, which contains Plato's account of the creation of the universe by the *demiourgos* (craftsman), pleasures and desires disturb the human body in ways that stir up sexual intemperance, or the vice of *akolasia*, like a deadly disease of the soul (*Tim.* 86C-D). Plato explains that a human being is not involuntarily bad by nature, but it becomes bad by reason of an ill disposition of the body and a bad education (*Tim.* 86E). Plato goes further to clarify his point. God determined the sovereign part of the human soul to be the divinity of the *nous*, which dwells at the top of the body, that is, the head (*Tim.* 90A). Through a lively desire of what Plato calls emission, which creates the love for procreation, the male organ of generation becomes rebellious and—like an animal disobedient to "reason" (*logos*) and maddened with

---

47. Vernon, "Plato," 205.
48. Tan, "Denial of *Eros*," 209.
49. Ludwig, *Eros and Polis*, 48-49.

the sting of lust—seeks to gain absolute mastery. The same behavior is experienced with what Plato calls the womb or matrix of women. The animal disobedient to reason within men and women is desirous of procreating children, but when remaining unfruitful beyond its proper time, the animal gets discontent and angry and wanders in every direction through the body and "brings them together, desire and love of the man and the woman" (*Tim.* 91B–C).[50] Without the practice of "self-control" (*enkrateia*) or "temperance" (*sōphrosunē*), the man's "desire" (*epithymia*) becomes "tyrannical desire" (*erōs*), and his "mind" (*nous*) becomes enslaved to erotic-passionate desire. The soul is entirely swayed by the indwelling tyranny of *erōs* (*Resp.* 573C–D) and by unsatisfied lusts (*Leg.* 870A).[51]

In his discourse, Plato speaks of three appetites—food, drink, and love (*erōs*)—and connects them and their accompaniments with the money-loving part because money is the chief instrument for the gratification of such desires (*Resp.* 580D–E).[52] Pleasures, desires, and passions can become a violent inner power when they become excessive and frantic. In the *Laws*, Plato clarifies the reason why a great number of people live without the virtue of temperance—it is either because of "ignorance" (*agnōsia*) or "lack of self-control" (*akrasia*) or both (*Leg.* 734A–C)—and in the *Republic*, Plato expresses the idea that the human "mind" (*nous*) has the power to master pleasures and appetites. He writes that the "expression self-mastery means the control or moderation of the worse by the part that is naturally better," that is, the mind (*Resp.* 431A). In his doctrine of the remedy of desire, therefore, Plato promotes *metriopatheia* (a doctrine followed by Middle Platonists), the moderation of desires and passion.[53] Indeed, Plato addresses the need to moderate sexual appetites, pleasures, and desires with "reason" (*logos*), the mind's aid (*Resp.* 431B–E). In *Resp.* 440A–B, Plato represents the inner struggle between reason and desire (*logos* versus *epithymia*) in the quest for the moderation of desire. He describes how reason fights against desire, and how reason is able to master the human body. All desires, including sexual desire, wait upon knowledge and reason before they pursue their pleasures in conjunction with them (knowledge and reason), and

---

50. See also Plato, *Leg.* 631D–632A.

51. Pieper notes regarding Lysias's speech about *erōs* that what is bad about this attitude is not the craving for sensual gratification, but the deliberate, systematic separation of sensuality from spirituality, of sex from love. Pieper, *Love and Inspiration*, 20.

52. See also Plato, *Leg.* 837C–D.

53. Plato, *Gorg.* 505A.

taking only those pleasures that reason approves, enjoy the truest pleasures (since they follow the truth) and the pleasures that are proper for them and their own (*Resp.* 586D–E).

THE STOIC DOCTRINE OF DESIRE: THE ELIMINATION OF A DEADLY PASSION

While "desire" (*epithymia*) appears first in Plato's writings, it is with the Stoic philosophers that desire receives a strong negative connotation. Like pleasure, grief, and fear, desire is an evil "passion" (*pathos*) of the soul. From the time of the founder of Stoicism, Zeno of Citium (fourth century BCE), the philosopher Diogenes Laertius (DL) notes that the Stoics coined desire as a deadly passion, "irrational" (*alogos*), and an "impulse" (*hormē*) that is "excessive" (*pleonazousa*) and disobedient to "reason" (*logos*) and contrary to "nature" (*phusis*).[54] As in the Platonic tradition, in Stoicism desire is closely connected with excessive impulse, irrational desire, and with excessive sexual desires, cravings, and yearnings.[55] However, the understanding of the relationship between "desire" (*epithymia*) and "excessive" (*pleonazousa*) desire is debated among the Stoic philosophers. For instance, while Plato's doctrine of desire (*Gorg.* 505A) proposes the moderation of desire and passions (*metriopatheia*), the Stoics opt for *apatheia*, which means a radical solution for the eradication or extirpation of desire and other passions.[56] Stoic philosophers followed the tradition of Zeno of Citium, who viewed "passions" (*pathē*) as always "excessive impulses."[57] Diogenes Laertius writes, "Passions or emotion is defined by Zeno as an irrational and unnatural movement in the soul, or again as impulse in excess" (*hormē pleonazousa* [*Lives* 7.110]). What is consistently clear in Stoic terms is that

---

54. DL, *Lives* 7.110. In the Stoic tradition, the term "impulse" (*hormē*) is considered one of the faculties or "powers" (*dunameis*) of the soul. See Gourinat, "*Akrasia* and *Enkrateia*," 221.

55. Stobaeus, *Ecl.* 2.90.19–2.91.9 (*SVF* 3:394). Epictetus often links *epithymia* with the irrational appetite, which is insatiable and never to come to rest. See Bonhöffer, *Ethics*, 33.

56. Translations of Stoic texts are from Long and Sedley, *Hellenistic Philosophers*, unless otherwise noted.

57. Stobaeus, *Ecl.* 2.88.8–2.90.6. Long and Sedley, *Hellenistic Philosophers*, 1:410. For a description of the Stoics on the extirpation of the passions, see Nussbaum, *Theory of Desire*, 359–401.

epithymia is subversive and must be eradicated to completely liberate the soul from its passion.[58]

In the Stoic tradition, both desire and passion are considered as always inherently bad and associated with immoderate or irrational impulses. However, the key question for the Stoics is not only *how* to explain desire's nature, as Thomas H. Tobin has pointed out,[59] but also *what* causes excessive impulse or desire. Indeed, Posidonius challenges Chrysippus with the question, "What is the cause of the excessive impulse or desire?"[60] Certainly, for these Stoic philosophers, there was not a clear distinction between desire and excessive or irrational desire. For example, the Stoic Andronicus claims that excessive desire is "an irrational stretching desire,"[61] and Chrysippus, another Stoic thinker (third century BCE) influenced by Plato's ideas, views "the excess of impulse" as an impulse that is excessive if it goes beyond the natural limits of reason.[62] But Chrysippus's interpretation follows a different course in that unnaturalness (what is not natural) and irrationality (beyond the limits of reason) consist in the immoderation of movement. For most Stoics, passion is always an excessive, uncontrolled "impulse" (*hormē*) due to an overestimation of indifferent things; but Chrysippus believed that there is also a correct impulse towards these things.[63] The answer lies in what is natural and what is unnatural; he explains this "natural-versus-unnatural" approach by using the analogy of running. When people run, triggered by their impulse, the movement of their legs exceeds their impulse. It is then when they are carried away and are unable to change and obey "reason" (*logos*). On the footsteps of Chrysippus, the Roman philosopher Cicero (first century BCE) later identifies desire as sexual lust and an immoderate desire that disobeys reason.[64] In this sense, when someone has the impulse to do something, the individual is not obedient to reason; instead, the individual's irrational impulses go beyond the rational proportion. Thus, for Chrysippus, the "excess in running" is called

58. Weisser, "Perils of Philosophical Persuasion," 96–97.

59. Tobin, *Paul's Rhetoric*, 229; Long, *Hellenistic Philosophy*, 56–59, 179–209.

60. Galen, *Hip. et Plat.* 4.3.2–5 (Posidonius, fr. 34). See Long and Sedley, *Hellenistic Philosophers*, 1:414.

61. Andronicus, *Pass.* 1 (SVF 3:391). See Long and Sedley, *Hellenistic Philosophers*, 1:411.

62. Galen, *Hip. et Plat.* 4.2.10–18 (SVF 3:462); see also DL, *Lives* 7.111. See Long and Sedley, *Hellenistic Philosophers*, 1:413.

63. Sandbach, *Stoics*, 63.

64. Cicero, *Tusc.* 4.7.14; see also 3.11.24.

contrary to the impulse, but the excess in the impulse is called contrary to reason.⁶⁵ In Chrysippus, the excessive quantity of irrational impulse (the unnatural) is inherently bad (contrary to reason). Hence, like Plato's idea, it is the "excessive impulse" (*pleonazousa hormē*) that has to be eliminated, and desire needs to be trained.⁶⁶

It is important to know that in the Stoic doctrine of desire, *epithymia* is the source from which irrational or immoderate desire and impulse derive. However, the Stoic philosophers argue among themselves about *what* would be the best remedy for desire and passions and thus eradicate excessive impulse and/or desire.⁶⁷ According to Brad Inwood, the Stoic thinkers, influenced by Plato's ideas, emphasize the connection between moderation and reason, for their ethics demand that human beings achieve perfect virtue and act accordingly,⁶⁸ that is, in accord with nature. Similar to Plato's doctrine of the temperate life in moderation (*Leg.* 734A–C) to eliminate "tyrannical desire" (*erōs*),⁶⁹ the Stoics propose "temperance" (*sōphrosunē*), a primary virtue and opposite to the main vice of "lack of self-control" or "intemperance" (*akrasia*), as the virtue to keep the impulses and desires balanced.⁷⁰ Following the tradition of Plato, the Stoics offer their interpretation of how "reason" (*logos*) struggles against the dangers of irrational passions in the inner soul. This is observed in Chrysippus's writings when he states: The rational animal moves towards and away from certain things in

---

65. Galen, *Hip. et Plat.* 4.3.5–4.3.9. See Long and Sedley, *Hellenistic Philosophers*, 1:413.

66. This is an important point that Svebakken has overlooked. See Svebakken, *Philo of Alexandria's Exposition*, 71–80.

67. Galen, *Hip. et Plat.* 4.7.24–4.7.41 (Posidonius, fr. 165), 5.6.22–5.6.26 (Posidonius, fr. 162), 5.2.3–5.2.7 (Posidonius, fr. 163). See Long and Sedley, *Hellenistic Philosophers*, 1:416–17. Seneca, *Ira* 2.3.1–2.4.

68. Inwood, "Rules and Reasoning," 95.

69. Plato, *Resp.* 430E–431B, 440A–B; see also *Leg.* 647C–D.

70. Stobaeus, *Ecl.* 2.63.6–2.63.24 (*SVF* 3:280), 2.59.4–2.60.2, 2.60.9–2.60.24 (*SVF* 3:262, 264); Cicero, *Tusc.* 4.30–4.31. As Gourinat notes, while there is no definition of *akrasia* in the Stoic ethical systems, *enkrateia* is a subordinate virtue together with other four subordinate virtues—"endurance" (*karteria*), "high-mindedness" (*megalopsuchia*), "good sense" (*euboulia*), and "shrewdness" (*agchinoia*). Under the main or generic virtue *andreia* are endurance and high-mindedness; under *phronēsis* are good sense and shrewdness; and under *sōphrosunē* is the virtue of self-control. *Akrasia* (lack of self-control), then, must be subordinated to the corresponding vice, *akolasia* (intemperance). Gourinat, "*Akrasia* and *Enkrateia*," 219–20. Interestingly, in Stobaeus, we find a full list of nineteen subordinate virtues; Stobaeus also explains to which of the primary virtues each of the subordinate virtues is subordinated. Stobaeus, *Ecl.* 2.7.5 (*SVF* 3:264).

a different way and pushes to excess in disobedience to reason. Passions as "irrational" and as "excessive impulses" refer to this movement, the movement contrary to nature, which occurs irrationally in this way, and to the excess in impulses. This irrationality must be taken to mean "disobedient to reason" and "reason turned aside"; with reference to this movement, the Stoic philosophers also speak in ordinary language, such as "being pushed" and "move irrationally, without reason and judgment."[71] Whereas there is no substantial exposition on sexual desire in the Stoic tradition as we find in Plato and later in Philo, what is clear is that, for most Stoics, any kind of desire is not only a deadly and evil passion but an impulse that must be eradicated (*apatheia*).[72] It is in this context that Stoics view sexual intercourse as necessary for procreation, never for pleasure alone![73] In the Stoic doctrine, like the virtue of *sōphrosunē*, "temperance" or "self-control" relates to sexual pleasures as opposed to "endurance" (*karteria*)—two kinds of subordinate virtues corresponding to two main forms of impulse in the Stoic ethical system—"desire" (*epithymia*) and "lack of self-control" or "intemperance" (*akrasia*), too, come to be related to sexual desires. Likewise, "desire" (*epithymia*), like other passions of the soul, triggers all kinds of pleasures, sexual desires, appetites, and lusts. Chrysippus shows particularity in his position; like Plato, he calls for the eradication of excessive impulse/desire, immoderate passions, or irrational desires and pleasures *only*. Thus, I argue that like Plato, he identifies only the *excessive* quantity of sexual desire as evil.[74] Chrysippus views sexual desire as a good human feeling;[75] it is the excess that has to be eradicated.

---

71. Long and Sedley, *Hellenistic Philosophers*, 1:413.

72. E.g., Musonius Rufus, *Fr.* 12–13. See Loader, *New Testament on Sexuality*, 412.

73. Loader, *New Testament on Sexuality*, 412. Both Stoics, Musonius Rufus and Seneca, who follow the earlier Pythagorean view, reject sexual desire altogether as a passion; sex is only all right within marriage, and even then, only for the purpose of procreation. See Gaca, *Making of Fornication*, 92–93.

74. Chrysippus considers the "abstinence from ugly women . . . to be a case of self-control (it is abstinence from sexual pleasure), but not as remarkable and praiseworthy." As Gourinat notes, "This is what may be inferred from a comparison with an excerpt from Chrysippus's *On Zeus* quoted by Plutarch, *Stoic. rep.* 13.1039A." Gourinat, "*Akrasia* and *Enkrateia*," 230. For further study on Stoic view of sexual immorality, see Gaca, "Early Stoic Eros."

75. Later Stoics follow Chrysippus's view; for example, Antipater (of Tarsus, ca. 133 BCE, or of Tyre, ca. 50 BCE), Musonius, Hierocles, Seneca, and Epictetus. These philosophers emphasize rational sexual relations within marriage, and sexual desire becomes problematic only when driven by excess and self-indulgence. Ellis notes that

PHILO OF ALEXANDRIA: DESIRE, THE WORST OF ALL PASSIONS

Philo of Alexandria, or Philo Judaeus, was a Hellenistic Jewish writer and philosopher who lived between the end of the first century BCE and the middle of the first century CE.[76] In his writings, Philo interprets the Jewish Scripture (the LXX), especially the Pentateuch, allegorically and using philosophical concepts and doctrines. He lived in the great ancient *polis* of Alexandria, Egypt, and he belonged to one of the wealthiest Jewish families in Alexandria. Philo had a privileged position that allowed him to receive probably the best Jewish and Greek educations of his time, as well as to be involved in political affairs on behalf of the Jews living in Alexandrian Greek diaspora.[77] Anyone who reads his treatises acknowledges the complexity and philosophical sophistication of his biblical interpretation within the Jewish and Greek traditions. Philo is considered a brilliant, first-century Hellenistic Jewish author, a contemporary of Jesus, Paul, and Rabbi Gamaliel, and certainly a good representative of Hellenistic Judaism. Significantly, most of his treatises were preserved by early Christians, not Jews.[78] In his writings, we can perceive great similarities in themes and concepts with those found in the New Testament books, especially in the Epistle to the Hebrews, the Gospel of John, Paul's letters, and the Gospel of Luke.[79]

Influenced by philosophical traditions, Philo gives great importance to the term "desire" (*epithymia*) and its cognates in his ethical discourse; particularly, this connection is explicit in his Allegory Commentary and the Exposition of the Law Series.[80] The noun *epithymia* itself is a common word; it is used 218 times! In the fourth book of *Special Laws*, which is devoted to virtues, the word appears twenty-two times more than in any

---

condemnations of sexual desire are quite rare in ancient philosophies. Far more common are condemnations of sexual immorality (in various forms) and excessive desire. Ellis, *Paul and Ancient Views*, 95. For full discussion, see 99–146.

76. Lévy, "Philo of Alexandria."
77. See Philo, *Embassy to Gaius*.
78. Runia, *Early Christian Literature*, 17–31.
79. Runia, *Early Christian Literature*, 63–82; Klauck, "Heilige Stadt"; Naveros Córdova, *God's Presence in Creation*.
80. In the Philonic corpus, the verbal form *epithymeō* appears fifteen times (*Leg.* 3.211, 3.250; *Sacr.* 24; *Migr.* 155; *Somn.* 2.266; *Ios.* 144, 216; *Mos.* 1.13; *Decal.* 136, 142; *Spec.* 3.66, 4.78, 4.90; *Praem.* 71; *QG* 4.173); the adjective *epithymētikos* ten times (*Leg.* 1.70 [3x], 71 [2x], 72 [2x]; 2.18; 3.115 [2x]) and *epithymētos* once (*Leg.* 3.250); and the noun *epithymēma* also once (*Conf.* 50); See Borgen et al., *Philo Index*, 141.

other Philonic work.[81] The word "desire" and cognates are quite common in Philo's Greek LXX, especially in 4 Maccabees,[82] a book highly influenced by Greek philosophy as we shall see below.[83] What is paramount for our purpose is the connection that exists between Philo's understanding of desire and the various interpretations of the concept studied in the traditions of Plato, the Stoics, and also Middle Platonist Plutarch.[84] Such connection is later reflected in Paul's view of desire when he deals with the vice of idolatry and sexual vices commonly practiced in the pagan world (see ch. 2).

In his definition of *epithymia*, Philo shows substantial knowledge of the Stoic doctrine of "passions" (*pathē*). According to him, desire is one of the four passions of the soul (desire, pleasure, grief, and fear). In his treatment of the tenth commandment, *ouk epithymēseis* (*Spec.* 4.78b–4.131),[85] Philo defines desire Stoically when he writes in his treatise, *On the Decalogue*, that desire is "subversive and enemy of the soul" (*Decal.* 142), and in the *Special Laws* 4 when he states that desire is the "most trouble and evil of all the passions" (*Spec.* 4.80).[86] Philo knows the Stoic interpretation of the dangers of desire, so he exhorts his audience "not to desire, because desire is the most difficult of all the passions" (*Leg.* 3.250; *QG* 2.37). Philo not only recognizes the evil nature of desire like the Stoics; he likewise connects desire with vices and pleasures of the body. Describing the nature of

81. *Spec.* 4.10, 80, 81, 82, 83, 84, 85, 86, 89, 92, 93, 95, 96, 113 [2x], 118, 129, 130, 131, 132, 215, 217.

82. E.g., *epithymein* in Wis 6:11, 13; 16:3; Prov 21:26; 23:3, 6; 10:24; 24:1; *epithymētos* in Wis 8:5; Prov 21:20; *epithymia* in Wis 4:12; 6:17 (2x), 20; 16:2, 21; 19:11; Prov 6:25; 10:25; 11:23; 12:12; 13:4, 12, 19; 21:25, 26; 4 Macc 1:3, 22, 31, 32; 2:1, 4, 5; 3:2 (2x), 11, 12 (2x), 16; 5:23. Hatch and Redpath, *Concordance to the Septuagint*, 1:520-21. For an overview of the use of *epithymeō* and *epithymia* in the LXX, see Bowden, *Desire*, 237–40.

83. In the Pentateuch, however, that part of the Greek Bible on which Philo almost exclusively focuses his exegetical interpretations, the term occurs eleven times only (Gen 31:30; 49:6; Num 11:4, 34, 35; 33:16, 17; Deut 9:22; 12:15, 20, 21) and its cognates fourteen times (Gen 31:30; 49:14; Exod 20:17 [2x]; 34:24; Num 11:4, 34; 16:15; Deut 5:21; 7:25; 12:20; 14:26 [2x]; 18:6).

84. For good studies on this topic, see Naveros Córdova, "Worst of the Passions."

85. See also *Decal.* 142–153, 173–174. Svebakken argues against Wolfson, who claims that Philo's tenth commandment deals only with desire for what belongs to another person. Svebakken, *Philo of Alexandria's Exposition*, 20–31. His argument opposes the argument of Gaca, who asserts that Philo understands the tenth commandment exclusively as a prohibition of sexual desire. When Philo hears the words "you shall not desire," he has in mind physical appetite, especially sexual appetite. Gaca, *Making of Fornication*, 196.

86. Translations of Philo come from Naveros Córdova, *Philo of Alexandria*; *Philo* (Colson and Whitaker).

epithymia, Philo states Platonically that desire must be moderated because uncontrolled desire can lead to "tyrannical desire" (*erōs*), "irrational desire" (*alogos epithymia*), and "immoderate desire" (*ametros epithymia*). Thus, in light of the traditions of Plato and the Stoics, Philo argues that to eliminate excessive desire and irrational impulses, the individual must control the passion of desire. It is important to note that Philo's definition of desire is expressed within the parameters of the Stoic doctrine of passions, and his description of desire is done within the parameters of Platonic interpretation of desire.

Desire and Its Sequels: Tyrannical and Irrational Desire

Stoically, Philo distinguishes each passion's negative characteristics and describes the human soul being trapped in passions. But he also Platonizes passions when he uses Plato's example of the mythical figure of Tantalus, who experiences desire without satisfaction (Plato, *Crat.* 395E), to represent the soul's miserable condition under the control of *epithymia* (*Crat.* 419B–E). It is in this context that Philo attributes to desire the quality of "tyrannical," representing Platonically the intrinsic evil nature of desire, which is also the Stoic position. When speaking of passion or desire, Philo considers the dangers of desire blameworthy (*Spec.* 4.79a) and stresses the notion that desire can become tyrannical (*Spec.* 4.113b). Clearly, the passion of desire in all its evil forms entailed a grievous slavery on the individual (*Her.* 271). Like Plato, the Alexandrian exegete believes that the cravings of desire, including sexual impulse and desire, can occupy the human "mind" (*nous*), which eagerly tries to satisfy them. What is dangerous for the soul is to become dominated and governed by unsatisfied or excessive (sexual) desire. This idea is explained by Plato's Socrates (see above). What is consistent in Philo is that "desire" (*epithymia*) is viewed Stoically as subversive and must be controlled to completely liberate the individual from excessive desire and immoderate impulses. Platonically, desire can become tyrannical and irrational without its moderation or control.

In Philo, desire is certainly a dangerous problem; it is the worst of all the passions, and if it is not controlled, it can lead to "excessive impulse" (*pleonazousa hormē*), "irrational desire" (*alogos epithymia*), "tyrannical desire" (*erōs*), and/or "immoderate desire" (*ametros epithymia*). Against the backdrop of Stoicism and Platonism, Philo shows how desire and passions are aroused by another bad passion: "love of pleasure" (*philēdonia*). In the

Allegorical Interpretation 3, for example, he claims that "desire comes into play through love of pleasure" and that "all the passions depend on pleasure" (*Leg.* 3.113). When desire overpowers the human soul, it leads the soul to pollution and the enslavement of the "mind" (*nous*).[87] In this way the impulse of irrational desire oversteps the bounds of "reason" (*logos*), and it is at this point that reason becomes a tyrant and irrational.[88] In his exposition of the tenth commandment (*ouk epithymēseis*), Philo articulates the detrimental dangers of irrational/excessive or tyrannical desire in a series of statements, which are in continuity with the tradition of Platonic interpretation. He writes,

> Desire breeds fierce and endless yearnings. . . . Desire constantly eluded and deprived struggles in vain, bringing the punishment of Tantalus on the wretched soul . . . that wretch who could never quench his thirst because the water withdraws every time he tried to take a drink. In the same way, whenever he reached for some fruit on the nearby trees, it all disappeared, making barren the fertility of the trees. For just as those unmerciful and relentless mistresses of the body, hunger and thirst, torture it with pains as great as, or greater than, those of the sufferers on the tormentor's wheel . . . desire makes the soul empty through oblivion of what is present, and then through memory of what is far away it produces fierce desire and ungovernable madness, and thus creates mistresses harsher than those just mentioned though bearing the same name, hunger and thirst. (*Spec.* 4.80–4.82)[89]

What is dangerous for Philo is that the passion of *epithymia* remains active in a state of continual arousal and in pursuit of bodily pleasures (*Spec.* 4.86–4.89). On the footsteps of the philosophical traditions of Plato and the Stoics, Philo views the excessive quantity or impulse of irrational desire as always inherently bad. He explains this condition using a plant metaphor in the *Allegorical Interpretation* 3 when he writes, "Using figures, he has given the name of thorny plants, which the irrational impulse, like a fire, meets first, and ranging herself with them burns up and consumes all the soul's possessions. . . . You see that the fire, the irrational impulse, when it has broken out does not set on fire the thorny plants but finds them. For being a seeker after the passions it finds what it desired to get" (*Leg.* 3.248–3.249).

---

87. Philo, *Prob.* 159; *Decal.* 151; *Ios.* 70; *Spec.* 4.127–4.130.
88. Philo, *Leg.* 2.91, 3.80; *Conf.* 164; *Her.* 245; *Agr.* 45–46; *Abr.* 242; *Prob.* 45.
89. See also Philo, *Gig.* 18; *Post.* 116; *Decal.* 149.

Philo's understanding of "excessive" (*pleonazousa*) is not only represented within the Platonic and Middle Platonic traditions, but it is also in continuity with the Stoic tradition (especially Chrysippus). Even though Philo's definition of desire is certainly Stoic, he does not encourage the elimination of desire because for him some human desires are good, e.g., desire to eat, desire to drink, desire for knowledge, desire for education, desire for sex, and desire in general. Indeed, sex and sexual desire in marriage are good and for procreation only.[90] As William Loader argues, Philo's objection is "uncontrolled and excessive passions" (e.g., *Leg.* 3.113–3.114; *Mut.* 72; *Spec.* 1.191).[91]

Philo proposes the "moderation of passions" (*metriopatheia*) as philosophers do in the Platonic and Middle Platonic traditions. In fact, Philo believes what must be eliminated is the excessive quantity of irrational impulse and passions that goes beyond the bounds of "reason" (*logos*). Like Plato (*Gorg.* 491D–E; *Symp.* 187D–E) and Middle Platonist Plutarch (*Mor.* 44C, 447D), Philo emphasizes both the "moderation of passions" (*metriopatheia*) and the eradication of the excessive quantity of passions.[92] He develops his theory of moderation of desire using philosophical language in light of the Greek ethical systems of Plato and the Stoics.[93] Philo promotes the practice of "self-control" (*enkrateia*)—the virtue opposite to "intemperance" or "lack of self-control" (*akrasia*)—and advocates sexual continence to control unrestrained pleasures and excessive desire. He considers sexual pleasure and desire in marriage as good and God's gift and views the irrational or excessive sexual desire/passion as sinful, and thus in need to be controlled.[94] Philo is aware of the ethical benefits of *enkrateia*;

---

90. Philo, *Opif.* 152; *Cher.* 43; *Her.* 164; *Abr.* 248–250; *Mos.* 1.28; *Spec.* 1.112, 3.113; *Virt.* 207; *Praem.* 139; *QG* 2.49; *Anim.* 48. On sex for procreation only, see Niehoff, *Philo on Jewish Identity*, 100–102.

91. Also Philo, *Det.* 112, 174; *Her.* 269; *Post.* 71; *Contempl.* 6; Loader, *New Testament on Sexuality*, 80–81.

92. Philo clarifies that the highest ideal for him is "insensibility" (*apatheia*), but he says that is reserved for the exceptional few, like Moses. For the majority of people, however, moderation or *metriopatheia* is sufficient (*Leg.* 3.129, 3.131–3.132, 3.144; *Abr.* 257; *Virt.* 195; *Leg.* 2.100, 2.102; *Plant.* 98; *Migr.* 67). See also Dillon, "Pleasures and Perils," 191.

93. For a Stoic catalog of virtues and vices, see DL, *Lives* 7.92–7.93 (*SVF* 3:265); Stobaeus, *Ecl.* 2.7 (*SVF* 3:264). See also Gourinat, "*Akrasia* and *Enkrateia*," 217; Jedan, *Stoic Virtues*, 158–59, 162–73. For a Platonic catalog of virtues, see *Resp.* 441C; *Leg.* 631C–D, 688A–B, 963A–965E; *Gorg.* 525. For an Aristotelian catalog of virtues and vices, see *Eth. nic.* 2.71107b–2.71108b1–10; *Eth. eud.* 2.2.1220b1—7.1223b1; *Rhet.* 1.1366b1–3.

94. E.g., Philo, *Opif.* 161–164, 158; *Leg.* 3.107; *Cher.* 71; *Prob.* 17–18, 151; *Sacr.* 26, 32,

for Stoic philosophers (e.g., Chrysippus), it is clear that this subordinate virtue consists of the capacity to abstain from pleasures, predominantly sexual pleasure and desires, and presumably also desires linked to food and drink.[95] This Greek virtue (self-control) is the opposite of desire; therefore, self-control has the power to both moderate desire and eradicate excessive impulses and desires. For Philo, bad or excessive desire is profane, unclean, and unholy, and can drive the individual away beyond the boundaries of virtue and reason. Hence, he sees the virtue of self-control as profitable for the individual's progress in the moderation of *epithymia*. To practice and acquire self-control, however, one must toil hard to achieve the greatest and the most perfect goodness (*Spec.* 1.149–1.150).[96]

Desire and Gluttony: Two Close "Friends"

When Philo describes the opposite characteristics of "desire" (*epithymia*) and "self-control" (*enkrateia*) in *Spec.* 1.149–1.150, he associates desire with the pleasures of the belly. He is faithful to the Platonic tradition (*Tim.* 70D–71A); but he also brings to the fore the dangers of "gluttony" (*gastrimargia*), an unchecked indulgence and a dangerous vice that stems from immoderate desire and pleasures of the belly. On the footsteps of Plato, Philo, too, develops a threefold relationship between "desire" (*epithymia*), "belly" (*koilia/gastera*), and "tongue" (*glōtta*). In *Migration of Abraham*, Philo states Platonically that "desire dwells in the belly" (*Migr.* 66),[97] and in *Special Laws* 4 he describes how "desire makes its way to the tongue and causes an infinity of troubles" (*Spec.* 4.90). When in activity, this threefold relationship (desire-belly-tongue) produces gluttony, which Philo calls "the most disgraceful pleasure" (*Ebr.* 222; *Spec.* 2.46; *QG* 4.234). As in Aristotle, Plato, and the Stoics, in Philo gluttony has two close "friends": food

---

105; *Her.* 245; *Ebr.* 101–102, 220; *Det.* 174, 176; *Somn.* 2.147; *Gig.* 44; *Fug.* 28, 153; *Abr.* 100, 148–149; *Ios.* 40–41; *Mos.* 1.296–1.297; *Spec.* 1.192, 1.282; *Agr.* 148, 153; *Migr.* 217; *Decal.* 142, 150, 173; *Spec.* 1.9, 2.163, 3.9, 3.33–3.36, 3.65–3.70, 3.79–3.81, 4.83–4.85, 4.79; *Virt.* 13, 28–31, 112; *Hypoth.* 6.10—7.20; *QG* 1.10, 1.28–1.29, 1.94, 2.1, 2.3, 2.46, 2.49, 3.41, 3.48, 4.154, 4.234; *Leg.* 2.71–2.74; *Cher.* 59, 113; *Plant.* 169; *Leg.* 3.140; *Migr.* 7, 9; *Agr.* 17; *Spec.* 1.173, 1.343, 3.9, 4.95. For a detailed analysis of these texts, see Loader, *New Testament on Sexuality*, 56–258.

95. Gourinat, "*Akrasia* and *Enkrateia*," 230.

96. See also Philo, *Spec.* 4.92–4.94.

97. See also Philo, *Mos.* 1.160–1.162; *Spec.* 1.168–1.182.

and drink (*Somn.* 2.155).⁹⁸ But the problem is not their close relationship; instead, the ethical issue is when the pleasure of eating becomes the desire to eat (*Virt.* 136–137), or in Platonic terms tyrannical desire (*Spec.* 4.100). Philo's philosophical view of irrational desire in connection with gluttony reveals an important ethical problem in discussion: that of immoderate sexual desire. Skillfully, Philo adopts the Stoic interpretation where sexual desire is classified under desire (Stobaeus, *Ecl.* 2.90.19–2.91.9 [*SVF* 3:394]), but his description of it is presented in Platonic terms (*Phaedr.* 237D–238E).

What is key in Philo is that the vice of gluttony is the gateway to sexual immorality and vices. He clearly states, "Gluttony is naturally followed by her attendant, sexual pleasure, bringing on extraordinary madness, fierce desire, and most grievous frenzy" (*Agr.* 37).⁹⁹ Philo follows further Plato's interpretation of "tyrannical desire" (*erōs*) and "passionate desire" (*pleonazousa [ametros] epithymia*) to denote the intrinsic connection between the indulgence in sexual pleasures and uncontrollable eating. In Philo's thought, the process of controlling daily diet (food and drink), for example, is a training that enhances a discipline of self-control or temperance.¹⁰⁰ Since certain animals (e.g., pigs) "provide a very appetizing and delectable repast" (*Spec.* 4.103), they can arouse a person's desires and produce gluttony (*Somn.* 2.155, 2.215).¹⁰¹ Philo argues that Moses was acting in the best interests of the Jews when he forbade them to eat pig, "the most delicious of the meats" (*Spec.* 4.101). In Philo, the practice of the food laws as part of the whole of the ethical commandments has the moral purpose of "improving the character of an individual" (*Spec.* 4.100–4.118).¹⁰²

---

98. See also Philo, *Somn.* 2.156–2.169, 2.181–2.184; Aristotle, *Eth. nic.* 3.5.1147b25–29. According to Vernon, for Aristotle, "People who first love themselves will then be able to love others, but he does not mean self-lovers in the sense of bodily pleasures. The kind of self-lover whom he thinks are those who desire what is best for themselves in terms of virtuous habits such as being just and moderate." Vernon, "Plato," 206.

99. See also Philo, *Leg.* 3.140–3.144; *Det.* 113; *Post.* 180; *Agr.* 37–38; *Congr.* 80; *Abr.* 133–136, 147–150; *Ios.* 26; *Mos.* 1.160–1.162; *Spec.* 2.49–2.50, 3.9–3.10, 4.85, 4.93–4.94, 4.100–4.101, 4.127–4.128; *Virt.* 136–137; *Contempl.* 55–56; *Prov.* 2.18–2.20; *QG* 2.46.

100. Philo, *Spec.* 4.100; *Somn.* 1.93–1.94; *QG* 4.167. In *Leg.* 1.69, self-control is the third virtue and takes the stand against pleasure/desire within Philo's "tripartite soul" (reasoning part: prudence; assertive part: courage; and desirous part: self-control). Philo follows the Middle Platonic view of the moderation of desires; as such, individuals can be under the control of "reason" (*logos*). See Wolfson, *Philo*, 2.228–29.

101. See also Philo, *Spec.* 1.50, 150; *Virt.* 134–144; *Contempl.* 55–56.

102. Philo sees the discipline of keeping the food laws as the moderation of desire; for him, such dietary regulations demonstrate Jewish superiority.

Philo is part of the philosophical discussions of passions and desires and is acquainted with self-control and its beauty to restrain irrational passions, gluttony, and immoderate sexual appetites. In light of Plato's tradition, Philo develops a link between self-control and both philosophy and the threefold relationship (desire-belly-tongue) in connection with improper sexual desire. He makes an interesting statement in his treatise *Preliminary Studies*: "Philosophy teaches self-control of the belly, self-control of the parts below the belly [genitals], and also self-control of the tongue" (*Congr.* 80). Attuned to the views of other Hellenistic Jewish writers (e.g., 4 Maccabees and the Letter of Aristeas),[103] he is aware of the ethical benefits of the practice of Moses's prescriptions of the food laws (*Spec.* 4.78b–4.131).[104] As an observant Hellenistic Jew and faithful to his Jewish tradition, Philo develops a doctrine grounded in his religion, Judaism. He describes the Mosaic law as the best law, indeed, equal to the natural law,[105] in order to present Judaism and its laws as more attractive than other Greek laws. Philo is able to either reconcile, or, as Cesar Motta Rios claims, "negotiate" with the complexities of his Hellenistic world.[106] The Mosaic approach provides the best course to practice self-control and acquire moderation of desire and the elimination of passionate, immoderate, or irrational desire. Philo's doctrine of moderation promotes a midway between the life of austerity and a life of daintiness to moderate "desire" (*epithymia*) and create a life of harmony and integrity (*Spec.* 4.102).[107] Through "practice" (*askēsis*), the human soul engages "reason" (*logos*) in a struggle against irrational desire

---

103. Let. Aris. 128–171. This Hellenistic Jewish literature, although important, is not addressed in this study because the term *epithymia* appears few times and is not used in the ethical sense. For this reason, the Letter to Aristeas will be mentioned when it is necessary only. For discussion, see Hadas, *Aristeas to Philocrates*; Svebakken, "Exegetical Traditions in Alexandria."

104. For a full exposition on Philo's tenth commandment, see Svebakken, *Philo of Alexandria's Exposition*, 109–83.

105. For studies on Philo's natural law, see Sterling, "Universalizing the Particular"; Vander Waerdt, "Original Theory"; Termini, "Dal Sinai alla creazione"; Koester, "ΝΟΜΟΣ ΦΥΣΕΩΣ"; Horsley, "Law of Nature."

106. Motta Rios argues that in his encounter with the larger world, Philo does not intend to reconcile Judaism with the "other" as some scholars have argued. Rather, Philo is engaged in what Motta Rios calls "tense intercultural negotiation" about what is his own (Jewishness) and what is common with the other. Motta Rios, "Philo of Alexandria." Scholars who suggest that Philo intends to reconcile both traditions are Sandmel, *Philo of Alexandria*, 4; Daniélou, *Philon d'Alexandrie*, 12; Winston, "Judaism and Hellenism."

107. See also Philo, *Opif.* 81; *Leg.* 2.23, 3.118; *Deus* 44; *Decal.* 153.

to obtain practical exercises of a positive command (eat clean animals), and thus inculcate "self-control" (*enkrateia*).[108] According to Philo's Moses, when the person avoids eating the meat of an unclean animal (e.g., wild beasts, pigs, and scaleless sea animals),[109] the irrational part of the soul is trained to literally avoid the temptation to immoderate passions, pleasures, and desires.

Two Opposite Powers: Reason and Desire

In the quest for moderation of "desire" (*epithymia*), the soul, with the help of reason, attains "self-control" (*enkrateia*) through the practice of the Jewish food laws. Philo, similar to Chrysippus and Plutarch (*Mor.* 449A),[110] allegorically depicts the internal struggle between two "enemies," reason and desire. These are two opposite powers fighting aggressively in the inner soul; if the dominant irrational power (desire) pushes, reason (*logos*), the rational power, pushes back; if chased, reason turns and charges.[111] Elsewhere Philo similarly emphasizes this struggle using the language of slavery; the soul "is driven toward desire or enticed by pleasure or turned away by fear, or shrunken by grief or overpowered by anger, it enslaves itself, and makes his soul a slave to a host of masters" (*Post.* 159).[112] He interprets these conflicting powers (reason *versus* desire) as symbols representing two powerful enemies, the lover of pleasure fighting against self-control and endurance, two important virtues in the Greek catalog of virtues.[113] For

---

108. In *Spec.* 4.103–4.117, Philo expounds in detail the ethical benefits to practice self-control. Stowers, "Paul and Self-Mastery."

109. Philo emphasizes the literal significance of unclean/savage/carnivorous and clean/gentle/herbivorous animals. When the human soul avoids eating the meat of an unclean animal, the irrational part of the soul is trained to literally avoid the temptation to passions and desires (*Spec.* 4.106–4.107). In *Spec.* 4.110–4.112, according to Philo, Moses identified aquatic animals permissible to eat as those that are distinguished by two signs, fins and scales. In *Spec.* 4.113–4.117, Philo asserts that Moses rejected those reptiles that have no feet and are four legged or many footed as unclean for eating, and birds that prey on other animals and/or human beings, those that are carnivorous, venomous, and those that use aggressive force of any kind.

110. Long and Sedley, *Hellenistic Philosophers*, 1:413.

111. Philo, *Leg.* 1.107–1.108; *Somn.* 2.276; *Spec.* 4.111; *Opif.* 79.

112. In some allegorical passages, Philo employs the language of the death of the rational faculty where passions and desires kill the soul (*Post.* 73; *Leg.* 3.52–3.53, 3.74). For discussion, see Wasserman, *Death of the Soul*, 63–64.

113. For a list of virtues and analysis of the Stoics' catalog of virtues in relation to Plato's virtues, see Jedan, *Stoic Virtues*, 81–93.

Philo, while the first (love of pleasure) is the easy road leading downhill until the soul reaches the lowest depths, the second (self-control/endurance) is uphill and a hard path leading to moderation. Although difficult, the second path is beneficial for the soul's reason to find the midway path.

Furthermore, Philo allegorically explains the process of how to control *epithymia*, giving emphasis on how the human soul is to become a virtue-loving soul, rather than a "lover of pleasure" (*Leg.* 1.90–1.106).[114] Therefore, when Philo defines the meaning of true "eating" (food and drink)—the two most essential necessities of the body (*Ios.* 154; *Mos.* 1.184; *Opif.* 38)—he declares that true "eating" is to eat "for food," not just "simply eat" (*Leg.* 1.99).[115] In this way, the soul finds true nourishment by "reason" (*logos*), which is necessary for the acquisition of virtues (*Leg.* 1.101).[116] Philo further explains that "eating for food" is when the soul eats like "an athlete does," that is, "masticates slowly" (*Leg.* 1.97–1.98). The act of "masticate slowly" is viewed by Philo as the training of the human soul to become virtuous. For him, this is the real meaning of God's command: "You shall eat 'for food'" in Gen 2:16. Allegorically, "eat" is a symbol for the nourishment of the soul, and the eating "for food" is the way the virtue-loving soul controls desires, passions, and vices by reason (*Leg.* 1.59). According to Philo, when the individual "washes out the entire belly," that is, overcomes the pleasures of the body through the practice of "self-control" (*enkrateia*), the perfect soul lives a life of virtue (e.g., piety) and is alive only to this life (*Leg.* 1.106). Likewise, for Philo, when the soul is overcome by the body's pleasures, the soul dies to the life of virtue and is alive only to that of vice.

Philo's doctrine of the moderation of *epithymia* has a twofold "goal" (*telos*): piety and immortality. Philo sees the contrast between gluttony (the "mother" of sexual desires and pleasures) and the benefits of piety: "To eat and drink . . . without delay would show gluttony, but refrain from taking

---

114. According to Tobin, Philo's allegorical interpretation of Gen 2–3 (*Leg.* 1–3) contains an inherent moral component at the very heart of "the allegory of the soul." Tobin writes, "It has to do with the way in which the human soul should function as it was intended by God, what it must do to live according to nature and to become more like God, to function in a way that leads to virtue and how it can avoid temptations to act otherwise." Tobin, "Philo's *Legum Allegoriae*," 19.

115. A similar take is found in Cynicism, where the principle of "living according to virtue" meant that "we should live frugally, eating food for nourishment only." It is said that some Cynics "at all events are vegetarians and drink cold water only" (DL, *Lives* 6.104).

116. Naveros Córdova, *Ethical Discourse*, 130.

them as food is an expression of piety" (*Spec.* 2.197).[117] In this sense, "piety" (*eusebeia*) teaches the mind not to put trust in what already stands prepared before the individual, as though it were the source of a healthy life. In his ethical teaching, Philo views "self-control" (*enkrateia*)—a subordinate virtue to the main virtue of "temperance" (*sōphrosunē*)—as a key virtue for achieving Jewish piety, the queen of all the other virtues (*Decal.* 52). He writes, "Moses . . . bridled them with ordinances, which are the best guide to self-control and to love of humanity and what is the greatest of all, piety" (*Spec.* 4.97).[118] The need to turn away from bodily self-indulgence in all kinds of passions and desires is a hopeful expectation, so that the person might live in truth and discipline and thus attain "true excellence" (*Spec.* 4.131b). Hence, Philo's exposition of clean reptiles that "leap from the ground" (*Spec.* 4.114) is a symbolic representation of the human soul's ability to move upward and free the soul's reason from enslavement to desire and to reach immortality.[119] There is, therefore, an ethical motive why individuals must practice self-control to avoid excessive (sexual) desire. In the context of the Platonic goal of life, "becoming like to God" (*homoiōsis theō*),[120] in Philo the human soul trained in self-control can certainly escape the body's passions and desires and ultimately reach God's heavenly realm (*Her.* 239).

4 MACCABEES: REASON, THE MASTER OF DESIRE

In the book of 4 Maccabees in the LXX (first century BCE–first century CE) the anonymous author provides a vivid account of the terrible time that the Jewish people faced under the control of the Seleucid kingdom, especially under Antiochus IV Epiphanes (175–164 BCE).[121] Using philosophical language, the author shows how through "reason" (*logismos*) and

---

117. See also Philo, *Abr.* 133–136, 150; *Spec.* 4.124; *Prov.* 2.70.

118. See also Philo, *Somn.* 2.186; *Mos.* 1.146; *Abr.* 60; *Mut.* 76; *Decal.* 100, 119; *Spec.* 4.135, 4.147; *Virt.* 95; *Praem.* 53; *QG* 1.10; *QE* 2.15b, 2.38a. For studies on Philo's treatment of piety, see Naveros Córdova, *Ethical Discourse*; Sterling, "Queen of the Virtues."

119. Philo, *Spec.* 4.114a; *Opif.* 164; *Leg.* 2.105.

120. Plato, *Min.* 88C; *Resp.* 613B; *Theaet.* 176–177A.

121. For the sake of consistency and since the author is unknown, I use "he," "the author," or the "author of 4 Maccabees." For a good commentary on 4 Maccabees and bibliography, see DeSilva, *4 Maccabees*; Hadas, *Books of Maccabees*; Collins, *Between Athens and Jerusalem*, 202–9; Barclay, *Jews in the Mediterranean*, 369–80. For a general overview on the ethics of 4 Maccabees, see Thompson, *Moral Formation*, 23–30.

faithfulness to the observance of the food laws, Eleazar, the seven brothers, and their mother are able to conquer torture and martyrdom and ultimately champion eternal life.[122] The book's topic centers its argument on the statement "Reason is the absolute master of the passions" (1:1).[123] DeSilva points out that passions are seen to cover a broad range of human experiences, including desires, emotional responses, and sensations, whether pleasurable or painful.[124] Andrew Bowden, who studied the semantics of desire and its functions in the argument and context of 4 Maccabees, explains that desire in the semantic level is associated with the passion script and also scripts of law and victory. Following the Platonic tradition of interpretations, "passion" (*pathos*) is what needs to be mastered, law is what enables this mastery, and victory entails control over passions rather than extirpation or annihilation.[125] The Greek term *logismos* is often used in Stoic texts to denote the human rational faculty as opposed to the passion of *thumos* (1:24), which refers to violent surges of desires, an equivalent of the Stoics' "governing faculty" (*to hēgemonikon*).[126] The question at stake is: How is the relationship between desire/passions/sexual vices and reason represented? Although the author does not give a detailed account of a sexual doctrine per se, the passion of desire holds a preeminent place in his account of the story of Eleazar, the seven brothers, and their mother.[127] The author speaks of passions and desires of both the body and the soul (1:20, 32) and identifies

---

122. See also 2 Macc 6–7. Barclay, *Jews in the Mediterranean*, 369; Collins, *Between Athens and Jerusalem*, 206. Unlike Philo, who views the food laws as a "moderation" (*enkrateia*) of "passion" (*pathos*), for the author of 4 Maccabees, the Jewish food laws have symbolic meanings that assimilate to the Stoics' view, the eradication of all pleasures and desires. The food laws teach the Jews self-control so that with the guidance of and obedience to the divine law, Jews overcome all pleasures and desires. The author uses the example of Eleazar, the seven brothers, and their mother to explain two things: that "reason" (*logismos*) dominates the emotions and all vices; and that *logismos* guides the virtues of courage and endurance, which led to the downfall of the Seleucid king Antiochus IV. Reason prevails over all passions, even over love for parents and children (2:9–14); the author emphasizes the role of the law and its compatibility with reason (7:7–10).

123. See also 4 Macc 1:7, 13; 2:7, 9. Translations of 4 Maccabees are from Pietersma and Wright, *New English Translation*.

124. DeSilva 4 *Maccabees*, 68. In his argument, Aune explains the four Stoic passions in 4 Maccabees and argues that the author's way of classifying passions is unique. Aune, "Mastery of Passions," 135.

125. Bowden, "Semantic Investigation," 409–24.

126. DeSilva, *4 Maccabees*, 69.

127. Barclay, *Jews in the Mediterranean*, 373; Collins, *Between Athens and Jerusalem*, 208.

sexual pleasures and desires as the passions of the body. However, reason can master the desires whether they are of the body or the soul (1:32).

Passions and Gluttony

At the beginning of the book, the author mentions the four Stoic passions of the soul: pleasure, desire, fear, and grief (1:22–28). The author classifies "desire" (*epithymia*) as the first passion when he writes, "Before pleasure comes desire" (1:22) and defines *epithymia* as the passion hindering self-control (1:3).[128] Both pleasures and desires are closely related to each other; indeed, Bowen rightly argues that desire belongs to the category of pleasure.[129] Passions and desires are, like in Plato and Philo, connected with the vice of "gluttony" (*gastrimargia* [1:3, 27–28]).[130] Although Bowden rightly notes that mastery of the physical desire is shown within the context of food, he does not develop the theme of gluttony in his argument.[131] In his presentation on the question of how desire can be defeated, the author of 4 Maccabees, like Philo, follows the Hellenistic Jewish tradition by highlighting the close relationship between the Mosaic law and reason.[132] Together, they represent the ideal weapon to defeat desire and its negative sequels. Specifically, the author claims that the practice of the food laws is meant to gain control of gluttony and desires through the power of reason (1:3) and the divine law (2:14).[133] Within the philosophical tradition, excessive eating, gluttony, and private gormandizing are presented as dangerous pleasures that jeopardize the cardinal virtues of justice, prudence, self-control, and the most important virtue, piety. The generic virtue of "prudence" or

---

128. Bowden, "Semantic Investigation," 414.

129. Bowden, "Semantic Investigation," 414–15.

130. Prov 23:6; Wis 16:2–3; 19:11. For a full analysis of Wisdom's reception in 16:1–4 of Num 11 LXX (Israel's desire for meat), see Bowden, *Desire*, 296–301.

131. See Bowden, "Semantic Investigation," 415.

132. The practice of the law takes a main role in the author's description of the mastering of desire. According to Redditt, the law is mentioned forty times, and it is presented in a way that reflects a method of teaching rational living. Redditt shows five functions of the law in 4 Maccabees: (1) to teach Jewish culture; (2) to enable rational living; (3) to encourage faithful perseverance in persecution; (4) to condemn or justify people for their behavior; and (5) to give commands for right living. Redditt, "Concept of Nomos."

133. In Ben Sirah's prayer (23:4–6), where the author asks for the removal of shameless passions from him, evil desire and gluttony are closely connected with sexual desire or lust.

"practical wisdom" (*phronēsis*), explains the author, signifies the ability to discern what is required for virtue in any context and to choose it.[134] Similar to the catalog of virtues in Greek ethical systems, the author singles out prudence as the chief of the four cardinal virtues.[135]

In the Greek philosophical ethical systems of Plato, the Stoics, and Aristotle,[136] *phronēsis* provides the foundation for all the other virtues. However, the author of 4 Maccabees chooses "piety" (*eusebeia*) and attributes to it the status of a cardinal virtue together with prudence, justice, and temperance. Thus, excessive appetites that are attracted to the body (e.g., pigs, seafood, fowl, quadrupeds) are forbidden by the food laws, which were prescribed by Moses, the lawgiver. With the help of reason, individuals are exhorted to abstain from these sorts of delicious foods; passions of the appetites are restrained by the temperate "mind" (*nous*), and, at the same time, the desires and passions of the body are bridled by "reason" (*logismos*). The practice of the Torah, particularly food laws, is the sign that reason can master passions and desires through the cultivation of self-control (1:34–35). The practice of the dietary laws proves that reason can master the inordinate craving for food (1:32–34). While in 1:32 the author explains that reason masters desires, in 1:33 he restates this thesis but substitutes *epithymia* with *orexis*.[137] Living a way of life in accordance with the ancestral law—even in the most terrible circumstances—is required to show fidelity to God and to his divine law.[138] In addition, faithfulness to the prescriptions of the Mosaic law is highlighted when the author claims that the Torah restrains the passions in unruly persons, as long as they obey its decrees.[139] Influenced by Greek philosophical traditions, the author teaches that "self-control" (*enkrateia*) or "temperance" (*sōphrosunē*) can help the individual to overcome pleasures and desires, as well as to exercise the individual not only in Jewish piety but also in the cardinal virtues (5:23–25).

---

134. DeSilva, *4 Maccabees*, 71–72.

135. "Prudence" or "practical wisdom" (*phronēsis*), "justice" (*dikaiosunē*), "courage" (*andreia*), and "temperance" (*sōphrosunē*) (Plato, *Prot.* 356D–357B; Plutarch, *Stoic. rep.* 1034C–E; *Virt. mor.* 440E–441B). Naveros Córdova, *Ethical Discourse*, 37–41, here 38.

136. Plutarch, *Mor.* 441A, 443D; Aristotle, *Eth. nic.* 2.7.1108b10.

137. Bowden, "Semantic Investigation," 415.

138. 4 Macc 2:20, 23; 4:23, 24; 5:16, 29, 33; 7:8–9, 15; 9:2; 15:9; 18:1, 4. For the author, keeping Jewish identity (the Jewish way of life) is crucial in times of persecution (4:19; 5:36; 18:5).

139. DeSilva, *4 Maccabees*, 92.

The author of 4 Maccabees, like Philo, is familiar not only with philosophical traditions but also with the Hellenistic Jewish tradition. Indeed, the author highlights the Jewish way of life as exemplified by Eleazar, the seven brothers, and their mother, a way of life that fulfills the highest ideals of Greek philosophical ethical systems.[140] The author views the practice of the food laws as the safe course to acquire "temperance" (*sōphrosunē*); it is the virtue akin to "self-control" (*enkrateia*), and, together with reason, temperance overpowers and defeats the desires of the body (1:31–32). The author defines the virtue of temperance in a similar way to what we find in Aristotle's definition. It is a "virtue" (*aretē*) that can restrain desire by reason when it is set on base enjoyments and pleasures and is resolute to endure natural want and pain (Aristotle, *Virt. vit.* 5.1.1250b12–15).[141] In other words, reason and temperance form together a powerful weapon to control passions and desires and eradicate excessive sexual appetites. Indeed, elsewhere, the author states, "Reason prevails not over its own passions but over those of the body and the soul. No one of us can eradicate such desire, but reason can provide a way for us not to be enslaved by desire" (3:1–2).[142] In this sense, "desire" (*epithymia*) as a dangerous passion has the power to enslave the body in a similar way we find in Philo when he speaks of irrational desire/impulse as the gateway leading to the enslavement of the soul's reason. At the same time, as Bowden has rightly noted, reason keeps the individual from being enslaved to desire.[143] Significantly, in 4 Maccabees, we find the sharp contrast between "desire" (*epithymia*) and "reason" (*logos/logismos*), and in Philo the sharp contrast between "desire" (*epithymia*) and "self-control" (*enkrateia*); both contrasts are seen as opposite powers in the human soul. For the author of 4 Maccabees, like in Stoicism, there is no middle point between desire and reason; in other words, it is an either-or situation, not a both-and situation. However, as Aune asserts, similar to Philo and (Middle) Platonists, the author exhorts the control or the master of desire and passions (*metriopatheia*) and not their extirpation (*apatheia*).[144]

---

140. DeSilva, *4 Maccabees*, 44.

141. DeSilva, *4 Maccabees*, 92.

142. In Proverbs, the author exhorts readers not to let desire for beauty conquer the individual (Prov 6:25)

143. Bowden, "Semantic Investigation," 417.

144. Aune, "Mastery of Passions," 136.

Watch Out! Irrational Desire Destroys the Body

Following the traditions of Philo and Greek philosophers studied in this book, the author of 4 Maccabees knows that desire and passions without moderation can become irrational and dangerous for the individual. When the author narrates the heroic piety of Eleazar, the seven brothers, and their mother, the language of "irrational desire" (*alogos epithymia*) appears. It is described allegorically in terms of the individual's experience of an internal torment, which when enslaved by it, inflames and consumes the individual's inner being (3:11).[145] Like Philo, Plato, and the Stoic philosophers, using the metaphor of war, the author depicts vividly the struggle between two powers, "desire" (*epithymia*) and "reason" (*logismos*): "When his armor-bearers complained bitterly over the desire of the king two staunch young soldiers, respecting the desire of the king, put on their full armor and, taking a pitcher, climbed over the enemy's ramparts" (3:12). Regarding this text, DeSilva notes, the author's Jewish audience in the Greek diaspora would likely identify it with the metaphorical burning of David's desire for something out of reach.[146] Reason is represented metaphorically by the full armor and intends to defeat desire, which is represented by the enemy (desire). The story of David's thirst (3:6), for example, reminds us of a parallel event earlier in David's life, when he conceived of a desire for unlawful sexual intercourse with a woman who was bathing on another man's roof.[147] For the author, like Philo and Socrates and other Hellenistic Jewish authors,[148] sexual desire in itself is good and God's gift; what is sinful is the improper or excessive sexual desire that goes against God's law.[149]

Moreover, like Philo in his exposition of the tenth commandment, *ouk epithymēseis* (*Spec.* 4.78b–4.131), for the author of 4 Maccabees "irrational

---

145. See also Prov 23:3.

146. DeSilva, *4 Maccabees*, 108.

147. DeSilva, *4 Maccabees*, 109.

148. See, for example, Wis 2:7-9; 7:1-2; 14:11-31; Let. Aris. 108, 142, 152, 250-251, 277-278; Ps.-Phoc. 3-8, 59, 67, 76, 175-217, 228; Sir 6:1-3; 7:19; 9:6-7; 18:30—19:3; 20:4; 42:8, 12-13; 23:4-6, 18-21; 25:2, 13-26; 26:5-6, 8-9, 13-21; 28:15; 37:11; Josephus, *A.J.* 1.165, 2.51-2.58, 3.274, 5.259, 5.279, 7.130-7.131, 7.169, 8.190-8.195, 15.29, 15.65-15.66, 18.345, 18.350; *C. Ap.* 2.190-2.219, 2.284; *B.J.* 2.120, 2.161; T. Jud 14:3; 15:1; T. Reu 1:10; 2:4, 8; 4:9; 6:4; T. Iss 2:3; T. Benj 6:2-3. For detailed analyses of these Jewish texts, see Loader, *Pseudepigrapha on Sexuality*, 398-476; Loader, *New Testament on Sexuality*, 259-435; Van der Horst, "Pseudo-Phocylides," OTP 1:574-82.

149. 4 Macc 2:1-6, 21-23; 3:2; 15:4-7; 16:6-11; 18:7-10. For a good analysis of these texts, see Loader, *Pseudepigrapha on Sexuality*, 440-56.

desire" (*alogos epithymia*) is associated with the tenth commandment (2:4). Interestingly, we find the same connection later in Paul's Letter to the Romans (7:7), as we shall see in the next chapters. The author of 4 Maccabees, however, highlights the negative emphasis on the commandment (you shall *not*); hence, for the author the divine law exhorts *not* to desire. Eleazar likewise assures the seven brothers and their mother that reason has the power to overcome desires of the body through the practice of the food laws. In addition, in 4 Maccabees there is an explicit connection between desire and excessive sexual desires and appetites (2:1–6),[150] and the fact that reason prevails not only over the "mad desire" (*oistron*) of one's passions but also over the frenzied urges for improper sexual gratification and over every desire of the soul. In this regard, Bowden states that while bodily desires evoke the mention of food, desires of the soul evoke a sexual context; specifically, desire towards union with beauty is set aside (2:1), as in the case of the temperate Joseph, who by means of the "mind" (*nous*) is able to master pleasurable passion (2:2).[151] The example of Joseph in Gen 39 and the case of forbidden sexual desire, given by the author, shows reason as the true master of any sexual desire (2:4). In 2:5, the author recites texts from the opening and closing of the LXX verbatim (Deut 5:21; Exod 20:17 NETS).[152] He writes, "For instance, the law says, Thou shalt not covet thy neighbor's wife, nor anything that belongs to thy neighbor."[153] In this sense, the focus is not the denigration of sexual desire; the author, like Philo, recognizes sex as part of God's creation. As Loader stresses, the focus is control and becomes

150. In her analysis, Gemünden ("Affekt der ἐπιθυμία") discusses the negativity of unlawful sexual desire in 4 Macc 2:1–6, distinguishing two social issues: sexual relations with outsiders (2:1–3) and eating food forbidden in the Torah (1:33–35). On the other hand, Loader points out that the major sexual wrongdoing in this text concerns both adultery and premarital chastity; these sexual vices are likewise found in Wis 10:13; T. Jos. 3–9; Jos. Asen. 4:7; 7:3, 5; Jub. 39:5–11. Loader, *Pseudepigrapha on Sexuality*, 443–46.

151. Bowden, "Semantic Investigation," 416. See also T. Jos 4:1–2; 6:7; 9:2–3; 10:2–3.

152. The Hebrew text reads: "You shall not desire your neighbor's house; you shall not desire your neighbor's wife, or male or female slave, or ox, or donkey, or anything that belongs to your neighbor."

153. As Bowden points out, the LXX switches the order from the Hebrew text, first forbidding desire for a neighbor's wife, followed by his house and his other possessions. The LXX also prohibits desiring a neighbor's field, which is not mentioned in the Hebrew text. Bowden, *Desire*, 242. Loader explores the comparison between the tenth commandment in the Hebrew text and the LXX and the reasons the author of the LXX made such changes to the order of the tenth commandment in Exod 20:17 and Deut 5:21. Loader, *Pseudepigrapha on Sexuality*, 9–11, 118–19. For a review of Loader's argument, see Bowden, *Desire*, 242–46.

effective with the practice of the Torah.[154] The prohibition against unlawful sexual desire begins with a clear negative command not to desire the wife of one's neighbor,[155] making an implicit connection between desire and sexual immorality. Here in 2:5, the Greek verb *epithymeō* refers to improper sexual desire (for a neighbor's wife), yet not exclusively as some scholars argued.[156] As Bowden rightly states, the prohibition applies to "all desires" and anything that belongs to a neighbor.[157] The author praises Joseph (2:1–4), indeed, his temperate character, through which he gained control over sexual desire by resisting the lustful advances of Potiphar's wife. When he was young and in his prime for intercourse, by his reason, he rendered powerless the frenzied desire of his passions, and apparently reason prevails over the frenzied urge for unlawful sexual gratification (3:18).

In 4 Maccabees, we find clear proof of the remedy for immoderate sexual desires and pleasures. Primarily, the practice of the ancestral Jewish laws (e.g., food laws) habituates the individual to become a master of the passions and gluttony, which in the Platonic and Philonic traditions is a vice and a secure gateway to excessive sexual desires. Through reason and in accordance with the law, the temperate mind eradicates not only *epithymia* but "irrational desire" (*alogos epithymia*), not only conquers the compulsions of the passions but quenches the flames of frenzied desires (3:17).[158] Loyalty to the law encourages individuals not to be compelled to taste, for example, pork (so delicious to the taste) and food sacrificed to idols (5:2). God's law teaches only self-control or temperance and how to overcome negative pleasures and desires, as well as how to train the individual in courage, justice, and piety in a way that befits the individual's ethical character and greatness (5:24).[159] The main virtue is not prudence of practical reason as in the Greek ethical systems. It is "piety" (*eusebeia*), the greatest and generic virtue in Hellenistic Jewish ethics. For Philo, too,

---

154. Loader, *Pseudepigrapha on Sexuality*, 456.

155. DeSilva, *4 Maccabees*, 95.

156. While a good number of scholars have argued that sex is not one of the possible objects of desire in Exod 20:17 and Deut 5:21, others support the contrary. For various discussions, see Gaca, *Making of Fornication*, 11–20; Wright Knust, *Abandoned to Lust*, 6–12. For a detailed analysis of *ouk epithymēseis* in 4 Maccabees, see Bowden, *Desire*, 246–78.

157. Bowden, "Semantic Investigation," 257–58, 277–78.

158. See also Wis 4:12.

159. The same four virtues are found in Xenophon, *Mem.* 4.6. DeSilva, *4 Maccabees*, 135.

piety is the queen and source of all the other virtues, as God is the source of all that exists (*Decal.* 52).

So, in his ethical teaching, the author of 4 Maccabees follows the same tradition of Philo; the author maintains the idea that a law-observant life (the practice of the food laws) is key to acquire the virtue of piety. Indeed, the author claims, everything is for the sake of virtue, piety (17:7)! In the story of Eleazar, the seven brothers, and their mother, the author writes, "Piety is at stake" (5:38).[160] It is also *piety* that leads Eleazar, the seven brothers, and their mother to *immortality* (9:22; 14:5; 18:23), which is the goal in 4 Maccabees. We have seen that Philo also makes this connection between piety and immortality. Eleazar, the seven brothers, and their mother demonstrate loyalty and faithfulness to the ethical commandments of the law, and as a result, they become "champions of virtue" (2:14), and that virtue is certainly piety (chs. 13–18). Similar to Philo, in 4 Maccabees, a combination of Stoic and Hellenistic Jewish elements is used in the author's understanding of "desire" (*epithymia*) and the verbal form *epithymein*. The important aspect in his understanding is that what rules over the impulsive in a human person is divine reason (1:13; 2:6; 5:23), and the impulsive includes all kinds of immoderate or excessive desires and the other three passions: pleasure, fear, and grief (1:22–23). The impulsive arises out of sensuality (1:3; 3:11–16) and sexual desires (2:4–5).[161]

CONCLUSION

In this chapter, we analyzed Paul's larger Greek philosophical and Hellenistic Jewish traditions. We have come to understand both traditions as the backdrop of the understanding of "desire" (*epithymia*) in the context of sexual desires and irrational/immoderate desires. What has been revealed is the problem of desire and its negative consequences in the lives of individuals. This is important because Paul, too, tries to explain and deal with this deadly passion threatening the virtuous life of believers. We explored how Platonists, Stoics, Philo, and the author of 4 Maccabees understood and dealt with the passion of desire, and the similar ways they tackled the dangers of desire, such as excessive impulse, pleasures, appetites, and irrational desire/impulse. Both Plato and Philo constructed a threefold

---

160. See also 4 Macc 7:18.
161. Büchsel, *TDNT* 3:170.

relationship (desire-gluttony-belly). For both authors, these are a powerful force that can lead to excessive sexual desires, vices, and passions.

Moreover, in terms of sexual desire, the authors, Plato, the Stoic Chrysippus (and later Stoics), and the Middle Platonist Plutarch share the same view that sexual desire is bad when it becomes irrational or immoderate desire, or in Plato's language, tyrannical desire. In both traditions—Hellenistic Jewish and Greek philosophical—"desire" (*epithymia*) and "reason" (*logos/logismos*) are viewed as two opposite powers. To control desire and eradicate excessive desire, especially in connection with sexual desire and impulse, the individual must be on the side of "reason" (*logos*) and its close "friend," the "mind" (*nous*). The remedy to either control or eradicate desire is moderation, which is acquired through self-control or temperance, and in Philo and 4 Maccabees through the practice of the food laws as prescribed by Moses. It is crucial to locate where Paul stands within these Greek philosophical and Hellenistic Jewish traditions. In the next chapters, we shall explore Paul's own understanding of *epithymia* and his treatment to control desire and eliminate excessive passions and desires within the context of the same traditions.

2

Paul's Reevaluation of Jewish Monotheism
Desire's Connection with Idolatry and Sexual Vices

NOW WE ENTER THE complex, first-century world of Paul to explore his view of "desire" (*epithymia*) and its cognates in connection with sexual vices in his seven genuine letters. For Paul, who was a Hellenistic Jew from Tarsus, a *polis* known for being the hub of Stoic philosophy, it is quite surprising to learn that the word *epithymia* and cognates are not common in his letters (see the introduction). I suggest that it is probably because Paul, like some of his Hellenistic Jewish contemporaries, was familiar with the pejorative understanding of the concept, especially in connection to the Stoic doctrine of "passions" (*pathē*).[1] Desire is a deadly passion of the soul! For this reason, perhaps Paul might have very well tried to intentionally avoid the

---

1. "Desire" (*epithymia*) as a bad vice appears in Sib. Or. 2:134 (inordinate desires). For a study of attitudes toward sexual behavior in the Sibylline Oracles, see Loader, *Pseudepigrapha on Sexuality*, 56–78. Desire in close association to sexual promiscuity is common in the Testament of the Twelve Patriarchs, e.g., T. Reu 5:7, 6:5; T. Jud 14:2; 16:2; T. Jos 7:7; 9:1. See Kee, "Testament of the Twelve." In the Letter of Aristeas the concept of *epithymia* appears twice in Eleazar's presentation of the law. See Hadas, *Aristeas to Philocrates*, 211 (*epithymēsai*) and 256 (*epithymiōn*); but not in connection with sexual immorality or vices. See Hadas, *Aristeas to Philocrates*, 183, 201. Similarly, in Josephus *epithymia* is mostly *vox media* (A.J. 11.176 17.352; Vita 70; B.J. 6.112), but it can also be used for sinful desire (A.J. 2.51). See Büchsel, *TDNT* 3:170.

use of *epithymia* or *epithymeō* in his letters. As we discussed in chapter 1, desire is one of the four passions of the soul in the Platonic and Stoic ethical systems, and in Philo and 4 Maccabees desire is a central concept in their discussions of the benefits of the Jewish law and the tenth commandment, *ouk epithymēseis*. An important question that scholars have overlooked and is worth asking is: At what point in his early career does Paul begin to expose the nature of "desire" (*epithymia*) as an evil passion (Stoic view) and relate it to sexual vices commonly practiced in pagan cities? Paul is familiar with specific texts from the LXX that deal with sexual commandments and prohibitions.[2] Certainly, as a faithful Jew, Paul had in mind biblical notions *before* his experience of the risen Christ. In this chapter, we shall see the extent of how Paul intends to reevaluate his biblical knowledge about sexual desires, pleasures, and experiences in relation to the Jewish law as he embarks on his missionary career in pagan territories.

Based on the information examined in chapter 1, Paul follows both Platonic and Stoic traditions in his use of the passion of *epithymia*. He treats desire as evil Stoically, but unlike the Stoic philosophers who implicitly connect desire with sexual desires and pleasures,[3] Paul does generally associate desire directly with sexual vices of the Greek world in close connection to idol worship or idolatry.[4] In the tradition of Plato's excessive and tyrannical desire or passion, Paul describes the dangers of *epithymia* as "sinful passions" (*ta pathēmata tōn hamartiōn* [Rom 7:5]), "sinful beyond measure" (*kath' hyperbolēn hamartōlos* [Rom 7:13]), and connects *epithymia* with "all kinds of desires" (*pasan epithymian* [Rom 7:8]). These include other pagan vices related to sexual vices, as we shall see below. Paul develops an interesting twofold relationship: *epithymia*–sinful passions/sinful beyond measure/all kinds of desire. This is something that Bowden has overlooked in his discussion. Thus, to answer the simple yet complex question posed above, we shall explore Paul's thought of *epithymia* and cognates (including *orexis*, a word akin to *epithymia*, in Rom 1:27) in his oeuvre within the context of his Christocentric approach in the advent of the Christ-event. Paul's own view of monotheism against the backdrop of the dangers of

---

2. Some major texts are Gen 1:26–27, 28; 2:24; 19; 39; Exod 20:17; Leviticus 18; 20; Deut 5:21; 22; Judg 19; 2 Sam 11; Job 31:1.

3. What I mean by the adverb "implicitly" is that the Stoic philosophers did not offer a detailed exposition of the close connection between desire and sexual immorality as we find in Platonism. See ch. 1.

4. On Greek religion and deities, see Koester, *History, Culture, and Religion*, 156–96.

pagan idolatry, the cause of sinful passions and sexual desires, are closely examined.

THE CHRIST-EVENT: PAUL'S CHRISTOCENTRIC APPROACH TO EVIL DESIRE

Paul's experience of his "prophetic call" needs to be placed within the broader picture—not just one event but an event that had multifaceted possibilities of interpretations—without completely detaching him from first-century Judaism. After his *experience* on the road to Damascus, he becomes a "Hellenistic Jewish believer," an apostle to the gentiles. The powerful experience Paul went through represents the most rewarding experience throughout his life; yet the experience of the risen Christ reaffirmed, too, his commitment to God and obedience to his call as an apostle to the gentiles. Monotheism was for him, as it was for all Jewish people, the highest standard of his being Jewish, his faithfulness to God, and his obedience to God's will.[5] Paul affirms how, in the power of God, he is able to preach his gospel. He writes in Romans, "For I am not ashamed of the gospel; for it is the power of God for salvation to everyone who believes, to the Jew first and then to the Greek" (Rom 1:16). Within the Jewish *tradition* of monotheism, Paul views God as the God of Israel first and then of Greeks; indeed, Paul always goes to the Jews first and then to the Greeks (Rom 1:16; 2:9–10).[6] He shares his understanding of God also with gentile believers in the wider world as he expands early Christianity westward during his missionary career; God is one and is the Father not only of Israel (Deut 6:4; Exod 20:3) but also of gentile believers. In this way, Paul envisions a universal and inclusive understanding of monotheism. Now, the role of the Jewish God as the Father, Lord, and Creator of all is that of inclusivity—salvation is open to all! God is a faithful and righteous God, and thus God brings into fulfillment what he has promised to Israel from the beginning: salvation to

---

5. Recently, Myers investigated the faithfulness of God in connection to Paul's call for gentile obedience in Rom 2; 7; 9–11. Myers developed his argument focusing on the themes of "obedience" and "faith" through the lenses of Greco-Roman notions of national diplomacy, military, civic, and home life. Using Greek and Latin sources, Myers shows how faithfulness to God implicates not only obedience to God but also to the gospel and Paul himself from the gentiles. Myers, *Paul*, 123.

6. Paul shares this distinctive Jewish belief with other Hellenistic Jewish authors, e.g., Let. Aris. 132; Philo, *Decal.* 65; *Spec.* 1.1–1.65; Josephus, *A.J.* 3.91; *C. Ap.* 2.167, 2.190–2.191.

all, and that includes gentiles (Rom 11)! It is important to recognize that Paul's vision of the inclusion of gentiles in salvation is reflected in some Jewish traditions that speak about gentiles coming to Zion (Isa 2:3-5; 25:6-9).[7] The notion of God as God of the gentiles was already, to some degree, present in strands of Israel's tradition, strands of it. Paul's rhetoric in Rom 3:29 does clearly suggest that this would have been an acceptable idea for some Jews and would have expected a positive answer. The Hellenistic Jewish believer and apostle writes, "Is God the God of Jews only? Is He not the God of Gentiles also? Yes, of Gentiles also" (Rom 3:29). Within this traditional Jewish understanding, Paul's christological understanding intends to innovate its theological implication. The point, for our purpose, is that within the tradition of his Jewish monotheism, Paul as a Hellenistic Jewish believer offers a new ethical praxis to Jewish and gentile believers alike. For Paul, it is crucial to maintain not only the survival but also the continuity of the new "religion," which is being challenged on all its fronts, especially in the ethical, political, religious, and social.

Paul's Christocentric Monotheism

Certainly Paul's personal understanding of the Christ-event permitted him to reconfigure his understanding of God and monotheism, a central mark of Judaism. His theological configuration maintains a continuity with his Jewish tradition as he finds a place for Christ the Lord in his monotheistic approach. While his monotheism remains rooted in his Judaism (what N. T. Wright called "Jewish-style monotheism"),[8] Paul recognizes Jesus as the Messiah (the Christ) who revealed himself to him and accomplished the salvation of all people with his voluntary death on a cross. Paul confesses that God raised Jesus from the dead and that he is now Lord of all. As Wright asserts, Paul took the divine title *kyrios* (Lord) of the LXX, and he used it in passages where he was well aware that in Jewish contexts *kyrios* referred to God, YHWH himself; now he understands it as a reference to Jesus (Rom 10:5-13).[9] What an innovative yet challenging change in Jewish

---

7. The same allusion may be reflected in Jesus' parable of the mustard seed where the "birds," a metaphor of gentiles, come and perch in the tree's branches, and also in the biblical quotation used at the temple expulsion (Matt 21:13; Mark 11:17; Luke 19:46 [Isa 56:7; Jer 7:11]) and even the promise to Abraham (Gen 17:3-5; 12:1-3; 15:4-5).

8. Wright, *Paul: In Fresh Perspective*, 90-91.

9. Wright, *Paul: In Fresh Perspective*, 92.

tradition! What a way to challenge a core belief in Judaism, though without rejecting Jewish monotheism! What a manner to envision Jewish monotheism on a new level! Paul writes extensively to the believers—Jewish and gentile—in Rome, a community he did not establish.[10] However, that does not prevent him from edifying and maintaining a good relationship with Roman believers. He expresses his deep longing to see them and hopes that he will eventually go to them (Rom 1:10–13). His genuine love for them as well as his hope for their reciprocal love for each other is revealed when he writes, "I am longing to see you [*epipothō idein hymas*] so that I may share with you some spiritual gift to strengthen you—or rather so that we may be mutually encouraged by each other's faith, both yours and mine" (Rom 1:11–12).

We encounter a particular perspective of Paul's way of reconciling both monotheism and Christology where the role of Christ in salvation and his association with God the Father come to be intrinsically connected. Jesus is not only Israel's Messiah (the Christ); he is also the Savior of the world. His status as Savior, given by God, raised Jesus as *kyrios* (Lord) to be or become somehow equal to God (high Christology).[11] In Phil 2:6–11, Paul writes,

> Who [*hos*], though he was in the form of God [*morphē theou*], did not regard to be equal with God [*to einai isa theō*] as something to be exploited, but emptied himself, taking the form of a slave, being born in human likeness. And being found in human form, he humbled himself and became obedient to the point of death—even death on a cross. Therefore God also highly exalted him and gave him the name that is above every name, so that at the name of Jesus every knee should bend, in heaven and on earth and under the earth, and every tongue should confess that Jesus Christ is Lord [*exomologēsetai hoti kyrios Iesous Christos*], to the glory of God the Father.[12]

---

10. Most commentators suggest that Paul wrote Romans in Gaius's home (Rom 16:23) between the years 54 and 59 CE. However, there are discrepancies in terms of the reasons why Paul writes to the Roman believers and what the situation and circumstances were at the time he writes the letter. For useful commentaries, see Fitzmyer, *Romans*, 68–84; Burns, *Romans*; Schnelle, *Letter to the Romans*; Schlatter, *Romans*.

11. See Fee, *Pauline Christology*, 237–88.

12. See also Col 1:15–20.

In this ancient hymn,[13] Paul views Jesus, the Lord (*kyrios*), as the one "equal" (*isa*) with the Creator God and who gives fresh expression to what that equality means by incarnation, humiliation, suffering, and death on a cross.[14] In Paul's Christocentric monotheism, Jesus is highly exalted; as having the same status as God, he shares the glory that the one God does not share with another being, only with the risen Christ.[15] This is an inclusive approach to make Jesus accessible to all believers, Jews and gentiles, and remarkably an ingenuity to describe the unconceivable union between God and Christ without fracturing the belief in one God, or the Jewish belief in monotheism. The Jewish-Christian Paul enriches further the Jewish understanding of monotheism among early Jewish and gentile believers.

A similar Christocentric monotheism appears in 1 Cor 8:5–6, a famous Pauline text highly debated among scholars. Here, Paul openly acknowledges the existence of other deities and the many so-called gods and lords (pagan polytheism). But he restates his Jewish monotheistic position and the primacy of the Jewish God, where God and Christ's role are juxtaposed. He writes, "Even if there are those who are called gods [*legomeoi theoi*] either in heaven or on earth—as in fact there are many gods and many lords [*theoi polloi kai kyrioi polloi*]—yet for us there is One God the Father [*eis theos ho patēr*] from whom [*ex hou*] are all things [*ta panta*] and for whom [*eis auton*] we exist, and one Lord Jesus Christ through whom [*di' hou*] are all things [*ta panta*] and through whom [*di' autou*] we exist" (1 Cor 8:5–6).[16] Paul's approach establishes an intrinsic relationship between

---

13. For details, see Murphy-O'Connor, *Paul*, 225–26.

14. Wright, *Paul: In Fresh Perspective*, 93.

15. Rom 14:10; Isa 45:23.

16. Scholars have analyzed the significance of the phrase "all things" (*ta panta*) in association to prepositional metaphysics in the NT. We find prepositional metaphysics and God (*ex hou; di' hou; di' on; eis auton*) in 1 Cor 8:6a (see also Rom 11:36; Heb 2:10), and prepositional metaphysics and Christ (*di' autou; en auto; eis auton*) in 1 Cor 8:6b (see also John 1:1–4, 10; Col 1:15–20; Heb 1:2). To bring anything into being needs all these conjointly: *di' organou* (through an instrument), *di' autou* (through himself/him), *en auto* (in him), *eis auton* (for him), *hyph' hou* (by which/whom), *ex hou* (from which/whom), *to di' hou* (through which/whom), *di' ho* (for which/whom). Sterling argues that Paul attempts to make a distinction between the God and Christ through the use of different prepositional phrases (*ex hou* versus *di' hou*). According to Sterling, the basis for prepositional metaphysics goes back to Aristotle's argument about "causes" (*aitia*) (e.g., *Phys.* 2.3.194b–2.3.195a, 2.7.198a; *Metaph.* 2.3–2.9 (194b–200b). Formulations of prepositional metaphysics found their way into Jewish synagogue liturgies with attempts to present God in philosophical categories and in wisdom speculations. Sterling, "Prepositional Metaphysics," 220–37. For further studies on the complexity of the origin

the Father and Christ in salvation history and in the creation of the world and humanity. Both God and Jesus Christ are connected with the phrases "all things" and "we exist" through prepositions: from whom/for whom/ through whom (two times). At the same time, Paul clearly acknowledges Jesus' subordination to the Father. So, Paul develops a creedal formulation in which he offers to the Roman believers an innovative construal of his view of monotheism rooted in Judaism yet reevaluated through the Christ-event.[17] His approach certainly intends to reconcile frictions and misunderstandings that might have created Paul's inclusion of Jesus Christ into his "new" monotheism, that is, Christocentric monotheism, in both Jewish and gentile believers.

The intimate relationship between God and his Son Jesus the Christ (*kyrios*) in the role as "creators" and God as "initiator" of all things in creation, including humanity, shows God's willingness to share his divine power in creation with Christ the Lord.[18] Faithful to his Jewish heritage, Paul clearly distinguishes the role of Jesus the Lord from that of God using prepositions—for God, "from whom" and "for whom"; for Christ the Lord, "through whom" (two times)—in order to highlight the primacy of God as the one God and Jesus as the Lord of "all things" (*ta panta*). In this well-articulated reevaluation of Jewish monotheism, Paul not only reconciles the role of God and that of Christ in his new Christocentric monotheism but also reaffirms his rejection of idolatry and its dangers at Corinth (1 Cor 10:1–22),[19] Thessalonica (1 Thess 4:1–9), and Rome (Rom 1:18–32). For him, the many so-called gods and lords to whom pagans offer sacrifices are *not* really God (1 Cor 8; 10:1–11:1); even though they exist, when compared to the Jewish God they are nothing (1 Cor 8:4b).[20]

---

and history of the metaphysics of prepositions in Hellenistic philosophy, see Cox, *By the Same Word*, 43–50; Theiler, *Vorbereitung des Neuplatonismus*, 1–60; Dillon, *Middle Platonists*, 137–39; Tobin, "Prologue of John."

17. In this regard, Fitzmyer explains that Paul gives a summary of the traditional Christian belief in one God, which nonetheless restates the monotheism inherited from Judaism but stands over against the polytheism expressed in 1 Cor 8:4b: "We know that 'no idol in the world really exists,' and that 'there is no God but one.'" Fitzmyer, *First Corinthians*, 342.

18. See Naveros Córdova, *God's Presence in Creation*, 145–50.

19. Fitzmyer, *First Corinthians*, 332.

20. Tobin, *Spirituality of Paul*, 73. Paul's language of "so-called gods" has led to different interpretations among scholars. I concur with Dunn, who offers a reasonable interpretation: Paul's intention "seems to maximize the force of the confession of God as one, which he shared with the Corinthians, by affirming it boldly in the face of these other

Within this theocentric understanding, which goes in continuity with his Jewish tradition, Paul's Christocentric approach, which is in discontinuity with his Jewish tradition, becomes a leading mark in his apostolic career throughout the gentile territories of the Greco-Roman world. His experience of the Christ-event transformed positively yet dramatically his way of "thinking Jewish" into an inclusive Christian understanding of seeing his new life in Christ rooted in his monotheistic understanding. One of the major aspects of this sui generis transformation has to do with his understanding of the Mosaic law and the ethical value of the practice of God's commandments (Decalogue). In other words, Paul's reevaluation of his Jewish monotheism moves forward together with his reevaluation of the value of the Jewish ethical prescriptions as we shall see in the next chapters. Within his Christocentric monotheism, Paul delivers his personal evaluation of the practice of the Mosaic law in the ethical life of the believers. As he does that, he also speaks of the passion of "desire" (*epithymia*) and sexual vices as dangerous for the believers' virtuous and holy life.

The Negative Sequels of Desire: Sexual Immorality and Vices

Having Paul's Christocentric monotheism in context, now we enter Paul's complex world to explore how he understands key terms related to "desire" (*epithymia*) and sexual vices. I take Rom 13:13–14 as the first Pauline text in our analysis. From the ethical perspective of a Hellenistic Jewish believer, Paul sees the need to address the problem of gratifying the desires of the "flesh" (*sarx*) in close connection with the expression "sinful passions" (*ta pathēmata tōn hamartiōn*) in Rom 7:5.[21] To avoid confusion, it is important to note that by *sarx* Paul does not refer to the physical flesh or body, but to the individual's sinful condition enslaved to all kinds of vices and excesses, as "the works of the flesh" (Gal 5:19–21) illustrate.[22] Speaking within

---

more common beliefs. So what if others so believe! It does not affect the truth given to us that 'God is one!'" Dunn, *Theology of Paul*, 37.

21. The Greek plural noun *pathēmata* appears only four times in the NT: Rom 7:5; 8:18; 2 Cor 1:5; 1 Pet 1:11 (the meaning is "suffering").

22. Matera, *Galatians*, 199–212. Matera argues that *sarx* means the "unredeemed humanity," and the "works of the flesh" are a manifestation of humanity turned in and upon itself. In this way, the whole persona (body and soul) is carnal (fleshly) because the individual's "doings" do not proceed from the Spirit. Fitzmyer explains that Paul uses *sarx* to denote a human being and to connote his or her natural frailty (Rom 6:19). With the expression "the works of the flesh," Paul refers to the material human existence in

the Greco-Roman context of sexual vices, which were common practices among pagans,[23] Paul exhorts Roman believers, saying, "Let us live [literally, walk] honorably as in the day, not in revelry [*kōmois*] and drunkenness [*methais*], not in illicit sex [*mē koitais*] and licentiousness [*aselgeiais*], not in quarreling [*eridi*] and jealousy [*zelō*]. Instead, put on the Lord Jesus Christ, and make no provision for the flesh [*sarkos*], to gratify its desires [*epithymias*]" (Rom 13:13–14). Paul's ethical exhortation emphasizes the avoidance of vices—especially Greco-Roman vices—and desires related to all kinds of sexual vices commonly practiced by pagans and idolaters; for example, revelry (*kōmois*), drunkenness (*methais*), illicit sex (*koitais*), and licentiousness (*aselgeiais*).[24]

The list of vices in Rom 13:13–14, which are commonly found in the Greek list of vices, highlights the "works of the flesh" (*ta erga tēs sarkos*) closely associated with sexual desires. After listing vices with sexual connotation, Paul indeed exhorts the believers, saying, "Make no provision for the flesh [*sarkos*], to gratify its desires [*epithymias*]" (Rom 13:14). Both Paul and Philo share the assumption that the "flesh" (*sarx*) has a powerful life of its own that expresses itself in its passions and desires.[25] In the footsteps of Marie E. Isaacs, I suggest that Paul was probably the first Hellenistic Jewish author to attribute to the term *sarx* a negative connotation in his ethical discourse.[26] When looking closely at each vice, we note that the vice

---

its weak and earthbound isolated condition (Rom 8:5) in a way similar to how he understands the phrase they "cannot please . . . God" (8:8). Fitzmyer rightly clarifies that Paul does not mean by "flesh" exclusively the "human sexual drive, for he identifies the *egō* itself with *sarx* and finds 'no good' in either of them" (7:18). Fitzmyer, *Romans*, 127.

23. Plato, *Resp.* 573B6–574E1; Greek nudity and genital nakedness: Plato, *Charm.* 154D; prostitution: Xenophon, *Mem.* 3.11; Plato, *Phaedr.* 240B; Aristotle, *Econ.* 3.3; Stobaeus, *Anth.* 2.7.5b9; Seneca, *Ep.* 95.24; pederasty (which involved sex and food excess): Dionysius of Halicarnassus, *Ant. rom.* 4.24.3–4.24.5; Plutarch, *Amat.* 751E. However, in Plato's *Leg.* 841D–E, sexual intercourse outside the household was prohibited, but sex with any woman bought or acquired in another way was still permissible. Westfall argues that Paul confronts the sexual licentiousness of Hellenistic culture and tries to maintain a double standard of sexual ethics, e.g., 1 Cor 6:18; Gal 5:19–21; 1 Thess 4:3–5; Col 3:5. Westfall, *Paul and Gender*, 10; Reno, "Pornographic Desire," 167. For ancient Rome sexual behavior, see Langlands, *Sexual Morality*, 18–19; Ludwig, *Eros and Polis*, 261–87. For a comprehensive study of sexuality in the Greco-Roman world, see Skinner, *Sexuality*.

24. See also 2 Cor 12:21.

25. Betz, *Galatians*, 290.

26. Isaacs, *Concept of Spirit*, 194–99. Westfall has claimed that Paul's condemnation of the flesh in relation to passions and desires has been taken historically to condemn sexuality and sex drives. Westfall, *Paul and Gender*, 179.

kōmos (revelry or reveling) in 13:13a denotes strong sexual connotation. Its original meaning was "merrymaking" in the sense of a riotous party, carousing, a debauched partying, or a drunken feast that hosted unbridled sexual immoralities.[27] In the Greco-Roman world, nocturnal and riotous processions were held by half-drunken and frolicsome fellows who paraded after supper through the streets with torches and music in honor of Bacchus or another deity, and who sang and played before the houses of their male and female friends. The unbridled drinking parties often indulged in "revelry" (*kōmos*) and were protracted until late at night.[28] It is attested that in ancient Rome, "sexual practice is characterized by excess and depravity, unfettered by the prudery of subsequent eras. One thinks of orgies, of slave girls dangling grapes into the mouths of reclining men, of classy courtesans in transparent dresses, of insatiable empresses and the incestuous desires and perversions of emperors."[29]

The second and last time that the vice *kōmos* appears is in Paul's Letter to the Galatians. In the list of vices in Gal 5:19–21, Paul opens with the vice of *porneia* (sexual immorality).[30] Reno points out that here Paul is drawing from his own accusations of salacious sexual deviancy and the excessive desire of the flesh (Gal 5:16–17).[31] As Paul redefines the Greek vices as "the works of the flesh" (*ta erga tēs sarkos*), in Gal 5:21a he places the vice of "revelry" (*kōmoi*) next to "drunkenness" (*methai*),[32] two vices

27. "*Kōmos*," LSJ 1018.

28. Bible Hub, "2970. kómos."

29. E.g., Juvenal, *Sat.* 6.115–6.132; Suetonius, *Nero*, 29. Langlands, *Sexual Morality*, 9–10.

30. See also Deut 22:21, 22, 24. The meaning of the Greek vice *porneia*, which in this study is interpreted as "sexual immorality" in general, has been a matter of many disputes among biblical scholars. The broad range of meanings are from sexual immorality, fornication, adultery, sex with prostitutes, unnatural sex, to even the various forms of homosexual relations. *Porneia* has also a close connection with the vice *moicheia* (adultery). The complexity of its meanings makes it difficult to pinpoint a clear definition when Paul used it, especially in 1 Cor 5–7. What is true is that in the first-century social systems, *porneia* was not considered "sinful," because it was not prohibited by law. In ancient Israel, such deviant sexual behavior included all the prohibitions listed in Lev 18. Malina and Pilch, *Social-Science Commentary*, 387. For a good study of the various uses of *porneia*, see Loader, *New Testament on Sexuality*, 141–42, 246–49; Reno, "Pornographic Desire," 164–65.

31. Reno, "Pornographic Desire," 183.

32. 1 Pet 4:3; Wis 14:23; 2 Macc 6:4. See Bible Hub, "2970. kómos." The original verbal meaning of the term *methē* (*methuō*) goes back to Homer, *Od.* 18.240. Its meaning was "to be drunk"; hence, *methuskō* meant "to intoxicate," to make drunk," or "to get drunk."

that surely lead to sexual immorality, though in Rom 13:13a, he places "drunkenness" (*methais*) next to the vice of "revelry" (*kōmois*).³³ In Paul (Romans and Galatians) both vices (revelry and drunkenness) are not only strongly associated with sexual desires and vices, but they appear together only in these two instances in Paul's oeuvre! Indeed, Paul knows that when he mentions the vice of *methē* (drunkenness), what his Roman readers or listeners would vividly visualize in their minds are images of drunkenness, intoxication, wine, and any kind of intoxicating drink. Like Philo, he is certainly aware that these vices often arouse the individual's sexual desires, lusts, appetites, the gateway to sexual immorality, and other vices.³⁴

Moreover, Paul's use of the Greek vice *koitais* in Rom 13:13b reinforces his emphasis on the relationship between sexual vices and *epithymia*. This vice, *koitē* (illicit sex), is a euphemism for sexual intercourse and in the ethical philosophical systems is understood as "repeated immoral sexual intercourse" and often used to speak of adultery and *porneia*, or unlawful sexual behavior in general.³⁵ Furthermore, the vice of *aselgeiais* (licentiousness and voluptuousness), also employed in Rom 13:13b, appears in the Greek catalog of vices. It was generally associated with debauchery and "excessive" sexual desires as in Gal 5:19 and 2 Cor 12:21.³⁶ The Greek word *aselgeia* usually means sensuality, lechery, licentiousness, and wantonness—clearly vices linked with outrageous or excessive sexual conduct considered shocking to public decency. An individual showing the conduct of an *aselgēs* (lecher) is identified as someone who engages in all kinds of sexual desires and vices such

---

By the time of Plato, the term *methē* became understood as "over-rich drinking" (*Resp.* 9.571C), "intoxication" and "drunkenness" (*Symp.* 176E; *Phaedr.* 256C); also in Aristotle, *Pol.* 2.12:1274b11; Epictetus, *Diss.* 3.26.5. In Plato's *Laws*, "drinking" is also a means of education to develop "temperance" (*sōphrosunē*) (*Leg.* 1.637–1.650). See Herbert Preisker, "μέθη, μεθύω, μέθυσος, μεθύσκομαι," *TDNT* 4:545.

33. See also Luke 21:34; Prov 20:1; Isa 28:7; Ezek 23:32; 39:19. In the NT, we find the vice *methē* (drunkenness) only in similar lists along with *kōmoi* (revelry or excessive feasting) here in Rom 13:13 and Gal 5:21. See Preisker, *TDNT* 4:547.

34. See also Philo, *Contempl.* 60–63, 74, 88–89. Loader points out that Philo, who speaks of the danger of excessive passion, generally depicts same-sex relations as the "outcome of excessive alcohol, leading to excessive and uncontrolled passion, which expressed itself in sexual promiscuity with both women and men" (e.g., *Abr.* 135; *Contempl.* 53–56). Loader, "Reading Romans 1," 126.

35. See also Rom 9:10; Luke 11:7; Heb 13:40.

36. In Greek literature, the vice *aselgeia* appears together with the term *sōma* (body) and *epithymia* (desire), e.g., Polybius, *His.* 36.15.4. See Otto Bauernfeind, "ἀσέλγεια," *TDNT* 1:490; Bromiley, *Theological Dictionary*, 83.

as unbridled lusts, licentiousness, lasciviousness, outrageousness, shamelessness, and even insolence. Jennifer Wright Knust stresses the distinction between men and women and how their sexual conduct was perceived in the Roman Empire. While the free, male citizens (the elite) practiced sexual penetration as an expression of being virtuous men who mastered others and thus their own passions, including desire for sex, women who engaged in sex to satisfy their insatiable lusts at every opportunity were considered bad, and by their sexual actions they shamed their families, their city, and themselves.[37] It is worth noting, too, that in Paul's Jewish and Christian traditions, *aselgeia* is also associated with the vice of gluttony,[38] carnality, lasciviousness,[39] and unchaste handling of males and females;[40] these vices are strongly connected with sexual desire and vices. In addition, the other two vices *eride* and *zēlos* (strife and jealousy) in Rom 13:13b do not have sexual connotations. Thus, of the six vices common in the Greek catalog of vices,[41] four of them (*kōmos, methē, koitē,* and *aselgeia*) have strong negative sexual connotations in their meanings, and likewise four of them (*kōmos, methē, aselgeia,* and *zēlos*) appear in the list of Gal 5:19–21 as the "works of the flesh."[42]

Within the context of the Christ-event, Paul's imperative to "put on the Lord Jesus Christ" in Rom 13:14 highlights his serious concern about the dangers of the passion of "desire" (*epithymia*) and its negative sequels, which mostly involve Greek vices related to sexual misconduct and promiscuity. Paul configures his understanding of sinful desires creating a dualistic, or opposite, taxonomy between virtues and sexual vices—the latter associated with the desirous *sarx* (eager to satisfy all carnal sexual desires) and the former with the Lord Jesus Christ.[43] René A. López points out that

37. Wright Knust, *Abandoned to Lust*, 28–52.
38. See also Jude 1:4.
39. Gal 5:19; 1 Cor 7:2; 2 Cor 12:21; Eph 4:19; 2 Pet 2:7.
40. Rom 13:13; see also Wis 14:26; 3 Macc 2:26. Bible Hub, "766. aselgeia."
41. Byrne, *Romans*, 402.
42. Josephus speaks of the Galileans' rapacity and excessive lechery and lawless desire characteristic of a brothel. In *B.J.* 4.562, he writes, "Not only the ornaments, but also the lust of women, and [they] were guilty of such intolerable uncleanness, and they invented unlawful pleasures of that sort. And thus did they roll themselves up and down the city, as in a brothel house, and defiled it entirely with their impure actions." Translation comes from *Works* (Whiston), 691. See also Reno, "Pornographic Desire," 176.
43. We shall see later that in 1 Cor 6:15–16 Paul creates a contrast between *pornē* (sexually immoral person) and Christ, the former associated with vices/desire and the latter with virtue.

Paul, in his preaching to the gentile believers, makes use of the catalog of vices to characterize the life from which they ought to depart, and which they as believers already left behind; that is, they left behind the pagan, lustful way of life. Paul exhorts the believers to depart from the works of the flesh (vices) and to let their position as believers in Christ enable them to live by the Spirit (Gal 2:16—5:26; Rom 6:1–23).[44] I argue, then, that Paul is thinking of and delivering his ethical message on desire and sexual vices Stoically, but also Platonically. He strongly believes that this deadly passion, *epithymia*, must be controlled to avoid excessive passions and desires (Rom 7:5, 8, 13), especially sexual vices (Rom 13:13–14). We shall see in the next chapter that because of the Christ-event, Paul comes to the realization that the commandments of the Mosaic law are no longer effective (Rom 7) to avoid sinful passions and desires, even though in some circumstances Paul is tolerant of some Jewish practices.[45]

Consistent with both the Greek philosophical (Stoicism and Platonism) and Hellenistic Jewish (Philo and 4 Maccabees) traditions of interpretations, Paul shows "passions" (*pathē*) in connection with negative desires and vices, and that includes sexual vices.[46] It is not surprising, then, why Paul uses *epithymia* in a positive way only twice (Phil 1:23; 1 Thess 2:17). In four Pauline texts—Rom 1:26–27; 7:5; Gal 5:24; 1 Thess 4:5—strictly speaking, Paul reflects both traditions (Greek philosophical and Hellenistic Jewish) by associating "passions" (*pathē*) with sexual vices prevalent in the gentile world.[47]

44. López, "Paul's Vice List," 66–67; see also López, "Study of Pauline Passages."

45. This is specifically clear in Paul's treatment of circumcision and food laws. These topics are analyzed in ch. 4.

46. The Greek word *pathos* (passion) appears in 1 Thess 4:5 (*pathei*; only here in the entire NT) and Rom 1:26 (*pathē*; only here in the entire NT); the word *pathēma* in Gal 5:24 (*pathēmasin*) and Phil 3:10 (*pathēmatōn*). The plural noun *pathēmasin* appears four times in the NT: Gal 5:24 (negative use of passion together with *epithymia*); *pathēmasin* (suffering) in Col 1:24; 2 Tim 3:11; 1 Pet 4:13; *pathēmata* (suffering) in Rom 8:18; 2 Cor 1:5; Heb 2:9; 1 Pet 1:11; *pathēmatōn* (suffering) in 2 Cor 1:6, 7; Phil 3:10; Heb 2:10; 10:32; 1 Pet 5:1, 9. For a detailed presentation of the history of research on passions in Paul's genuine letters, see Aune, "Passions in Pauline Epistles." Aune argues that Paul uses the Stoic term *pathē* (passions) exclusively to connect with sexual immorality and vices related to the pagan society, and the term *pathēmata* and the cognate verb *paschō* are used to describe various sufferings rather than "passions" that needed to be subdued (222).

47. Aune mentions the same texts. Aune, "Passions in Pauline Epistles," 236. However, Aune (222) and Bowden agree in that Rom 1:26 does not relate to sex only as the list of vices show. Bowden expands his argument, saying that Paul clarifies that desire and passion manifest themselves in numerous ways in addition to illicit sex. Bowden,

For this reason God gave them over to degrading passions [*pathē atimias*]. Their females exchanged natural intercourse for unnatural [*tēn phusikēn chrēsin eis tēn para phusin*]. Similarly, also the males, having abandoned the natural intercourse [*tēn phusikēn chrēsin*] with females, were burned in their desire [*orexei*] for one another. Males committing indecent acts [*aschēmosunēn*] with males and receiving back in their own persons the penalty for their error. (Rom 1:26-27)

For when we were in the flesh [*en tē sarki*], our sinful passions [*ta pathemata tōn hamartiōn*], were at work through the law [*tou nomou*] in our members, so as to bear fruit for death. (Rom 7:5)

And those who belong to Christ Jesus crucified the flesh [*tēn sarka*] with its passions [*pathēmasin*] and its desires [*epithymiais*]. (Gal 5:24)

Not with desirous passion [*en pathei epithymias*] like the Gentiles [*ta ethnē*] who do not know God [*mē eidota ton theon*]. (1 Thess 4:5).[47]

I want to point out some general ideas before these texts are examined in greater detail. First, from the perspective of common sexual practices in the larger Greco-Roman world, often disapproved by Hellenistic Jewish authors, Paul refers to homosexual relations between women as "degrading passions" (*pathē atimias*), adding the statement, "Females exchanged natural intercourse for unnatural" (*tēn phusikēn chrēsin eis tēn para phusin* [Rom 1:26]).[48] The same reference is explicit about men when Paul writes, "Also the males, having abandoned the natural intercourse [*tēn phusikēn chrēsin*] with females, were burned in their desire [*orexei*] for one another. Males committed indecent acts [*aschēmosunēn*] with males" (Rom 1:27).[49]

Desire, 482-83. My point is not that in Rom 1:26 passion and sexual desire are connected in relation to sexual immorality only; in light of 1:18-32, Paul has in mind sexual vices and other vices in connection with idolatry common in the Greek world. What Bowden has overlooked, however, is the fact that in Rom 1:26 the Greek word *epithymia* does not appear at all, and Paul's connection between passion and sexual immorality is explicit, as passion appears together with "unnatural" intercourse.

48. On homosexual relations in Rom 1:26-27, see Loader, "Reading Romans 1," 125-27.

49. The Greek term *chrēsis* (literally, use or function) has sexual overtones. Rejection of homosexual relations is found in Hellenistic Jewish tradition, e.g., Sib. Or. 5:162-78 (the Sibyl speaks of Roman homosexual acts); Ps.-Phoc. 187-194 (Phocylides speaks of

Second, in the context of his Hellenistic Jewish tradition, Paul believes that while living "in the flesh" (*tēn sarka* [Gal 5:24]; *en tē sarki* [Rom 7:5a]), "passions and desires" (*pathēmasin kai epithymiais* [Gal 5:24]) and "sinful passions" (*ta pathēmata tōn harmartiōn* [Rom 7:5b]) are aroused by the works or through the practice of "the law" (*tou nomou* [Rom 7:5c]). Third, within both Hellenistic Jewish and Greek traditions, Paul connects the phrase "desirous passion" (*pathei epithymias*) with both "Gentiles and the lack of knowledge of God" (*ta ethne ta mē eidota ton theon* [1 Thess 4:5]).

Remarkably, in 1 Thess 4:3–6, for the first time, Paul seemingly creates a clear connection between *porneia* and both "desirous passions" (*pathei epithymias*) and pagan sexual vices, which endanger the holiness of believers. Paul writes,

> For this is the will of God, your sanctification [*ho hagiasmos*]: that you abstain [*apechesthai*] from sexual immorality [*tēs porneias*]; that each one of you knows how to control [*ktasthai*] your own body in holiness [*en hagiasmō*] and honor [*timē*], not with desirous passion [*en pathei epithymias*], like Gentiles [*ta ethnē*] who do not know God [*ta mē eidota ton theon*]; that no one wrongs [*pleonektein*] or exploits a brother or sister in this matter, because the Lord is an avenger in all these things [*pantōn toutōn*], just as we have already told you beforehand and solemnly warned you.

The phrase *pantōn toutōn* (all these things) in verse 6 alludes to the infinitive *pleonektein*, which can refer to "covet," "desire," or "defraud" like the lexeme *pleonekteō*, an irrational desire, especially lusting for what belongs to someone else, as in the term *pleonexia* (covetousness or desire for advantage). So, when Paul writes the term *pleonektein* (to exploit) in the context of verses 3–6, he might have in mind "desirous passions" in connection with the sexual vice of *porneia*. Paul's contemporary, Philo, also speaks within the same, wider Hellenistic world against sexual immorality in terms of exploitation, especially of minors (*Prob.* 124; *Her.* 274; *Abr.* 135–136; *Spec.* 3.37–3.42; *Virt.* 20–21; *QG* 2.49).[50] Thus, Bowden has rightly argued that in this particular case "desire" (*epithymia*) relates to "sexual immorality"

---

shameful ways of intercourse, such as sexual union with irrational animals and unlawful sexual practice between men). For the various interpretations of the meaning of "unnatural and unnatural" in Rom 1:26, see Malina and Pilch, *Social-Science Commentary*, 229–31; Martin, *Sex and Single Savior*, 55–60; Fredrickson, "Natural and Unnatural Use"; Bock and Del Rosario, "Table Briefing," 225–26.

50. Other sexual vices where Philo draws from the larger Greco-Roman world are found in *Spec.* 1.325, 2.50, 3.37; *Contempl.* 60. Loader, "Reading Romans 1," 126.

(*porneia*), and by pursuing holiness and honor and avoiding the passion of desire (4:4-5) believers in Thessalonica *will distinguish themselves from gentiles* who do not know God.[51] Whether single or married, Thessalonian believers must control their sexual urges (1 Thess 4:4) in contrast to their pagan fellow citizens who pursue sexual partners with "desirous passion" (*pathei epithymias*).[52] I would, however, add that in 1 Thess 4:1-6, Paul writes to the Thessalonian believers influenced by his Christocentric monotheism. Therefore, in 1 Thess 4:5, the Greek concepts of "passion" (*pathos*) and "desire" (*epithymia*) appear together to speak about forbidden desires and their associations with gentiles, who lack both knowledge of God and self-control, because they do not know the true one God. Significantly, in ancient Greek ethics, especially in the Stoic tradition, knowledge (*epistēmē*) and self-control or temperance (*sōphrosunē*) are contrasted with lack of knowledge (*agnoia*) and intemperance (*akolasia*).

The Vice of Idolatry Versus Monotheism and Knowledge of God

During Paul's time, idol worship was a common practice throughout the Greco-Roman world, but for him it was above all the greatest threat to

---

51. Konradt argues that Paul's exhortation in 1 Thess 4:1-6, within the eschatological context, is meant to strengthen the believers' ethical identity in order to establish "boundary markers" from the ethos of the pagan environment, and thus avoid vices. I argue, not only "vices"; Paul especially emphasizes the avoidance of *porneia* and other sexual vices. Konradt, *Gericht und Gemeinde*, 93-128.

52. In this regard, I agree with Bowden's interpretation of 1 Thess 4:1-8. He states that in this passage Paul explains that, for Thessalonian believers, holiness implied they should abstain from sexual immorality (4:3), which, among other things, includes avoiding the passion of desire, in this instance, desire for sex (4:5). See Bowden, *Desire*, 375-78, 381-82, 386-89. Similarly, Wright Knust, in her analysis of 1 Thess 4:4, points out that early believers claimed pagans were enslaved to desire, and believers have gained control of their desires and rejected all impure, unnatural sexual behavior. Wright Knust viewed a close connection between desire and slavery, self-control, and sexual immorality. Wright Knust, *Abandoned Lust*, 51. On the other hand, Weima claims that *skeuos* (vessels) in 1 Thess 4:4 is a metaphor that originally was interpreted to mean either one's own wife or one's body. In recent times, *skeuos* refers euphemistically to a particular part of one's body, e.g., the male sex organ. Weima further states that the passage is an exhortation to married men in the Thessalonian church to treat their wives with respect in the context of sex, that is, "with holiness and honor," and not as sex objects or a means to satisfy their passions and desires, "like Gentiles, who do not know God" (4:5). Weima, *1-2 Thessalonians*, 268-70.

monotheism.⁵³ Like in the writings of most Hellenistic Jewish authors (e.g., Philo of Alexandria, Wisdom of Solomon, 4 Maccabees, Josephus) who defended Jewish monotheism against the threats of polytheistic societies,⁵⁴ in Paul the vice of "idolatry" (*eidōlolatria*) is a direct path to moral depravity and all kinds of sexual vices (Rom 1:18–32; 1 Cor 5–7; 6:9–18; 1 Thess 4:1–5). For instance, Loader claims that in light of the Jewish and Christian tradition, Paul associates sexual immorality and idolatry already represented in the "idolatrous ways of the Canaanites and Egyptians" (Lev 18).⁵⁵ Most of Paul's audience were gentiles who participated in festivities of pagan deities before becoming believers.⁵⁶ Living in a world influenced by Hellenistic Judaism and the philosophical thought of his day, especially Stoicism and (Middle) Platonism,⁵⁷ Paul adopts monotheistic notions to express his own understanding of God and God's role in the ethical life of believers. The notion that God is one—an idea that goes back to Xenophanes (ca. 500 BCE)—is especially something that Paul as a Hellenistic Jew takes very seriously.

In Rom 1:26–27,⁵⁸ Paul follows the tradition of other Hellenistic Jewish authors when he links both passions and sexual vices with the vice of

---

53. See 1 Thess 1:9–10; 1 Cor 8:5–6; 2 Cor 6:19; Gal 5:20; Rom 1:23.

54. Tobin, *Paul's Rhetoric*, 105. We have, though, important exceptions. In the Letter of Aristeas (16) God is identified with Zeus and Dis. Also, Artapanus (fr. 3 in Eusebius, *Praep. ev.* 9.27.1–9.27.37) uses the term "god" for pagan deities and attributes Egyptian cults and idolatry to Moses. Artapanus regards the animal cults of the Egyptians as harmless and beneficial for human beings. See Collins, "Artapanus," 2:889, 898–99.

55. Loader, "Reading Romans 1," 124.

56. E.g., 1 Thess 1:9; 1 Cor 5:10–12; 6:9–11, 13–18; 12:2; Rom 1:18—2:16. Cousar, *Letters of Paul*, 72.

57. 1 Cor 15:35–49; 2 Cor 5:1–10. Malherbe, *Paul and Popular Philosophers*, 76.

58. This text has lately received much attention in biblical scholarship, especially in terms of homosexual behavior. Like most scholars, I argue that Paul does not present his rejection to same-sex relations; instead, I argue that he *speaks of* pagan homosexual practices and does not offer his personal reflection on homosexuality and/or homosexual behavior. This is the view of Manoly who, in light of Gen 19:4–5; 2 Pet 2:6; and Jude 7, links Rom 1:26–27 with "the sins of the flesh," such as adultery and homosexual acts. Manoly also argues that the expression "men committed shameless acts with men and received in their own persons the due penalty for their error" in v. 27b "can be better understood as incurable diseases contracted by those people who engage in such practices" (*peut être mieux compris aujourd'hui en raison des maladies presque incurables contactées par ceux et celles qui s'adonnent à de telles pratiques*). Manoly, *Histoire du salut*, 23. For other studies, see Sprinkle, "Paul and Homosexual Behavior"; Banister, "Ὁμοίως"; Kuhn, "Natural and Unnatural Relations"; Kalin, "Romans 1:26–27 and Homosexuality." For helpful information about homosexual behavior in the NT, see West

idolatry and the lack of knowledge of God.⁵⁹ At first glance the passage in Rom 1:26–27 is viewed as a reference to Paul's criticism of homosexuality and homosexual acts, as some scholars argued;⁶⁰ however, this is not the case. Thomas Stegman writes,

> In response to the Gentiles' choice to worship creatures instead of the Creator, Paul declares three times that "God gave them up"—to unruly desires in their hearts (v. 24), to dishonorable passions (v. 26) and to a base mind (v. 28). Abandonment of God results in the *entire* person being adversely affected. There is a progression from disordered passions to calculated insolence that rips apart the fabric of human community.⁶¹

According to Greco-Roman expectations on sexuality, men and women should exercise proper sexual roles. However, in Paul's time Greeks were known for their "lack of self-control" (*akrasia*; Latin, *continentia*) and their free rein for irrational sexual pleasures.⁶² In Rom 1:26–27, Paul then cap-

---

and Shore-Goss, *Queer Bible Commentary*, 622–25; Dunning, "Same-Sex Relations"; Scroggs, *New Testament and Homosexuality*. For a good summary of Scroggs's work, see Smith, "Ancient Bisexuality."

59. E.g., Wis 11:15–16; 13–15; Philo, *Spec.* 1.21–1.22; Sib. Or. 2:255–64; 3:8–45; Josephus, *C. Ap.* 1.225, 1.239, 1.244, 1.249, 1.254, 2.66, 2.81, 2.86, 2.128–2.129, 2.139. Tobin, *Paul's Rhetoric*, 109.

60. See Martin, *Sex and Single Savior*, 52–64; Fitzmyer, *Romans*, 285.

61. Stegman, "Saint Paul on Homosexuality." Similarly, Bowden (*Desire*, 481) writes, "It would be wrong to use the term 'homosexuality' to describe the sexual relations Paul describes in 1:26–27, since this word was first used in the second half of the 19th century." Grieb argues that "Romans 1:18–32, one of the two biblical texts most clearly prohibiting homosexuality (cf. Lev. 18:22; 20:13), is sometimes tragically misread as calling for the punishment of death to those who engage in same-sex relations. There is, however, no support for that interpretation, either from Paul's vantage point or from our own. In fact, that misreading is, in Paul's words 'without excuse' (Rom. 2:1)." Grieb, *Story of Romans*, 29. Ward, who analyzed Plato, Philo, and Phocylides traditions, notes that the language of Rom 1:26–27 does not derive from Lev 18:22 or Lev 20:13, and unlike Plato, Philo, and Pseudo-Phocylides, does not speak of same-sex female relations. Paul, however, is certainly influenced by Plato's tradition, particularly the *Timaeus* and *Laws*. There is also a possibility that Rom 1:26–27 represents an antihedonistic, procreation argument typical of Hellenistic Jews (e.g., Philo and Pseudo-Phocylides) who wish to set themselves apart from the pleasure-oriented Romans. The fact is that the abundant evidence for women loving women in the Roman world may well reflect the increasing sexual freedom that women were experiencing, despite the criticism of some male moralists. Ward, "Why Unnatural?" See also Martin, "Heterosexism."

62. In the Stoic list of vices, *akrasia* is listed as one of the many vices subordinated to the main four vices—imprudence (*aphrosunē*), injustice (*adikia*), cowardice (*deilia*),

tures the (homo)sexual milieu in which he and his mixed audience lived; it was a world where homosexual behavior was believed to be the result of excessive lust and uncontrollable sexual desire.[63] It is important to underline that in this text Paul does not have in mind Old Testament (OT) examples of homosexual behavior.[64] I argue that it is from this Hellenistic milieu that Paul speaks of the disapproved sexual behavior among gentiles—generally connected with Greek sexual vices—to emphasize *not* his personal view about homosexual behavior but the evil nature of the sin of "idolatry" (*eidōlolatria*) and its consequences. Paul turns to homosexual behavior practiced among pagan men and women, who exchange "natural intercourse for unnatural" (Rom 1:26–27), as an example to address the Roman believers about his main topic, "idolatry" (*eidōlolatria*).[65] Trent Rodgers states that the connection between the sin of idolatry and sexual immorality was a common theme in Hellenistic Jewish idol polemics.[66] Within this pagan context, Paul aims to show the connection between idolatry and sexual vices, and the close association between "desire" (*orexei*) and both idolatry and sexual vices. Similar to other Hellenistic Jewish authors, Paul expresses his critique of idolatry by telling Roman believers (Jewish and

---

and intemperance (*akolasia*)—(DL, *Lives* 7.92 [*SVF* 3:265]) in opposition to the four main or generic virtues—prudence (*phronēsis*), justice (*dikaiosunē*), courage (*andreia*), and temperance (*sōphrosunē*). However, in Diogenes Laertius, *akrasia* is listed as a subordinate vice, without specifying to which primary vice it is subordinated (DL *Lives* 7.93 [*SVF* 265). Inwood, *Ethics and Human Action*, 136–39. See also Philo, *Opif.* 158; *Abr.* 135; *Spec.* 3.43; Plato, *Leg.* 836C; Plutarch, *Alex. fort.* 3.336d; *Conj. praec.* 16.140b; Seneca, *Ep.* 95.21. Aristotle's discussion of *akrasia* is found in bk. 7 of the *Nicomachean Ethics*. See also Reno, "Pornographic Desire," 175; Rorty, *Essays on Aristotle's Ethics*, 267–84. For studies on *akrasia* in Greek philosophy, see Bobonich and Destrée, Akrasia *in Greek Philosophy*.

63. This is also the view of Sprinkle in "Paul and Homosexual Behavior," 500. See Dio Chrysostom, *Discourses*, 4.9, 7.149, 7.151–7.152; Plato, *Leg.* 636C; Musonius, *Diss.* 12 (translation in Musonius Rufus, "Lectures and Fragments").

64. Gen 19:1–29; Judg 19:1–21; Lev 18:1–30; 20:13. For a short analysis of these texts, see appendix A.

65. A good number of scholars have supported the view that in this passage Paul targets gentiles and not Roman believers (Jewish and gentile); for example, Sloan, "Paul's Jewish Addressee," 524. Stowers also suggests that the original readers of the Letter to the Romans were gentiles who understood Paul's progressive discourse about "gentile wickedness," especially in Rom 1:18—2:16. Stowers, *Rereading of Romans*, 159, 83–100; also Swancutt, "Sexy Stoics."

66. Rogers, "God and the Idols," 269.

gentile) that they (pagans) are worshipers of idols instead of the true living God.⁶⁷ Paul hopes to prevent the Roman believers from God's punishment.

Bowden, who like other scholars supports the view that Paul has in mind gentiles not Roman believers (Jewish and gentile) as his audience, puts God's punishment in this way: "God gives the Gentiles over to same sex relations as punishment for idolatry" (Rom 1:24–28).⁶⁸ Paul is acquainted with Greco-Roman culture, where homosexual practice is quite acceptable and even highly regarded.⁶⁹ In the Jewish literary tradition, especially in texts composed in the Greek diaspora, as Loader argues, "Same sex relations commonly feature in condemnation of pagan cultures."⁷⁰ Like other Hellenistic Jewish authors,⁷¹ Paul regards such relations as a quintessential vice proper of gentiles and idolaters, *not* of believers.⁷²

---

67. The same criticism is found in other Hellenistic Jewish literature, e.g., Let. Aris. 152; Wis 15:8–27; T. Reu 3:10—4:11; Ps.-Phoc. 31.

68. Bowden, *Desire*, 481.

69. E.g., Plato's *Symposium*; Plutarch's *Lycurgus*. Dunn, *Theology of Paul*, 122. See Greenberg, *Construction of Homosexuality*, 141–60, 202–10. Dodson asserts that sexual licentiousness, e.g., heterosexual, homosexual, bisexual activities, and pederasty, often occurred at the *convivia* and that might have been in Paul's background when he was writing Rom 1:26–27 (see also Philo, *Spec.* 3.37; *Contempl.* 50–52; *Hypoth.* 7.1; *QG* 4.37). Dodson provides a broad range of Greek and Roman examples of the widespread association of sexual perversion associated with Roman banquets to interpret Rom 1:26–27, such as male homosexual acts and men's habits of molesting slave boys and abusing male prostitutes and children. Dinner parties associated with these carnal activities would include women taking part in all kinds of warped behavior. Dodson, "Convivial Background," 112–13.

70. For Philo's example, see n34; Sib. Or. 3:185–87, 596–99; 4:33–34; 5:166–68, 387, 430; Let. Aris. 108, 130, 152; Josephus, *J. A.* 3.275, 4.290–4.291, 15.25; *C. Ap.* 2.269, 2.273–2.275; *B.J.* 4.561–4.562; Ps.-Phoc. 3:190–92. While Roman critics declared homosexual relations a Greek disease, the Greeks in turn condemned the Romans for tolerating such relationships beyond when young men reached marrying age at around thirty years old. See Loader, "Reading Romans 1," 125–26, 132.

71. Wis 14:26; Let. Aris. 152; Philo, *Abr.* 135–137; *Spec.* 3.37–3.42; Sib. Or. 3:184–86, 764; Ps.-Phoc. 3:190–92; 3:213–14; Josephus, *C. Ap.* 2.273–2.275. See Dunn, *Theology of Paul*, 122.

72. I argue against scholars who suggest that Paul stands on his Jewish tradition (see Lev 18:22; 20:13) and is reacting against homosexual practices as contrary to nature (Rom 1:26; 1 Cor 6:9). This is the view of Dunn, *Theology of Paul*, 122. Like in Rom 1:26, in Sib. Or. 3:575–90, 657–710, 762–66, there is a clear denunciation of idolatry and its connection with sexual aberration and immorality in the pagan world (see Let. Aris. 152). See also denunciation against Roman sexual vices in Sib. Or. 5:162–78, 386–96. Collins, "Sibylline Oracles," 1:362–80.

Indeed, as Stegman notes, in Rom 1:26–27 "same-sex relations are not the main issue."[73] Therefore, Paul's focus is on "sinful passions" (*ta pathēmata tōn hamartiōn*), "idolatry" (*eidōlolatria*), the source of all vices, especially sexual vices and their relation with the failure to recognize and honor God or lack of knowledge of God; these were common characteristics among gentiles (Rom 1:21–23, 25, 28a).[74] As David M. Coffey denotes, it is the gentiles (not believers) who knowingly refused to worship God and gave themselves up to sophistry, exchanging the glory of the immortal God for images of men, birds, animals, and reptiles.[75] In Rom 1:28–32 Paul writes,

> Since they did not see fit to acknowledge God [*ton theon echein en epignōsei*], God gave them up to a debased mind [*adokimon noun*] and to things that should not be done [*poiein ta mē kathēkonta*]. They were filled with every kind of wickedness, greediness, and evil. Full of envy, murder, strife, deceit, and malice. They are whisperers, slanderers, God-haters, insolent, arrogant, boastful, inventors of evil things, disobedient to parents, senseless, faithless, heartless, and merciless. They know God's decree, that those who practice such things [*ta toiauta prassontes*] deserve to die—yet they not only do them but even applaud others who practice them.

As in the vice lists in 1 Cor 5:10–11; 6:9–10; and Gal 5:19–21, the vices and improper conduct in Rom 1:28–32 are characteristic among nonbelievers and commonly listed in the catalog of Greek philosophical ethical systems (especially in Stoicism) and in Jewish ethics.[76] Paul lists four items that function as main or generic vices deriving from idolatry (Rom 1:18–23): unrighteousness (*adikia*), wickedness (*ponēria*), greediness (*pleonexia*),

---

73. Stegman, "Saint Paul on Homosexuality."

74. See Tobin, *Paul's Rhetoric*, 108.

75. Coffey, "Natural Knowledge of God," 676–77. The author states that Paul does not refer to animal worship among his contemporaries/believers; rather, he is alluding to Ps 106:19–20 and Deut 4:15–18, the descriptions of the idolatrous behavior of the Hebrews in the wilderness. So, in describing the idolatry of the gentiles, Paul is borrowing the language that the OT uses to describe the same sin committed by the Hebrews in the wilderness.

76. Bowden stresses the notion that in Rom 1:28–32, Paul speaks of non-Jews who honored foreign gods, and because of that "God gave them over to their sins." That is, God punished gentile idol worshipers by allowing them to be enslaved to the "passions" (*pathē*) and "desires" (*epithymiai*) of their bodies. Bowden, *Desire*, 40–41. See also Stowers, *Rereading of Romans*, 36–37.

and evil (*kakia*).⁷⁷ Then, Paul identifies types of sinful individuals "who practice such things" (*ta toiauta prassontes*) because they (gentiles) do not know God (Rom 1:28): those who are full of envy (*phthonou*), murder (*phonou*), strife (*eridos*), deceit (*dolou*), and malice (*kakoētheia*); those who are whisperers (*psithyristas*), slanderers (*katalalous*), God-haters (*theostygeis*), and boasters (*alazonas*); the insolent (*hubristas*) and arrogant (*hyperēphanous*); those who are inventors of evil things (*epheuretas kakōn*), disobedient to their parents (*goneusin apeitheis*); those who are without sense (*asynetous*), without faith (*asynthetous*), without humanity (*astorgous*), and without mercy (*aneleēmonas*) (Rom 1:29b–31). In Rom 1:26–27, Paul relates "passions" (*pathē*) with unnatural sex; however, none of the vices listed next in 1:29–31 includes sexual vices or *porneia*. Recently, this detail has been addressed by Bowden;⁷⁸ but he has overlooked the fact that in this passage Paul is connecting these vices and conduct with the lack of knowledge of God, which in Paul's mind is closely linked with idolatry, the focus of his argument.

In light of Greek and Hellenistic Jewish traditions, Paul depicts these ungodly individuals as being overpowered by all kinds of vices which are against God's commandment. The greatest vice of idolatry is understood as the failure to worship the one true God in the midst of "other deities" of the Greco-Roman world, suggesting it is the practice of idols worship that fits with the lack of the knowledge of God.⁷⁹ Although he recognizes the celestial beings as "gods" (1 Cor 8:5)—although "no idol in the world really exists because there is no God but one" (1 Cor 8:4)—for Paul, the worship of these pagan deities is the source of all kinds of vices and sins, which includes sexual vices (Rom 1:24–32).⁸⁰

---

77. The Textus Receptus inserts the vice *porneia* before *ponēria, pleonexia*, and *kakia*. However, it seems unlikely that Paul would have included *porneia* within the list itself because he argues in Rom 1:24–25 that such vices as listed here issue from the licentious practice of idolatry. See Metzger, *Textual Commentary*, 506.

78. Bowden, *Desire*, 510.

79. The complexities of Greek deities and the nature of Greek religion are explained well by Despland, *Education of Desire*, 88–98.

80. Moo, *Epistle of the Romans*, 117. In his study of Rom 1:24–28, Bowden states that "God responds to Gentile idolatry by giving the people over παραδίδωμι to three things": "God gave them up because of their desires of their hearts to uncleanness" (v. 24a); "God gave them up to disgraceful emotions" (v. 26a); and "God gave them up to a debased mind" (v. 28b). Bowden, *Desire*, 479. Bowden fleshes out these three things in *Desire*, 479–81.

Alec A. Lucas argues that Rom 1:22–32 concentrates on the sexual immorality that results from idolatry, and that the multitude of vices resulting from idolatry implies that idolatry is the source or cause of all kinds of vices.[81] Particularly, scholars have found strong commonality between Paul's language in Rom 1:18–32 and Wis 13:1–9, arguing that in both God has made himself known through what he has made; thus, from the things in creation, God's character ought to have been discernible.[82] Likewise, human beings failed to glorify God or to give him thanks. As Dunn says, "Knowledge of God is a lie if it is not an acknowledgment of him. Hence, as in Wis. 13.8–9, they are without excuse (1.20). And the consequence, again as in Wis. 13.1—futility of thinking and a foolish heart darkened (1.21)."[83] Frank J. Matera, who finds explicit similarities between Rom 1:18–32 and Wis 13–15, argues that Paul differs from the book of Wisdom's critique of gentile idolatry in two ways: whereas Wisdom supposes that gentiles do not attain a knowledge of God from creation (Wis 13:1), Paul assumes that gentiles know something about God from creation and affirms that they will not sin because they know that God acknowledges them (Wis 15:2).[84] Loader shows the close connection between sexual immorality and idolatry within the Greek social context (Wis 14:23–26), arguing that "the major focus appears to be sexual wrongdoing in the context of drunken partying and similar activities in the public sphere."[85]

Furthermore, in Rom 1:26–27 Paul highlights the negativity of "degrading passions" (*pathē atimias* [v. 26]) in connection with the passion of desire, using the Greek term *orexis* (strong desire, lust, appetite) in verse 27 instead of *epithymia*. Martin underlines the idea that Paul's use of *orexis* intends to represent sexual desire as burning or feelings of strong lust.[86] Joseph A. Fitzmyer notes that *orexis* "expresses a human or animal desire, but often used in a pejorative sense." Thus, in the context of Rom 1:27, *orexis* denotes strong sexual impulses.[87] Significantly, Paul does not speak in the context of

81. Lucas, *Evocations of the Calf*, 144.
82. Loader, "Reading Romans 1," 124.
83. Dunn, *Theology of Paul*, 91.
84. Matera, *Romans*, 44.
85. Loader, *Pseudepigrapha on Sexuality*, 425. The sexual promiscuity might have referred to adultery, prostitution, or illicit sexual relations, such as between a barren woman and a eunuch. Interestingly, there is no explicit reference to male same-sex relations. On this see Loader, *Pseudepigrapha on Sexuality*, 398–426.
86. Martin, *Sex and Single Savior*, 66.
87. Fitzmyer, *Romans*, 286; see also H. W. Heidland, "ὀρέγομαι, ὄρεξις," *TDNT* 5:447–48.

biblical tradition. Rather, he has in mind his Christocentric monotheism, rooted in his Jewish monotheism, and the believers' positive response to God's sovereignty in the new era of the Christ-event: God is one and Jesus Christ is Lord. Paul's explicit ascription to same-gender sexual relations in Rom 1:26–27 is then in reference to idolatry, a cultural practice that Paul is well aware of. Idolatry, as the root of vices, is equivalent to sinful passions, vices, and desires that enslave the flesh.

Unlike gentiles, who are idol worshipers and practice vices, Paul exhorts early believers that idolatry must be avoided; for "the wrath of God" (*orgē theou*) is revealed against the unrighteousness of gentiles who suppress the truth about God and the knowledge of God. The language of *orgē theou* (a divine quality), which Paul inherited from his Jewish tradition (2 Kgs 22:13; 2 Chr 12:12; Ezra 10:14; Ps 78:31; Isa 13:13; 26:20), is closely linked to monotheism and idolatry.[88] And the expression "the knowledge of God" (*epistēmē theou*) in Paul is linked to "virtue" (*aretē*).[89] Indeed, in Stoic tradition, "virtue" (*aretē*) is "knowledge" (*epistēmē*), and vice is the "lack of knowledge" (*agnoia*). In this sense, Paul's association of vices with the lack of knowledge of God goes closely in line with the philosophical notion of the contrast between virtue and vices and knowledge and lack of knowledge of God. Therefore, Paul's central point of discussion is idolatry and its dangerous consequences, and he explains it within the context of Greco-Roman sexual vices and other vices well known to his audience.[90] Sexual vices are not only a gentile failure to acknowledge or *know* God but are also juxtaposed against God's righteousness and Paul's understanding of his Christocentric monotheism.

---

88. In Paul's Jewish tradition, *orgē theou* "denotes the expected reaction to human sin and evil"; it is linked not only to monotheism but also to the "covenantal relationship of God with Israel, expressing the justifiable reaction of a loving and faithful God toward his disobedient people and their proneness to idolatry, to evil, and to sinful conduct. It denotes God's steadfast attitude as a judge of Israel's breach of the covenant (Ezek 5:13; Hos 5:10; 2 Chr 36:16)." Fitzmyer, *Romans*, 107.

89. On the understanding of virtue as knowledge, see Jedan, *Stoic Virtues*, 66–80, 97–102.

90. Against Malina and Pilch, who state that Paul is condemning homosexual relations. Malina and Pilch, *Social-Science Commentary*, 231.

Sexual Vices Endanger the Lives of Believers

In several passages, Paul provides sexual instructions and/or his advice regarding sexual matters in the gentile Christian communities he founded. In 1 Thess 4:1–5, Paul uses the language of "passion" (*pathos*) in connection with his exhortation about how to control one's body, avoiding "desirous passion" (*pathei epithymias*), which is often connected to excessive sex and uncontrolled sexual desire.[91] In the context when Paul is reminding the Thessalonian believers what he, Silvanus, and Timothy already told them (4:6)—about what "the will of God is" (4:3)—the topic of sexual vices in connection with "the lack of knowledge of God" (*agnoia theou*) and gentiles is in view.[92] Particularly in 1 Thess 4:3–6, the association of "desire" (*epithymia*) with "passion" (*pathos*) is explicit and is presented in terms of a contrast between "holiness" (*hagiasmos*) and "sexual immorality" (*porneia*). "Sexual impurity" (*akatharsia*) in all its forms is a distinguished characteristic in Paul's gentile and idolatrous world.[93] Because of the mystery religions and cults in Thessalonica, where fellow citizens engaged in all kinds of sexual promiscuity and idolatry,[94] Paul worried about the pressure from these individuals to compromise the believers' stance on *porneia*. What is revealing as well as significant in 1 Thessalonians is that Paul does not focus on a single sexual vice endangering the believers' holiness and honorable lives; Dunn says, the view in 1 Thess 4:5 is unspecified sexual indulgence, thus it probably covers a whole range of unlawful sexual

---

91. Fredrickson, "Passionless Sex," 27, 29. For similarities between 1 Thess 4:1–8 and Rom 1:18–32; 12:1–2, see Kim, "Paul's Common Paraenesis," 133–35.

92. In 1 Thess 4–5, Paul (with Silvanus and Timothy) writes about various ethical instructions that they previously taught the Thessalonian believers, topics for which the believers probably needed clarification in order to please God (4:2, 6, 11, 15); for example, holiness in the midst of pagan sexual immorality, mutual charity (the commandment to "love one another," which they say God taught them), the believers' death before Jesus' coming, and the believers' own resurrection. Paul and his coworkers used this opportunity to give them miscellaneous exhortations about how to remain faithful as they wait for Jesus' coming while living in a complex pagan world, how to show respect toward those who minister to them in love and in Christ, how to help one another, and how to be at peace and in joy. The letter ends with a list of "dos" and "don'ts," characteristic behavior that conforms with faithfulness, holiness, and the will of God.

93. In Col 3:5, the term "desire" appears together with sexual immorality (*porneia*), passion (*pathē*), evil (*kakos*), covetousness (*pleonexia*), and idolatry (*eidōlolatria*).

94. Such pagan cults would have included those of Cabirus, Dionysus, Isis, and Aphrodite. See Bowden, *Desire*, 375; Donfried, "Cults of Thessalonica."

relations.⁹⁵ Certainly, the unspecified sexual vices (*porneia, akatharsia,* and *pathei epithymias*) derive from idol worship and are related to gentiles who do not know God (1 Thess 1:5–9). Paul views the dangers of *porneia* and its sequels as threatening to many of his Thessalonian gentile believers who had turned away from idols and sexual vices (1 Thess 1:9).

Similarly, 1 Cor 5–7, for which detailed analysis goes beyond the scope of this study, cannot be overlooked.⁹⁶ In this unit (5:1—7:40), Paul does not rebuke the Corinthian believers for tolerating *porneia*;⁹⁷ instead, Paul is responding to questions about sexual desire and behavior raised by the believers at Corinth, a pagan and idolatrous city known for its bad reputation for sexual promiscuity.⁹⁸ In 1 Cor 7, Paul advises believers to control excessive or uncontrolled sexual desires in marriage and celibacy.⁹⁹ Bowden makes a good observation—the word *epithymia* is not mentioned in 1 Cor 5:1—7:40, which is his discussion of *porneia*;¹⁰⁰ Paul waits to

95. Dunn, *Theology of Paul*, 121.

96. See also Lev 18:8; 20:11. For good analysis of this topic, see Martin, *Corinthian Body*, 198–228.

97. I concord with most of Bowden's argument in *Desire*, 416–32, especially 429. However, I think Bowden goes too far suggesting that, in 1 Cor 5:1—7:40 and 8:1—11:1, Paul is alluding to the decisions of the Jerusalem Council, instructions given to him by James at the end of the council about abstaining from "sexual immorality" (*porneias* [1 Cor 7]) and avoiding "meat sacrificed to idols" (*eidōlothytōn* [1 Cor 8:1—11:1]). Wright Knust asserts that because sexual morality pervaded Christian discourse, Paul worried about marriage practices, sexual renunciation, incest, adultery, intercourse with prostitutes, and other sexual practices he identifies as *porneia* (e.g., 1 Thess 4:1–7; Gal 5:16–26; 1 Cor 5:1–13; 6:9–20; 7:1–40; 10:7–22; 11:2–15; 2 Cor 6:14–18; Rom 6:12–23). Wright Knust, *Abandoned Lust*, 52. For an argument against Wright Knust, see Bowden, *Desire*, 27–27.

98. Ancient Corinth was historically known for the practice of fornication and sacred prostitutes who served at the temple of Aphrodite. See Murphy-O'Connor, *St. Paul's Corinth*, 53–57. According to Westfall (*Paul and Gender*, 194), prostitution in Corinth was a predominantly male activity. An honorable woman's sexuality was severely restricted in the culture; men, however, had the option of accessing prostitutes in a temple or in a brothel or forming liaisons with women or men who were marginalized for various reasons and had multiple sex partners. See also Wright Knust, *Unprotected Texts*, 82. For prostitution at Corinth, see Lanci, "Stones Don't Speak," especially 113–52.

99. For a good analysis of 1 Cor 7 within its Hellenistic context, see Deming, *Paul on Marriage*. Westfall claims that the Stoic view in the Stoic-Cynic debates on marriage is often seen to influence Paul's views on the advantages of celibacy. Westfall, *Paul and Gender*, 197. See also "Sinful Body," in Engberg-Pedersen, *Paul and Philosophy*, 309–29.

100. Bowden explains that behind Paul's statement in 1 Cor 10:6a in reference to *epithymētēs* is Num 11 LXX and Israel's desire for meat. Indeed, Israel's problem was that they allowed their desires to cause them to weep for the food they had enjoyed in Egypt

mention it until 1 Cor 10:6 when he exhorts the Corinthian believers on whether they could eat meat that had been sacrificed to idols (8:1—11:1), as we shall see below.[101] He makes use of the phrase *epithymētas kakōn* (one who desires evil things) and the aorist verb *kakeinoi epethumēsan* (those who desired). In light of the Stoic and Hellenistic traditions, Paul articulates his personal advice as follows: if married, have sex regularly so as to avoid *porneia* (7:2), and if possible, avoid marriage unless (you have) "lack of self-control" (*akrasia*) and/or (your) sexual passion is unmanageable (7:5, 9, 36).[102] At this point, it is important to note that for Paul sexual desire is not in itself sinful; what is sinful is the *excessive* passion/desire that goes in the wrong direction (Rom 1:27; 1 Cor 7:9).[103] His personal advice, then, follows the tradition of most Jewish writers who consider sexual desire and pleasure within the context of marriage and procreation as something positive, and sexual desire in excess like wine in excess (see also Philo, *Spec.* 1.192; Sir 26:8–9; 32:5–6; T. Jud 14:1), as dangers that need to be controlled and/or directed.[104]

Within the same traditions, Paul also offers a set of explicit instructions regarding the importance of "self-control" (*enkrateia*) and self-mastery in response to sexual behavior "done in pursuit of pleasure, in the passion of excessive desire, and without the protective guard of moderating self-control."[105] J. Edward Ellis is right to suggest that for Paul the real issue is not the elimination of sexual desire, but its control to avoid excessive

---

as slaves (Num 11:4a; 34 LXX). Bowden, *Desire*, 278. For the whole analysis of 1 Cor 10:6, see Bowden, *Desire*, 278–89, 422–30.

101. In his analysis, Bowden (*Desire*, 422) focuses on the phrase *epithymētas kakōn* in 10:6a only and overlooks in his discussion the term *epethumēsan* in 10:6b.

102. Ps.-Phoc. 175–206. See also Wright Knust, *Unprotected Texts*, 109. On the central arguments of a debate on marriage in Stoicism and Cynicism as Paul's background, see Deming, *Paul on Marriage*, 50–107. Deming (*Paul on Marriage*, 213) suggests that the fact that Paul employs in 1 Cor 7 a number of similarities with popular maxims from the general philosophical milieu of the Hellenistic world (e.g., maxims attributed to Menander, Euripides, Plato, and Crates) indicates that Corinthian believers were probably exposed to a syncretistic or popularized form of Stoicism at Corinth.

103. Loader, "Reading Romans 1," 133.

104. See discussion in ch. 1.

105. The same exhortation is found in Paul's Hellenistic Jewish tradition: Sib. Or. 2:130–31, 142, 145; T. Reu 1:6; 4:7–8; 5:3–4; 6:1; T. Lev 9:9; 14:6; 17:11–12; T. Sim 5:3; T. Iss 4:4; 7:2; T. Jud 11:1–5; 12:1–9; 13:5–8; 17:1–3; 18:2–6; T. Dan 5:7; T. Jos 3:10; 10:2–3; Ps.-Phoc. 59–69, 76, 98. On the concept of *porneia* in 1 Cor 5–6, see Wheeler-Reed et al., "Can a Man Commit."

desires.[106] Thus, in order to inculcate sexual self-mastery among the Corinthian believers, Paul recommends celibacy for the strong and marriage for the weak.[107] He connects *porneia* and "lack of self-control" (*akrasia*), two vices among gentiles, when he advises the believers to marry if they cannot control their sexual urges or lack self-control (1 Cor 7:1–9). Loader puts it in this way: "Paul would have shared disapproval of excessive passion and been suspicious of the dangers of strong passion, although he can accommodate strong passion such as in his advice that those with strong passion should marry and not feel guilty for doing so (1 Cor 7,9; similarly 7,28)."[108] According to him, Paul is not so much concerned with the intensity or excess of sexual desire, but "the *misdirection*" (emphasis added).[109] Because Paul is aware of the realistic power of sexual desire in the pagan environment, he assures them that it is better to marry than to be burned with passions (1 Cor 7:5, 9; 7:37).[110] Along this line, Reno has suggested that "these two concepts [*porneia* and *akrasia*] refer to a single problem: Paul alleges that the Corinthians lack [the] self-control necessary to be celibate, a point made evident ostensibly by the acts of lechery among them."[111] In this text, Paul shows his preference of singleness to marriage (1 Cor 7:7), which he views as a gift from God given to him, using the philosophical language of *erōs* (love), or Platonically speaking "tyrannical desire" (1 Cor 7:8–9, 38). However, unlike Philo and other authors, Paul does not consider procreative intent as a cure-all for sexual passions. Actually, marriage helps to protect those believers of weak self-control from the dangers of excessive sexual passions and desire.

Moreover, in 1 Cor 6:9–11, a passage where Paul challenges those who fail to control desire or "lack self-control" (*akrasia*), his main concern is sinful sexual vices and *not* his personal evaluation of homosexual behavior,

---

106. Ellis, *Paul and Ancient Views*, 168–69.

107. Wright Knust, *Unprotected Texts*, 85.

108. Loader, "Reading Romans 1," 134. Ellis argues that the issue is not the elimination, but the control of sexual desire to avoid excessive desires. Ellis, *Paul and Ancient Views*, 168–69.

109. Loader, "Reading Romans 1," 134. Similarly, Martin argues that Paul is concerned not with a "*disoriented* desire, but with an *inordinate* desire" (emphasis original), namely the excessive quantity of sexual desire. Martin, "Heterosexism," 342.

110. Dunn, *Theology of Paul*, 121; Reno, "Pornographic Desire," 181.

111. Reno, "Pornographic Desire," 183. I interpret Reno's statement, "Corinthians lack self-control," as a reference to pagan Corinthians and not to the Corinthian believers. For further study, see Deming, *Paul on Marriage*.

as in Rom 1:26–27. Paul emphasizes Greek vices (*agnoia*) and again the lack of knowledge of God among nonbelievers and warns the Corinthian believers not to go back to what they used to be. He writes, "Do you not know that wrongdoers [*adikoi*] will not inherit the kingdom of God? Do not be deceived! Sexually immoral persons [*pornoi*], idolaters [*eidōlolatrai*], adulterers [*moichoi*], male prostitutes [*malakoi*], sodomites [*arsenokoitai*], thieves, the greedy, drunkards [*methuroi*], revilers, robbers—none of these will inherit the kingdom of God. And this is what some of you used to be" (1 Cor 6:9–11a).[112] Again, the main issue is idolatry and its close association with the "failure to recognize and honor God."[113] Paul treats both idolatry and lack of knowledge of God along the same vein as sexual vices and other vices strongly connected with sexual vices. He does the same thing as in Rom 1:29–31, identifying individuals who engage in vices, but in this case most of the vices are specific (or vices that lead to) Greek sexual vices, such as sexual immorality, idolatry, adultery, male homosexuality, sodomy, and drunkenness. In Rom 2:17–24, Paul delivers a criticism to those (Jews) who rely on the practice of the commandments of the law. In it, Paul reflects a clear contrast between knowledge of God/truth and adultery/idolatry, two vices closely connected with *epithymia*. Particularly, the four sexual vices in which individuals engage in 1 Cor 6:9—*pornoi* (sexually immoral persons), *moichoi* (adulterers), *malakoi* (effeminates), and *arsenokotai* (drunkards)—are directly correlated to the vice of "idolatry" (*eidōlolatria*) and "those who are idolatrous" (*eidōlolatrai*).

Furthermore, the same construction is previously found in 1 Cor 5:9–11 where Paul writes,

> I wrote to you in my letter not to associate with sexually immoral persons [*pornois*]—not at all meaning the sexually immoral

---

112. The Greek word *arsenokoitai*, here translated as "sodomites," is difficult to translate (see also 1 Tim 1:10). It can be also translated as homosexual sex or men who have sex with men. For the various possible meanings, see Martin, *Sex and Single Savior*, 37–50. According to Martin (*Sex and Single Savior*, 40), *arsenokoitai* "had a more specific meaning in Greco-Roman culture than homosexual penetration in general, a meaning that is now lost to us. It seems to have referred to some kind of economic exploitation by means of sex, perhaps but not necessarily homosexual sex." Similarly, the term *malakos*, often translated as "effeminate" or "male prostitute," did not always refer to the sexual act itself. Martin notes that the category of effeminate men was much broader than that. For example, *malakoi* are those people who cannot put up with hard work, men who take life easy, and men who are cowards. Martin, *Sex and Single Savior*, 44–45. For other interpretations, see West and Shore-Goss, *Queer Bible Commentary*, 640–43.

113. Stegman, "Saint Paul on Homosexuality."

persons [*pornois*] of this world, or the greedy and robbers, or idolaters [*eidōlolatrais*], since you would then need to go out of the world. But now I am writing to you not to associate with anyone who bears the name of brother or sister who is sexually immoral [*pornos*] or greedy, or is an idolater [*eidōlolatrēs*], reviler, drunkard [*methysos*], or robber. Do not even eat with such a one.

There are clear connections between sexual vices and idolatry in 1 Cor 5:9-11 and 6:9-10. For example, idolatry is generally placed with sexual vices like sexual immorality, intoxication or drunkenness, homosexuality, and male prostitution.[114] These pagan (sexual) vices flow from "excessive/immoderate desire" (*pleonazousa/ametros epithymia*), which was once indulged and practiced by gentile believers in their pre-Christian lives, and now Paul urges them to avoid associating with their former pagan pals (1 Cor 5:11).[115] Indeed, in 1 Cor 5:1-6, Paul shows his strong intolerance of a man sleeping with his father's "woman" (*gynē*).[116] In this case, he imparts his personal and radical disagreement combining Stoic concerns for marital duty and Jewish-Christian concerns of the dangers of *porneia*.[117] For Paul, members of the Corinthian community must neither associate with any brother guilty of "sexual immorality" (*porneia*) nor even share table fellowship with such sexually immoral individuals, for they will likewise behave like pagans and idolaters.

Interestingly, in 1 Cor 6:15-16, we find the only use of *pornē* (sexually immoral person) in Paul's oeuvre employed in the sense of a comparison between the "flesh" (*sarx*) belonging to lustfulness and another to the Lord.[118] In other words, Paul contrasts a *pornē* with the Lord Christ, posing two rhetorical questions: "Do you not know that your bodies are members of Christ [*christou*]?" in verse 15; and "Do you not know that whoever is united to a *pornē* becomes one body with her?" in verse 16. It is at this point

---

114. In the NT, we find the Greek term *methysos* (drunkard) only in the lists of vices here in 1 Cor 5:11 and 6:10. See Preisker, *TDNT* 4:547.

115. Sexual depravity in ancient Greek culture is amply described in Plato, *Resp.* 5 (e.g., 457D1-2; 459A-457B; 462C; 464C-D). For details, see Ludwig, *Eros and Polis*, 305-18. It is also well known that in the ancient Greek and Roman cultures, sexual desire exceeding acceptable levels was addressed by philosophers and moralists, as Despland has demonstrated in *Education of Desire*, 157-62. See also Deming, *Paul on Marriage*, 31.

116. Wright Knust, *Unprotected Texts*, 85. For discussion on this passage, see McNamara, "Share the Incestuous Man."

117. Deming, *Paul on Marriage*, 213.

118. Gal 5:24; Rom 7:5; see also Sir 18:30—19:3. Stowers, *Rereading of Romans*, 42-82.

(v. 18) that Paul reinforces his main point of discussion—the dangers of idolatry and sexual vices—urging the believers with the imperative, "Flee [*pheugete*] from *sexual immorality*!" Paul exhorts believers not to become slaves to excessive sexual desires (vices; *sarx*) but to the Lord (virtues; *pneuma*). Later in his discussion against idolatry in 1 Cor 10:14–22, Paul again stresses his exhortation directed to the Corinthian believers with the imperative, "Flee [*pheugete*] from *idolatry*" (v. 14). In this text, as we shall see below, Paul contrasts those who participate in the blood and the body of Christ with those who are participants in eating meat sacrificed to idols, calling them "demons" (1 Cor 10:20–21).[119] Paul has in mind his Christocentric monotheism, not his former Jewish monotheism. Thus, to avoid failure in his Christocentric monotheism, Paul speaks of the dangers of idolatrous behavior in terms of common pagan sexual vices: the lustful indulgences in unnatural intercourse and sexual immorality, such as prostitution, adultery, and fornication.

A Lesson from the Past: Gluttony, Idolatry, and Sexual Immorality

In his missionary career as apostle to the gentiles, Paul knew how to navigate in the larger Greco-Roman world, especially in terms of his belief in Christocentric monotheism. He follows the traditional Jewish belief in God, the supreme and only God.[120] But Paul's exposition of the sinful dangers to his Christocentric monotheism revolved around the themes of the primacy of God, the righteousness of God through faith, the fidelity of God, and the grace of God given to those who believe in Christ the Lord. As part of the discussion about pagan idolatry, especially Egyptian idolatry, Paul expresses his rejection of polytheism and idol worship in Rom 1:23, 25.[121] He writes, "They change the glory of the immortal God for images of

119. On the topic of eating meat sacrificed to idols, see Bailey, *Paul Through Mediterranean Eyes*, 229–41, 283–92.

120. Gal 3:20; 1 Cor 8:4; Rom 3:30.

121. Criticism of Egyptian idolatry is found in various Hellenistic Jewish literatures, e.g., Philo, *Decal.* 78–80; *Spec.* 1.21–1.22, 1.24; *Legat.* 139; Josephus, *C. Ap.* 1.225, 1.239, 1.244, 1.249, 1.254, 2.66, 2.81, 2.86, 2.128–2.129, 2.139, 2.145–2.286; Let. Aris. 134–138; Wis 13–15; Sib. Or. 3:8–45, 184–87, 594–600, 764; 4:6–23; 7.1–15; 8:377–98; T. Reu 4:6; T. Jud 19:1–4. Fitzmyer (*Romans*, 283) suggests that in Rom 1:23 Paul alludes to Ps 106:20 MT, which reads, "They exchanged their glory for the image of a grass-eating bullock" (translation mine). According to Fitzmyer, this is an allusion to the worship of the golden calf in the wilderness (Exod 32:1–34).

mortal humans, birds, beasts, and reptiles," and "they exchanged the truth about God for a lie and worshiped and served the creature rather than the Creator, who is blessed for ever! Amen."[122] In continuity with his Jewish tradition, Paul appropriates as his own the creed of monotheism (the one true God over against the gentile deities) and claims that God's temple has no common ground with idols (2 Cor 6:16).[123]

Paul's ancestors in the wilderness (1 Cor 10:1-17), too, created an idol (golden calf)[124] and worshiped it while Moses was still on Mount Sinai (Exod 32).[125] So Paul does not wish the believers to fall into the same sins because they were baptized in Christ (Rom 6:3-4). Within this real Jewish experience, Paul exhorts the Corinthian believers, "Do not become idolaters [*eidōlolatrai*] as some of them did; as it is written, 'The people sat down to eat and drink [*ekathisen ho laos phagein kai pein*], and they rose up to play [*paizein*]'" (1 Cor 10:7).[126] Malina and Pilch point out that the word *eidōlolatrai*, translated as "idolaters," means to "show respect to deities revealed in the presence of images." Respect for these deities, like servants show to their masters, entailed eating (*phagein*), drinking (*pein*), and playing (*paizein*). Similar to the Greek vice *koitē* (illicit sex) in Rom 13:13b, which is a euphemism for sex, the "play" language is a euphemism for sexual promiscuity, a sexual behavior prohibited in the Torah;[127] thus, the term would have been familiar to Paul and his Corinthian audience.

For Paul, just like for Greek thinkers and Philo, "gluttony" (*gastrimargia*) was "too much eating."[128] This is clearly reflected in his discussion concerning the resurrection of the dead (1 Cor 15:12-58). He exhorts,

---

122. See also Martin, *Sex and Single Savior*, 54.

123. See also Aristob., 124-169; Jos. Asen. 11:10-11; Philo, *Spec.* 1.208; *Leg.* 2.1-2.2; *Legat.* 115; Josephus, *A.J.* 8.91, 5.335-5.337.

124. Paul does not explicitly mention the "golden calf" in his letters by name. However, he alludes to the incident in 1 Cor 10:7 ("Do not become idolaters as some of them did; as it is written, 'The people sat down to eat and drink, and they rose up to play'"), which is a direct reference to Exod 32:6 LXX, where the Israelites worship the golden calf: "And early the next day, he brought up whole burnt offerings and offered a sacrifice of deliverance, and the people sat down to eat and drink, and they arose to play" (NETS).

125. Malina and Pilch, *Social-Science Commentary*, 100; Bailey, *Paul Through Mediterranean Eyes*, 270.

126. Paul quotes Exod 32:6 where the Israelites in the wilderness fashioned a golden calf and offered burned offerings to it. Bailey, *Paul Through Mediterranean Eyes*, 270. In 1 Cor 10:23-33, Paul provides instances when early believers might eat what had been offered to idols without sin.

127. Malina and Pilch, *Social-Science Commentary*, 101.

128. Martin, *Sex and Single Savior*, 57.

> If with merely human hopes I fought with wild animals [*ethēriomachēsa*] at Ephesus, what would I have gained by it? If the dead are not raised, "Let us eat and drink [*phagōmen kai piōmen*], for tomorrow we die." Do not be deceived [*mē planasthe*]; "Bad companionship ruins good morals [*phtheirousin ēthē chrēsta homiliai kakai*]." Become sober [*eknēpsate*] like upright men, and sin no more [*mē hamartanete*]; for some people have no knowledge of God [*agnōsian gar theou tines echousin*]. I say this to your shame. (1 Cor 15:32–34)

It is worthwhile to mention four points: in this text (1) Paul exhorts the gentile believers at Corinth like a *philosophos*; (2) he makes a contrast between virtues ("good morals") and vices ("sin no more"); (3) he likewise links gluttony with both vices ("sin no more") and lack of knowledge (*agnoia*); and (4) he puts in perspective the close connection of idolatry with excessive eating and drinking (gluttony), lack of self-control, vices of the flesh, and lack of knowledge of God.

In line with Philo and the Platonic doctrine of "gluttony" (*gastrimargia*), Paul knows that "excessive" (*pleonazousa*) eating and drinking leads to "idolatry" (*eidōlolatria*), "sexual immorality" (*porneia*), and other sexual vices.[129] In 1 Cor 10:1–17, Paul relates gluttony with idolatrous worship and Stoically with both sexual vices and "lack of self-control" (*akrasia*), which is closely associated with the primary or generic vice, *akolasia* (intemperance). The Stoic Epictetus, for example, shows the relationship between sexual desires, pleasures, and lack of self-control when he speaks of "carnal intercourse" (*ēttēthēs . . . sunousia*) and "lack of self-control" (*akrasia*) in *Diss*. 2.18.6.[130] In Paul's Jewish tradition, eating and drinking played a role in their ancestors' feasting with the golden calf and in their "play," or sexual debauchery (Exod 32). Now, Paul encourages his audience not to become idolaters as some of his ancestors did and compares the idolatrous behavior and his ancestors' sexual vices with that of gentiles and idolaters. Paul gives an instruction in the next verse: "We must not indulge in sexual immorality [*porneuōmen*] as some of them did [*eporneusan*] and were destroyed by serpents" (1 Cor 10:8).[131] Paul expands the consequences of the idola-

---

129. Fitzmyer, *Romans*, 290. It is attested that in ancient Rome, sexual desire or immoderate sexual intercourse was strongly associated with food and wine. See also Langlands, *Sexual Morality*, 134.

130. Epictetus, *Diss*. 1–2.

131. Paul hopes to prevent the believers at Corinth from falling into the same disgrace as their ancestors; thus, he appeals to "his Jewish tradition as a textual basis for his ethical

trous and sexual sins committed in the wilderness; he writes, "God was not pleased with most of them," thus "they were struck down in the wilderness" (1 Cor 10:5). For Paul, the practice of "such things" (*toiauta* [Rom 1:32; 2:2, 3; 16:18; 1 Cor 5:1; Gal 5:21]) has ethical implications and refers to sexual sins; hence, they have negative consequences: punishment and the fury of God (Rom 1:18), which involves feelings of anguish and distress. "Those who do such things [*toiauta*]," Paul writes, "will not inherit the Kingdom of God" (Gal 5:21b; see also 1 Cor 6:10).

Paul knows that idol worship or idolatry could be a freeway to *methē* (drunkenness) and *kōmos* (revelry or reveling), two vices that lead to unbridled sexual appetite.[132] These vices are a gateway to sexual vices; therefore, Paul, drawing from the experience of the Israelites' sinful behavior in the wilderness (sexual promiscuity) and its golden calf (idolatry), commands believers to "Flee [*pheugete*] from the worship of idols [*eidōlolatrias*]!" (1 Cor 10:14).[133] Earlier they were also urged to "Flee [*pheugete*] from sexual immorality [*porneian*]" (1 Cor 6:18). In both cases, Paul makes a contrast: in 1 Cor 10:14-22, "participants in the altar" and "participation in the blood and body of Christ" versus "participants with demons"; in 1 Cor 6:15-20, *porneia* versus "Christ the Lord." The imperative *pheugete* in both occurrences is used in relation to idol worship at Corinth, and that involves "sacred prostitution" or *porneia*.[134] Therefore, in the context where Paul is dealing with "eating meat sacrificed to idols" (*peri de tōn eidōlothytōn* [8:1—11:1]) and worrying that the Corinthian believers may repeat the same sinful behavior—that is, sexual promiscuity and vices—as the

---

warning." In this way, Paul tells them the "gravity of idolatry in a wordplay: 'They were destroyed by the destroyer' (v. 10)." See Naveros Córdova, "1 Corinthians 10:1-4," 250.

132. For further study on the relationship between idol food and homosexual behavior, see Olson, "Idol Food."

133. As Paul emphasizes the ethical character of monotheism, Paul intends to universalize his view of monotheism. That is, salvation is for both Jews and gentiles, apart from the observance of the Mosaic law (Rom 3:4-25); the one God is also the God of all Jews and gentiles (Rom 15:9), for all those who have faith in Christ receive God's promises that were made to the patriarchs of Israel (Rom 9-11). Tobin, *Paul's Rhetoric*, 320-82. In Acts, there is a different depiction of Paul's attitude toward idolatry in Athens (Acts 17). Elliott and Reasoner have noted that in the book of Acts Paul gives ostensible respect to the piety of the Athenians, whose streets are filled with temples and altars and who even worship an "unknown god" (Acts 17:23). He takes the opportunity to present himself as the herald of this unknown god who is the true Creator of all things—"in him we live and move and have our being" (Acts 17:28). N. Elliott and Reasoner, *Documents and Images*, 87.

134. Bailey, *Paul Through Mediterranean Eyes*, 276.

Hebrews in the wilderness, he speaks of *epithymia* as a bad passion. He writes, "These things occurred as examples for us, so that we might not desire evil things [*epithymētas kakōn*] as they [their ancestors] did [*kakeinoi epethumēsan*]" (1 Cor 10:6).[135] Here, Paul strengthens the pejorative meaning of "these things" (*tauta*) and "evil things" (*kakoi*) with their relation to the passion of *epithymia*;[136] interestingly, previously, he used the expression "such things" (*toiauta*) with an implicit reference to sexual vices. To encourage the avoidance of such evil pagan practices (vices), gentile believers at Corinth, like those gentile believers at Thessalonica (1 Thess 1:9–10), are exhorted to turn away from idols and to worship the one God only.[137] In 1 Cor 10:1–17, "desire" (*epithymia*) is linked to "idolatry" (*eidōlolatreia*), "sexual immorality" (*porneia*), and sexual vices (*tauta, kakoi,* and *toiauta*). We depict a clear description of Paul's desire–sexual vices relationship; using Bowden's words, "Paul categorizes 'not being idolaters' (10:7), 'not engaging in sexual immorality' (10:8), 'not testing the anointed one' (10:9),

---

135. The noun *epithymētas* as well as the verb *epethumēsan* appear only here in the entire NT. Bowden points out similarities among Wis 16:1–4; Philo, *Migr.* 155–163; and 1 Cor 10:6. He argues that the three Hellenistic authors have in their background Num 11 LXX, the Israelites' faults in the wilderness, which included their desire for meat from Egypt and led them to the sin of idolatry (see also Ps 77:28–29; 105:13–15). In light of this connection, Bowden concludes his argument saying that, unlike 1 Thess 4:5, in 1 Cor 10:6 the phrase *epithymētas kakōn* (he does not include *epethumēsan* in his conclusion) is desire for meat, and not a reference to desire for sexual immorality. That Paul does not mention a cognate of *epithymia* in relation to *porneia* in 1 Cor 5:1—7:40 is for Bowden evidence to state that the objects related to sex were not the primary objects of desire and cognates in Paul. Bowden explains that the reason why Paul uses *kakōn* as the object of *epithymētēs* in 10:6 is because he, like other Roman imperial authors, recognizes that *kakōn* and related lexemes stood at the top of the paradigmatic tree when discussing objects of *epithymia* and cognates. Paul continues by reminding the Corinthian believers not to be idolaters (10:7), not to test Christ (10:9), and not to grumble (10:10), all of which he classifies as specific expressions of "those who desire bad things" (10:9). Certainly, Bowden's connection between 1 Cor 10:6 and Num 11 LXX in relation to desire for meat is right. However, I do not find his statement convincing because 1 Cor 10:6 must be read within the context of 1 Cor 10:1–22. The question whether or not desire relates to sexual immorality is a narrow view of Paul's argument in the whole passage. Paul is concerned with the *dangers of eating food sacrificed to idols and idolatry because they are a direct gateway to sexual immorality and sexual vices* (10:8). Thus, viewing both *epithymētēs* and *epethumēsan* in 10:6, what Paul has in mind is the connection of "these things" or "evil things," such as (sexual) desire, sexual immorality and vices, and idolatry. Bowden, *Desire*, 312, 322, 329, 429–32.

136. The language of "these things" is an inference to the golden calf.

137. See also Rom 14:11; 1 Cor 14:25; 2 Cor 9:13.

and 'not grumbling' (10:10) as specific expressions of 'those who desire bad things' (10:6)—the vice that introduced the list."[138]

Christocentric monotheism is essential in Paul's thought in the configuration of his understanding of desire and excessive (sexual) desire. It is true that in Romans, as in Galatians, Paul speaks of the ethical character of the law and works of the flesh within the theme of "the righteousness of God" (*dikaiosunē theou*).[139] In Romans, too, Paul presents the ethical character of *epithymia* within the theme of "the righteousness of God" (*tēn tou theou dikaiosunēn* [Rom 1:16-17]), and the "fruits" in the context of the unrighteousness of gentiles and the law (Rom 1:18—2:11).[140] But he also speaks of desire in relation to his Christocentric-monotheistic view in the context of "excessive" (*pleonazousa*) or "immoderate" (*ametros*) sexual desire, "sexual immorality" (*porneia*), "flesh" (*sarx*) and vices (*kakai*), "excessive" (*pleonazousa*) indulgences in food and drink ("gluttony" or *gastrimargia*), and, as we shall see, in relation to the tenth commandment, "you shall not covet" (*ouk epithymēseis* [Rom 7:7c]).[141] Paul shares with his Jewish tradition the notion that *epithymia* is a dangerous passion; perhaps this may be the reason why he focuses on the tenth commandment of the Decalogue.[142]

In 1 Cor 10:1-4, Paul reinterprets the work of the figure of "wisdom" (*sophia*) in the Jewish tradition,[143] and, governed by his Christocentric monotheism, Paul delivers a sui generis statement: "They drank from the

---

138. Bowden, *Desire*, 427.

139. The meaning of the expression *dikaiosunē theou* in Paul is much debated, especially around the word *theou*; whether the genitive *theou* is subjunctive or possessive, referring to God's own righteousness, or is an objective genitive, expressive of the righteousness communicated by God to human beings. For a summary of the major arguments, see Fitzmyer, *Romans*, 105-7.

140. According to Bowden, in Rom 1:18-32, Paul provides a description of gentile evil, and Paul develops a rhetorical strategy in Romans to persuade his Roman audience that the self-mastery they seek is not to be found in the Jewish law. Bowden, *Desire*, 474.

141. Lyonnet argues that in Rom 7:7 Paul refers to Gen 3, the fall of Adam, which is clearly mentioned in Rom 5. Lyonnet, "Histoire de salut," 133.

142. E.g., Apoc. Mos. 19:3 (desire is the origin of every sin); Philo, *Decal.* 142, 150, 153, 173; *Spec.* 4.84-4.85; Jas 1:15. See Dunn, *Theology of Paul*, 98.

143. The figure of *sophia* is an important concept in Hellenistic Jewish speculation. Unlike the *logos* in the prologue of the Gospel of John, *sophia* (wisdom) was never replaced by the *logos*. Indeed, even though the cosmic attributes given to *sophia* in Jewish wisdom literature are similar to those of the *logos* in the hymn of the prologue, the *logos*'s role goes beyond Jewish wisdom literature. For a good article on this topic, see Tobin, "Prologue of John."

spiritual rock that followed them, and the spiritual rock was Christ!" (1 Cor 10:4b).[144] In the new covenant coming with the Christ-event, it is now Christ who follows them (now believers). Therefore, if they have Christ accompanying them, they "must not indulge in [*porneia*]" as some of their ancestors did in the wilderness (1 Cor 10:8). Then, within the traditions of Plato and Philo, in a threefold relationship—desire-gluttony-idolatry—Paul develops his ethical message against "desire" (*epithymia*): the passion of desire, gluttony, and idolatry working together in the flesh bring forward excessive sexual desire and sexual vices;[145] "the sinful [behavior] beyond measure" (*kath' hyperbolēn hamartōlos*) is what believers ought to avoid. Likewise, in light of philosophical and Hellenistic Jewish traditions, for Paul, *epithymia* and "sinful passions" (*ta pathēmata tōn hamartiōn*) are "fruits" of death and are associated with slavery to the law, "lack of knowledge" (*agnoia*) of God, and idolatry. Such sinful behavior (expressed in the language of *toiauta, tauta, kakoi*) put God (Jewish monotheism) to the test in the wilderness *then*; with the Christ-event, such sinful behavior puts Christ (Christocentric monotheism) to the test *now*, for Christ was the spiritual rock.

CONCLUSION

Several important points have been explored in this chapter. Paul's Hellenistic Jewish and Greek philosophical traditions are at the fore as important components in his development of his understanding of "desire" (*epithymia*) and its connection to idolatry, sexual vices, gluttony, and lack of knowledge of God. His understanding of *epithymia* as a passion reflects certain knowledge of philosophical notions and doctrines found in Philo and 4 Maccabees. In particular, Paul shows familiarity with the Greek philosophical and Hellenistic Jewish traditions when he encourages believers to avoid idolatry, the root of excessive sexual desire and sexual vices. He used specific vices characteristic of the Greek catalog of vices and spoke within the context of pagan language of sexual vices. Significantly, as Paul exhorted the believers to avoid (excessive) desire and idolatry, for these lead to sexual vices, he did not rely on the authority of Jewish Scripture

---

144. See also Num 20; Pseudo-Philo, *LAB* 10.7; Harrington, "Pseudo-Philo," *OTP* 2:317; Tg. Onq. on Num 21:16–20 ("Song of the Well Legend"); Tg. Onq. on Exod 17:5–7; Wis 11:1–4; Philo, *Leg.* 2.21. Fitzmyer, *First Corinthians*, 383.

145. In Plato and Philo, the threefold relationship is composed of desire-gluttony-belly.

(LXX).¹⁴⁶ Indeed, he is silent about the sexual prescriptions found in the Jewish Scripture (LXX). Instead, Paul found appealing the ethical benefit of the Greek understanding of *epithymia* and its connection to sexual vices and other vices. The presence of sexual language is strong; the language of the wrath of God and wickedness allude to Paul's notion of impiety or ungodliness in close connection with (sexual) desires of the flesh and idolatry. The unnatural intercourse and other sexual vices prominent in the gentile world, as understood by Paul in his first-century context, arise from "degrading passions" (*pathē atimias*) and excessive "desire" (*orexei*). Paul's exhortation against the dangers of excessive food and drink, idolatry, lack of knowledge of God, and their contributions to excessive or uncontrolled sexual desires and appetites reflected Greek philosophical and Hellenistic Jewish understandings of the vice of "gluttony" (*gastrimargia*). Indeed, alongside the traditions of Plato and Philo, he developed a threefold relationship: desire-gluttony-idolatry. At the heart of his view of desire and sexual vices was his reevaluation of his Jewish monotheism, now Christocentric monotheism, in light of the Christ-event and the practice of gentile idol worship. While the "fruits" of *idolatry*—gluttony, excessive sexual desires/vices, and lack of knowledge of God—come from feasting on idol meat at temple precincts and worshiping idols, the "fruit" of *monotheism*— God's righteousness (Rom 1:17; 3:5; 6–8; 2 Cor 5:20–21; Phil 3:9) and his faithfulness (Rom 3:1–4)—must come in agreement with the Christ-event (Christocentric monotheism).

Paul's experience of the risen Christ dramatically changed his understanding of the Mosaic law and the ethical commandments of the Decalogue. Within the framework of his ethical discourse centered in the Spirit and not in the law—further expounded in the next chapters—God imparted to believers his grace and righteousness and his faithfulness to all who believe in Christ. Desire and its sequels—sinful passions beyond measure—threatened the believers' holy lives, and idolatry with its evil comrades—desire, gluttony, and sexual vices—destroyed their relationship with God. Influenced by both his Hellenistic Jewish and Greek philosophical traditions, Paul approved appropriate and controlled sexual desire within marriage; the excessive/immoderate sexual desire was sinful because it led to sexual immorality and vices. This was a particular issue tackled and

---

146. For the most comprehensive study on Paul's use of Jewish Scripture and his understanding of Jewish Scripture, see Koch, *Schrift als Zeuge*.

addressed in 1 Cor 5:1—7:40. His advice and exhortation showed the appropriate way to handle sexual passions.

Thus, Paul had the urgency to deal with the passion of desire and eradicate sinful or excessive (sexual) desire. We shall see next that Paul does not espouse the solutions offered by Philo and 4 Maccabees; although he shares their assumption that (sexual) desire, like other desires (e.g., hunger and thirst), belongs to how God created people, the problem is excess and immoderation, expressed by Paul as "sinful passions," "sinful beyond measure," and "all kinds of desires." So, in the next chapter, Paul moves beyond Jewish Scripture to present the believers his own understanding of the problem of desire and its negative sequels by offering them a new way of avoiding desirous passions and vices and instead possessing righteousness, knowledge of God, faith in Christ, and the works (virtues) of the Spirit of God outside the practice of the commandments of the law. These are key ethical elements to help Jewish and gentile believers to experience the grace of God.

3

Paul's Reevaluation of the Mosaic Law
The Problem of Desire and Sinful Passions

AS A FORMER PHARISEE, Paul was a zealous observer of the Jewish religion;[1] he was certainly familiar with the ethical benefits of the practice of the Mosaic law and with the passages regarding sexual laws and prohibitions instructed in the Jewish Scripture (LXX).[2] He was aware of the knowledge of God's covenantal demands on sexuality and sexual behavior and what constituted sexually immoral conduct. Paul also had in mind the notion that obedience to God's commandments related to sexuality ought to be practiced and required constantly; otherwise, the penalty could be death! Zeal for God's sake was the ideal; morally speaking it was a clear expression of a virtuous and noble character. Thus, in Paul's thought, the passion of "desire" (*epithymia*) is a threat to the faithful observance of God's commandments, and it is associated with ungodly desires often connected to wickedness and disobedience to God's covenant. Now, the practice of the Mosaic law and the commandments of the Decalogue are no longer the right avenue to a healthy ethical life, which, theoretically speaking, involved the possession of righteousness, faithfulness to God's covenant, and his commandments.

---

1. Betz, *Galatians*, 67.
2. E.g., Gen 1:26–28; Exod 20:17; Lev 20:10; Deut 6:5–6; 22:13–30. For a short analysis of these texts, see appendix B.

Influenced by the Christ-event and his becoming apostle to the gentiles after his prophetic call, Paul's strict, black-and-white Pharisaic viewpoint dramatically began to change. However, I want to be clear: Paul does not become a rejecter of Judaism; he does not leave Judaism! Paul, who sees himself as the "last of all" and "least of the apostles," becomes an "outlier," a "Hellenistic Jewish believer," an apostle hoping to offer Jewish and gentile believers, with whom he communicated through letters, an appealing reevaluation of the Mosaic law. While scholars may never agree in identifying Paul's Jewish identity or provide a satisfactory proposal, the important aspect is that in his treatment of *epithymia* Paul moves in continuity with his Hellenistic Jewish tradition and expands his Christian thought outside the practice of the law in accord with the philosophical traditions of Plato and the Stoics.

Even so, what exactly does Paul's reevaluation of the Mosaic law or the commandments of the Decalogue mean in relation to his Jewish-Christian audience and what effects does it have? Vincent J. Genovesi notes that "Paul's perception of the Mosaic Law would naturally shock the Jews for whom this Law was indeed the very word of God and, as such, revealed treasures of wisdom and knowledge." Genovesi adds, "Once he becomes a follower of Christ, his vision of the Law of Moses is radically recast and he begins to remind us that as Christians we live no longer under the Law but under grace (Rom 6:14)."[3] Paul's conviction about ethical matters and the question of what makes a believer holy and righteous becomes the primary topics of his new gospel given to him by the risen Christ himself. In Paul's mind, the period of the law is over; with the Christ-event, it came to an end (Rom 10:1–4).[4] There are two epochs in Paul: *tradition*—his being a Jew, a "defender" of the Jewish law on the footsteps of his fathers and ancestors (2 Cor 12:22; Phil 3:5–6)—and *experience*—his becoming a "believer" (Hellenistic Jewish), who comes to see new ways of understanding the law as a whole in light of the Christ-event. This dual interaction (*tradition* and *experience*) reflected throughout this and the next chapter, I suggest, marks the basis for his religious and human sensibilities, personal struggles, and even his ambivalence as he begins to internalize the dichotomies of being Hellenistic Jewish and a believer in Christ underneath the Jewish umbrella.

At the heart of Paul's inner thought and struggle is certainly the role of the Mosaic law. The reevaluation of the commandments of the law and

---

3. Genovesi, *In Pursuit of Love*, 51.
4. See Tobin, "Romans 10:4."

the Decalogue permitted Paul and other believers who agreed with him (Gal 1:2) to bring to the fore questions like, What is the ethical value of the Jewish law as a whole? Does the practice of the commandments and the food laws lead believers to righteousness and thus salvation? How to deal with the law and explain the conviction that the ethical commandments of the law are no longer necessary to be holy and righteous to his audience in the different communities of gentile territories was not an easy task for sure (Gal 2:11—6:10); it was something that probably kept him awake for endless nights (Gal 3:1–5). The inquiry at stake and that Paul must respond to his Jewish-Christian brothers and sisters about is, What, then, if not the law, makes one holy and righteous? In other words, What is another option, if any, by which Jewish believers should live ethically? Paul constantly argues that the Jewish laws (e.g., circumcision, food laws) were meant to last for a limited time only (Gal 3:15—4:7) because they reached their goal in the coming of Christ (Rom 10:4; Gal 4:1–7). This idea, key to his understanding of "desire" (*epithymia*), is his starting point of persuasion that eventually led him to break away from the central viewpoint held by most Jewish believers of his time (Gal 1–2).

The close association of the passion of "desire" (*epithymia*) with sinful passions, sexual immorality and vices, and idolatry strongly reflects the understanding of desire and excessive or irrational desire in the Greek philosophical tradition, especially (Middle) Platonic and Stoic. Using key Pauline passages, we shall endeavor to explore the relationship between desire and the negative sequels of this deadly Stoic passion. Within his understanding of the practice of the commandment (e.g., food laws) and the tenth commandment, *ouk epithymēseis* (Rom 7:7c) from the Decalogue, the reevaluation of the ethical value of the Mosaic law is restructured in close cooperation with his understanding of the problem of desire and its negative sequels. In particular, I flesh out Paul's old understanding of the "practice" (*askēsis*) of the commandments in a way that reflects the struggles and challenges among Jewish and gentile believers in the wider Greco-Roman world. We analyze Rom 7:7–8 and 13:9, two texts from Paul's Letter to the Romans, which is his mature letter, theologically speaking. We shall focus on the connections of these two texts with the other texts where the term "desire" (*epithymia*) and its verbal form (*epithymeō*) explicitly appear.

PAUL'S CHANGE OF ATTITUDE TOWARD DESIRE AND SEXUAL VICES

In Paul's ethical exhortation, his Christocentric view comes to the surface as he replaces the role of the Mosaic law in the ethical life of the believers. The passion of "desire" (*epithymia*) and its connection with sexual vices are presented as a real threat in the early Christian communities, particularly because the believers are living at the height of pagan sexual promiscuity and idolatry (Rom 2:22–24). Paul uses the word "desire" (*epithymia* and *orexei*) and cognates only fourteen times in negative terms. In comparison to Philo and 4 Maccabees, Paul's use of the word in connection with sexual vices is modest. Yet it is crucial for his argument and understanding of the law, and sexual immorality, and vices (see ch. 2).[5] Paul's complex discourse in Rom 7 employs the technique of "speech-in-character" (*prosōpopoiia*), a Greek way of persuasion used to demonstrate his position about the role of the Mosaic law and the practice of the commandment. His poetic-rhetorical technique would prove wrong "those who know the law [*ginōskousin nomon*]" (Rom 7:1). From his Jewish tradition (like Philo and 4 Maccabees), Paul takes the tenth commandment of the Decalogue, *ouk epithymēseis*, as an example to dramatically represent his reevaluation of the Mosaic law (Rom 13:9) and assure the believers that the practice of the law incites people to sin and to know passions and desires.

Paul challenges the law's ethical position by identifying the practice of the law as the source of the knowledge of sin (Rom 3:19–20; 7:7). Even though "the commandment is holy, just and good" (Rom 7:12), its practice produces "all kinds of desires" (*pasan epithymian* [Rom 7:8]). Significantly, it is at this point in his argument that Paul connects "sin" (*hamartia*) directly with "desire" (*epithymia*) in its verbal form (*epithymēseis*).[6] In light of

---

5. The Greek terms *epithymia* and *epithymein* are rare in the four Gospels. They are more common in the Epistles, but they are also often a *vox media*, or neutral word. Similar to the Greek tradition, they are used for the natural desire of hunger (Luke 15:16; 16:21), desire for longing (Acts 20:33; 1 Thess 2:17; Jas 4:2; Rev 9:6); desire for the divine mysteries (Matt 13:17; Luke 17:22; 1 Pet 1:12; see also Wis 6:11–13; Sir 1:26; 6:37); and desire for anything good (Phil 1:23; 1 Tim 3:1; Heb 6:11). See Büchsel, *TDNT* 3:170.

6. Some scholars capitalize *hamartia* (Sin) because they interpret it not as a sin per se, but as a heinous power, a negative entity in sharp opposition to God's grace and Spirit. For matters of simplicity, in this study I use "sin"; the use of either "sin" or "Sin" does not affect the central argument in this study. For a good summary of the various interpretations of "sin" in Rom 7, see Wasserman, *Death of the Soul*, 83–89; Dunn, *Theology of Paul*, 111–24.

this understanding, Paul recognizes the dangers of desire and assures the believers that through the practice of the commandment working in the flesh, sin becomes not only "sinful passions" (*ta pathēmata tōn hamartiōn* [Rom 7:5]) but, as he writes, also "sinful beyond measure" (*kath' hyperbolē harmartōlos* [Rom 7:13]). In the previous chapter, we discussed that in sexual matters the real problem for Paul is not sexual desire itself but the immoderate or "excessive" (*pleonazousa*) (sexual) passion/desire, especially, as Loader says, when it is "wrongly directed."[7] Like Philo and the author of 4 Maccabees, who follow the traditions of Plato and the Stoics, Paul believes that "passions" (*pathē*) and "desire" (*epithymia*) are the most dangerous of the soul's irrational part. For Paul, *porneia* or sexual immorality connotes excessive desire and passionate disorder often associated with the subordinate vice—"lack of self-control" (*akrasia*)—and the primary or generic vice—"intemperance" (*akolasia*)—in the Stoic list of vices.[8] Hence, he develops his discourse within the context of the Greek ethical systems of Plato and the Stoics where desire, excessive desires, and passions are cataloged as dangerous to the human soul.

Romans 7:7–8 and 13:9—A Change of Perspective

Paul's view on (sexual) desires is formed and influenced by his Jewish tradition and his Christocentric understanding of faithfulness to the commandments of God. Considering the impact of the Christ-event on his thought and Jewish identity, Paul internalizes the obedience and practice of the ethical commandments regarding sexual vices in a way that changed his traditional Jewish viewpoint. The centrality of his (Christocentric) theological approach within the Jewish umbrella is governed by his new understanding of Christ and his death on the cross. It can be safely said that Paul was probably the first among early believers (the church of God) to speak boldly that Jesus, the Messiah, died crucified on a cross.[9] As we turn to Romans, there are two key texts that connect the passion of "desire" (*epithymia*) and the ineffectiveness of the Mosaic law and its practice (Rom 7:7–8; 13:9). In these texts, desire and its verbal form are mentioned four times: interestingly, the noun "desire" (*epithymian*) appears twice in Rom

---

7. Loader, "Reading Romans 1," 119.
8. See ch. 2. See also Reno, "Pornographic Desire," 166–67.
9. E.g., 1 Cor 1:17–18, 23; 2:2; Gal 5:11; 6:12; Phil 2:8; 8:34.

7:7a and 7:8, and the verbal form (*epithymeseis*) appears also twice in Rom 7:7b and 13:9.¹⁰

In the context of Rom 6–9, where Paul presents his view of sanctification, he dramatically expounds his ethical exhortation, focusing on the freedom from the law's condemnation (Rom 7), explicitly referring to the sinful aspect of the practice of the law. This is an important topic in the Pauline oeuvre (especially Galatians), and a topic that has led to continuous debates among biblical scholars.¹¹ In Paul's first-century, Greco-Roman context, it was the "practice" (*askēsis*) of the law that gave Jews social and religious security, personal and religious identity, and assurance to righteousness through faith (Rom 9:30–33) and salvation. But the notion that a believer in Christ could achieve freedom from the Mosaic law was a possibility never considered in the mind of a Jew, and even in (some) Jewish believers who also zealously defended some teachings of Judaism (e.g., food laws, table fellowship, and circumcision).¹² It was simply a topic off the radar in the life of a Jew, for the law constituted the central mark of the covenantal relationship between Jews and God. Surprisingly, it is the brave Paul, a former Pharisee, now a Hellenistic Jewish believer and apostle, who brings up central issues for discussion (e.g., circumcision and table fellowship or food laws) to the authorities of the nascent church in Jerusalem (Acts 15; Gal 2). For Paul, it is important that the two parties—Jewish believers who defended with zeal the practice of the law, and gentile believers who did not follow the law—come to good terms and learn to live harmoniously in light of the Christ-event. He believes that those who profess faith in Christ can continue to live that faith without the observance of the law. Thus, as he reevaluates the ethical role of the law, his actions and words will also challenge the fundamental ethical practices of a religion—Judaism—which had more than two thousand years of tradition.

The question regarding the "law" (*nomos*) in Rom 7:7ab ("What then should we say? That the law [*nomos*] is sin? By no means!") has had different interpretations. Scholars have questioned whether *nomos* refers to the Mosaic law or law in general. In this book we follow the view of the majority of scholars, who opt for the Mosaic law as the immediate context

---

10. Bowden claims that the reason why Paul uses *epithymia* and cognates in Rom 7 is because these lexemes "fit into the broader metaphor *slavery to the master of the sin and freedom from this master*, which Paul develops in Rom 6:1—8:39" (emphasis original). Bowden, *Desire*, 496. See also his essay, "Sklaverei, Gesetz," 17, 23, 28, 29–30, 37–38, 45.

11. See Fitzmyer, *Romans*, 454–79.

12. Acts 22:3; 26:4–5; Rom 2:17–24; Gal 1:14.

(Rom 7:2, 3, 4b; 5:20; 6:12, 14). In Galatians and Romans, Paul shows the notion that through Christ believers are freed from the law and how that freedom also liberates them from the Mosaic law.[13] Paul launches rhetorical questions that would help his mixed Roman audience (Jewish and gentile believers) pinpoint what he might have visualized as the problem in the ethical life of the believers that needed to be resolved. For example, Paul poses the following rhetorical questions: "Do you not know, brethren . . . that the law is binding on a person only during his life?" (Rom 7:1); "What then shall we say? That the law is sin?" (Rom 7:7); and "Did that which is good, then bring death to me?" (Rom 7:13). These rhetorical queries illumine Paul's personal reevaluation of the role of the "practice" (*askēsis*) and observance of the Mosaic law. Clearly the problem is not the law itself and its various commandments and prohibitions (directed to Jewish believers). As a matter of fact, Paul acknowledges the law's divine provenance and its goodness and holiness when he boldly claims, "The law is holy, and the commandment is holy and just and good" (Rom 7:12; see also 7:22). In Paul's statement, the mixed community of believers perceive that the problem is not "human beings themselves," as some scholars have suggested,[14] but it is the indwelling of sin in human nature that came through the practice of the commandment.

Paul spends time conversing with the defenders of the law—Jewish believers—about the place of the law in their ethical lives. Influenced by his Jewish *tradition* and in continuity with Jewish beliefs before his prophetic call and along the lines of Philo and the author of 4 Maccabees (and Letter of Aristeas), Paul, too, supports the Jewish belief that the purpose of the Mosaic law was to foster virtues; it was the law that led human beings to God. His *experience* of the risen Christ, however, changed that point of view; in discontinuity with his Jewish tradition, he began to consider the practice—although he does not explicitly use *askēsis*—of the ethical commandments of the law as the manipulative force to rise passions, desires, and pleasures in the flesh (Rom 7:5). In order to make such a strong and challenging statement, Paul had probably experienced it and saw it firsthand among the Jewish believers in the early communities he founded. At this point, Paul moves away from other Jewish authors (e.g., Philo and 4

13. Fitzmyer, *Romans*, 454–55.

14. Fitzmyer points out that Paul finds that the problem is "with human beings themselves"; they are carnal, made of flesh that is weak, and prone to succumb to attacks of sin. He overlooks the practice of the Mosaic law, which is against what Paul is arguing. Fitzmyer, *Romans*, 472–73. See also Matera, *Romans*, 16.

Maccabees) who praised the practice of the Jewish law as the instrument to control or moderate "desire" (*epithymia*) and eradicate "excessive" (*pleonazousa*) and "irrational" (*alogos*) passions and desires.

In a "speech-in-character" (*prosōpopoiia*) form, Paul writes to Roman believers, "I was once alive apart from the law, but when the commandment [*tēs entolēs*] came, sin revived and I died" (Rom 7:9).[15] In his ethical discourse Paul is not a philosopher in the strict sense of the word; he is "a lover of wisdom" (*philosophos*) in his own way. As I have argued elsewhere, Paul is an "eclectic" Middle Platonist of the first century CE.[16] In one way or another, believers are being influenced by the cultural complexities of the time, including sexual vices in ancient Rome as well as in Corinth, Thessalonica, and the territory of Galatia (see ch. 2). As Darrell L. Bock and Mikel Del Rosario state, "While Rome was one of the most sophisticated cultures, it was also of the most depraved; hedonism was rampant. Indeed, many forms of sexual expression were commonplace that were outside the norm of Paul's Jewish background."[17] What is at stake is that Paul's critical observation regarding immoderate or "excessive" (*pleonazousa*) desire led him to associate the phrase "sinful passions" (*ta pathēmata tōn hamartiōn*) in Rom 7:5 with the tenth commandment, "You shall not covet" (*ouk epithymēseis* [Rom 7:7c]) and with the practice of "the commandment" (*tēs entolēs* [Rom 7:8–12]). We have seen that in Rom 1:18–32 Paul deals with the issue of

---

15. In the last century, scholars have offered a plethora of interpretations on Rom 7. Particular attention has been given to the identity of the "I." A group of scholars have documented the most relevant studies of the various different approaches and perspectives on Rom 7: see Krauter, *Perspektiven auf Römer 7*; Seifrid, "Subject of Rom 7:14–25"; Kümmel, *Römer 7*. Lyonnet develops his argument in light of the tenth commandment of the Decalogue in relation to the pronoun "I," who represents all of humanity. Lyonnet, "Histoire de salut." Bowden assumes that the "I" in Rom 7 refers to the gentiles in Rome. Bowden explains that in Rom 7:7–12, "Paul puts on the mask of an imaginary Gentile," describing their metaphorical slavery to sin because of the coming of the law and their need for freedom in order to illustrate that the law brings about recognition of sin (Rom 7:7). Bowden, *Desire*, 494–505. On the other hand, Käsemann claims that in this passage Paul has in mind pious Jews who are under the law. Käsemann, *Commentary on Romans*, 195. I do not accept Bowden and Käsemann's interpretations; instead, I argue that in Rom 7:1–12 Paul is speaking to (Roman) Jewish believers who are still practicing the commandments of the law.

16. See Naveros Córdova, *Live in the Spirit*, 152–55.

17. Bock and Del Rosario, "Table Briefing," 222. In the Jewish tradition, the Sibyl condemns Rome as an "effeminate and unjust, evil city" and "unclean" for its "adulteries and illicit intercourse with boys" (Sib. Or. 5:116–68), in association with incest, prostitution of its virgins, and bestiality (Sib. Or. 5:387, 430). See Loader, "Reading Romans 1," 125.

"*corrupted* passions," a language that echoes the phrase "having been *filled*" (v. 29). In the context of Rom 1:18-32, certainly, both phrases are carried on in the strong sexual connotation reflected in the expressions "sinful passions" and "beyond measure" in Rom 7:5, 13. Clearly, his treatment of the problem of *epithymia* is a demonstration that he, too, is navigating within the larger Greco-Roman world like Greek philosophers, Philo, the author of 4 Maccabees (and other Hellenistic Jewish authors). I would affirm that Loader offers a valuable point when he states that Paul has "some familiarity with discussions about the danger of passions."[18]

It is understood that for most Jews, as we find in Philo and 4 Maccabees as well as in the Letter of Aristeas, the practice of the food laws—a Jewish commandment—prevented them from falling into the passion of desire, pleasures, and sexual vices. With the help of "reason" (*logos* or *logismos*) and the practice of the commandment, they could attain the virtue of "self-control" (*enkrateia*) or "temperance" (*sōphrosunē*). In the Jewish tradition, as we have seen in Philo and 4 Maccabees in chapter 1, the practice of the food laws helps Jews to be obedient to the tenth commandment and avoid desiring what is forbidden; this is what (some) Jewish believers continued believing and practicing. I presume that the pre-believer Paul was aware of the Hellenistic Jewish traditions found, for example, in Philo, 4 Maccabees, and the Letter of Aristeas, and that knowledge (tradition-continuity) remained with him as a Hellenistic Jewish believer after his prophetic call. Then, by associating "sinful passions" (*ta pathēmata tōn hamartiōn*) with the tenth commandment (*ouk epithymēseis*), Paul might have had in mind the *practice* of the food laws when he referred to "the commandment" (*tēs entolēs*), which interestingly appears six times in Rom 7:8-13.

According to Paul, it is in the practice of the commandment that human nature becomes carnal and a slave to "every kind of desire" or "all kinds of desire" (*pasan epithymian* [Rom 7:8]) and its negative sequels or excessive desires. In light of the connection of *epithymia* with both sexual vices and the language of *toiauta*, *tauta*, and *kakoi* discussed in chapter 2, the expression *pasan epithymian* certainly alludes to sexual vices. Following Philo's Hellenistic Jewish tradition and the Platonic and Stoic traditions, Paul's understanding of the expressions "sinful passions" (*ta pathēmata tōn hamartiōn* [Rom 7:5]) and "sinful beyond measure" (*kath' hyperbolēn hamartōlos* [Rom 7:13]) involve the immoderate (*ametros*),

---

18. Plato, *Phaedr.* 253D; *Symp.* 210-212; *Tim.* 43C-D; *Leg.* 775D-E. Loader, "Reading Romans 1," 131.

irrational (*alogos*), and excessive (*pleonazousa*) quantity of sexual desires that leads to every kind of sexual vice. Indeed, Paul identifies sin becoming sinful beyond measure through the practice of "the commandment" (*tēs entolēs*), here interpreted as the food laws, in order to observe the tenth commandment (*ouk epithymēseis*).[19] More precisely, in his view there is nothing good dwelling within the human body; as he writes, "I am of the flesh, sold into slavery under sin" (Rom 7:14b). Therefore, Paul does not see the human body as being naturally bad as some scholars have argued;[20] likewise, Paul does not condemn sexual desire, as long as it is reasonably controlled by the mind of the Spirit, which I call in the next chapter the divine "enabler." In Paul's eyes, that practice (of a commandment) is what leads the human body to sin and death, and not to the observance of the tenth commandment. His identification of the power of sin as "another law"—the law of sin—enslaving human nature and corrupting the mind (Rom 7:23) is a proof that the law itself is not sin (Rom 7:7ab). Now in light of the Christ-event, he envisions that the dangers of sinful, excessive, or irrational passions and desires are aroused through what (the commandment [*tēs entolēs*]) is good, just, and holy. The identity of first-century Christianity as an illegal "religion" changed from being mainly Jewish to being mostly gentile; thus, some important aspects of Judaism needed to be reevaluated and reoriented. For Paul, the Christ-event brought about the parameters for such necessary changes. Hope was not lost, for he assured Jewish believers, or "those who know the law" (Rom 7:1a), that they "have died to the law" (Rom 7:4ab) and are also "discharged" from the commandment's practice and the law's observance, which had held them in captivity to desire (Rom 7:6ab).

Therefore, Paul directs his speech to Jewish believers, the defenders of the practice of the law: the commandment is good, holy, and righteous. However, his statement that the law and its commandments are no longer the best channel to salvation sounded appealing to gentile believers, who probably saw the observance of the law as unnecessary. Paul is compelled to persuade his mixed audience living in a complex world to come to terms with one another and have the same mind, have the same love, live in the same Spirit, and be one with Christ.[21] Thus, using the Greek rhetorical-poetic technique as his weapon in Rom 7:7–25, Paul launches a dramatic

19. For the analysis of Rom 14–15, Paul's view on the food laws, see ch. 4.
20. Wasserman, *Death of the Soul*, 96.
21. 2 Cor 4:13; Phil 2:2–4; see also 1 Cor 12:4–7.

performance of the sinner in despair. He does this, not only as a persuasive rhetorical strategy but as a reinforcement to the claim he previously made to Jewish believers in Rom 7:1–6—the practice of the ethical commandments of the law functions to expose sinful passions in the flesh.[22] Paul employs both the technique called "speech-in-character" (*prosōpopoiia*) and images from Plato's moral psychology to recreate for his mixed audience a real experience of the purpose of the practice of the Mosaic law and the freedom from its authority.[23]

Paul especially wants to convince "those who know the law" to stop defending and practicing the commandments of the Mosaic law.[24] What Paul offers in Rom 7 is not a defense of (or "apologia" for) the law, though this is often held to be the case by most scholars.[25] Rather, I argue that this passage vividly provides Paul's representation of the defenders' or Jewish believers' present life under the practice of the ethical commandments of the law. The Jewish laws represented a negative thwart against which to set more effectively the freedom received in the grace of God through Christ.[26] As we shall see in the next chapter, the phrase "the grace of God" (*charis theou* or *charis tou theou*) is understood by Paul as Jesus' salvific death on a cross, the so-called Christ-event.[27] Paul believes that it is Christ who guides

---

22. For a helpful study on Paul's use of dramatic performance in Rom 7, see Selby, *Not with Wisdom*, 59–79. On Paul's use of personification to describe sin in this text, see Dodson, *"Powers" of Personification*.

23. Loader, "Reading Romans 1," 130. The classical rhetorical technique of *prosōpopoiia* (making a mask) refers to a form where the speaker produces speech that represents another person or type of character (Theon, *Prog.* 8.116; Aphthonius, *Prog.* 11.35; Quintilian, *Inst.* 9.2.30). Its translation as "speech-in-character" is from Butts, "*Progymnasmata* of Theon." For an excellent treatment of speech-in-character in relation to Paul, see Stowers, *Rereading of Romans*, 16–21, 269–72.

24. The same emphasis is found in Rom 2:17–24.

25. Byrne, *Romans*, 209.

26. The phrase "the grace of God" is Paul's favorite word and appears throughout his genuine letters: *charis theou* in 1 Cor 3:10; 2 Cor 6:1; 8:1, 9 (of our Lord); 9:14; Gal 2:21; *charis tou theou* in Rom 5:15; 16:20 (*tou kyriou*), 24 (*tou kyriou*); Phlm 1:25 (*tou kyriou*); see also Phlm 1:3; *charis autou* (his grace) in 1 Cor 15:10 (2x); *charis tou kyrios* in 1 Cor 16:23; 2 Cor 13:14; Gal 6:18; Phil 4:23; 1 Thess 5:28; *hē charis mou* (my grace) in 2 Cor 12:9.

27. In his analysis of the language of "atonement" (Rom 5:1–11) and "sin" (Rom 8:3–4), Breytenbach rightly argues that, for Paul, "the grace of God" (*charis tou theou*) refers to the shedding of Jesus' blood and his death on the cross. Breytenbach, *Versöhnung*, 166–68. On the other hand, Manoly argues that the meaning of *charis* correctly expresses the notion of "unmerited favor or gift," for the "entire process of salvation flows

the members of the nascent church, showing them how to navigate ethically through the sexual complexities of the larger Greco-Roman world of the first century CE.

THE PROBLEM OF DESIRE AND ITS NEGATIVE SEQUELS

It is worth noting that Paul's letters emphasize three ethical points regarding the passion of "desire" (*epithymia*): (1) vices, passions, and pleasures of the flesh are associated with desire; (2) the problem that must be solved is desire; and (3) the practice of the food laws and self-control (Philo's proposal) have not yet solved the problem of desire. Significantly, in the first two points Paul shows continuity with his Jewish tradition; Paul converges with other Hellenistic Jewish writers, especially Philo, 4 Maccabees, and Eleazar in the Letter of Aristeas (139–170). Like these writers, Paul is familiar with the four Stoic passions of the soul (fear, grief, pleasure, and desire), and like the Stoics and Philo, he views "desire" (*epithymia*) as a deadly passion. When uncontrolled, it becomes the source of "all kinds of desires" (*pasan epithymian* [Rom 7:8]), "sinful passions" (*ta pathēmata tōn hamartiōn* [Rom 7:5]), and "sinful beyond measure" (*kath' hyperbolēn hamartōlos* [Rom 7:13]). Contrary to Philo and the author of 4 Maccabees, Paul believes that "the commandment" (*entolē*) still is a problem, that the practice of the food laws (to observe the tenth commandment) has not solved the problem of desire.

Thus, for Paul, the food laws are not the best solution or remedy to resolve the problem of desire and its negative sequels. Believers are still (weak) in danger of sinful, excessive, or irrational (sexual) desires and vices, and thus live enslaved to the power of sin. Paul's reevaluation of the ethical commandments of the Mosaic law allows him to view its practice, not the law itself, as a secure avenue to "bear fruit for death" (Rom 7:5). His negative view of *epithymia* concords with Philo and the Stoic philosophers who believe that desire as a passion is a deadly evil; most Stoics, however, seek

---

from the marvelous mercy of a loving and holy God (Titus 2:11)." Manoly further argues that the actualization of grace is visible in the cross; thus, grace is not merely a theoretical element in the nature of God, but in "the love of God poured out" in abundance upon those who did not deserve it (Rom 5:5, 20–21). Paul further describes *charis* as the power operating in the believers' (and our) lives to bring victory over sin. What is clear in Paul is the fact that (a gift that does not give us) the right to misuse it (Rom 6:1, 15). Manoly, *Histoire du salut*, 7.

its extermination, which is *apatheia*. In this regard, the task of suppressing the passions and desires of the flesh confirms the ideal of their complete elimination. In this account, the distinction is that in the Stoic tradition the aim of being "without passions" (*apatheia*) was contrasted with the ideal of "moderation in passion" (*metriopatheia*) in the (Middle) Platonic tradition.[28] In his position about excessive sexual desire, Paul shares much in common with Philo, 4 Maccabees (and other Jewish writers), Plato, Chrysippus, and later Stoics (see ch. 1). What Paul intends to extirpate is the "excessive" quantity of sexual passions and desires (Rom 1:27) and to control or moderate sexual desire and passions.[29] As Loader says, for Paul "the issue was not passions but their excess."[30]

Paul presents to his Jewish and gentile believers the law's limitation to overpower sin and proves the practice of the commandment ineffective. He rejects the practice of the food laws to observe the tenth commandment (*ouk epithymēseis*), and instead he opts for an appealing emotional argument of persuasion. Paul is able to transport his audience—particularly "those who know the law" (*ginōskousin nomon*), or Jewish believers (Rom 7:1)—into a dramatic experience that would take them from past (7:7–11) to present (7:14–23), leading to the climactic cry of despair in the future tense: "Who will rescue me from this body of death?" (Rom 7:24b). Skillfully, Paul "vividly" (*enargōs*) represents for his audience the present situation of the tortured sinner who is enslaved to the power of sin by setting the scene "before their eyes" as if they were eyewitnesses.[31] The dramatic performance allows Paul and his mixed audience to picture in their minds the "real" situation of the sinner in despair as a representation of those Jewish believers who defend and uphold the observance of the ethical commandments of the law. Like Philo and within the philosophical

---

28. The contrast between *apatheia* and *metriopatheia* was later adopted by Peripatetics in dependence on Aristotle, who argued that it was wrong to feel either too little or too much fear, anger, pleasure, or desire. See Sandbach, *Stoics*, 63.

29. In this regard, Gaca argues that Paul approves only marriage between believers, and only God-fearing believers (husband and wife) may have sexual relations. Gaca, *Making of Fornication*, 147–52.

30. Loader, "Reading Romans 1," 132.

31. Especially in 7:14–25, Paul provides a mimetic performance in which he represents the sinner in despair, engulfed in self-condemnation, and then miraculously freed from the law's domination by the grace of God. Selby argues that Paul's dramatic performance of the anguished sinner "played a crucial role in his broader attempt to bring about the unity of Jews and Gentiles in the Christian Church." Selby, *Not with Wisdom*, 59. For Selby's whole analysis, see 59–79.

tradition, Paul moves further to echo Plato's description of the tyrannical man who is miserably ruled by passions and appetites (*Resp.* 9.574E–577A). He assures his audience—Jewish believers—that the practice of the commandment proves to be death and not life (Rom 7:10), claiming that it is in the practice of the *entolē* that sin finds opportunity to deceive and kill the individual spiritually (Rom 7:11) and to commit "all kinds of desires" (*pasan epithymian* [Rom 7:8]).

Philosophically, sin operates as a malevolent power that lies in wait for an opportune time to incite passions and all kinds of desires in human beings. Consistent with Plutarch's view of vice's power to invade the human body,[32] Paul depicts sin as a powerful force invading human nature. Like Philo and the author of 4 Maccabees, Paul does not disapprove of the goodness of the Mosaic law. Yet he consistently considers its practice (e.g., food laws) an instrument for sin to enslave and lead human beings to death (Rom 7:13b–14),[33] as he tells his audience that through sin "a sinner might become sinful beyond measure" (*kath' hyperbolēn hamartōlos* [Rom 7:13b]), that is, "excessive" (*pleonazousa*) sinful (sexual) desires. Strikingly, Paul's language—"sinful beyond measure"—points directly to Philo's philosophical expressions "excessive impulse" (*pleonazousa hormē* [*Spec.* 4.79]), "excessive and irrational passions" (*alogous kai pleonazousas tōn pathōn* [*Conf.* 90]), "irrational desire" (*alogos epithymia* [*Somn.* 2.276]), and "excessive pleasure" (*pleonazousēs hēdonēs* [*Spec.* 1.9]) when speaking of sexual desire. Both Hellenistic Jewish authors are influenced by Plato's notion of the "tyrannical man." Thus, in the context of Plato's doctrine of excessive and irrational desire, Paul, too, proves once again not only the inefficiency of the practice of the commandment but also desire's strong connection to sexual immorality and vices, commonly known and practiced in the pagan world, as well as excessive, immoderate, or irrational (sexual) desires.

Desire as "Sinful Beyond Measure"

Appealing to his rhetorical-poetic skills and Platonic tradition, in a soliloquy Paul develops a drama of sin becoming "sinful beyond measure" (*kath' hyperbolēn hamartōlos* [Rom 7:13b]), which represents the present situation of "those who know the law" (Rom 7:7a). He vividly and repetitively

---

32. Plutarch, *Am. prol.* 498d.

33. Philo, too, employs the language of the death of the rational faculty where passions and desires kill the soul (e.g., *Post.* 73; *Leg.* 3.52–3.53, 3.74).

performs the inner struggle between what the anguished sinner in despair wants to do, what he hates to do, and then ends up doing the latter:

> I do not understand my own actions. For I do not do what I want, but I do the very thing I hate. Now if I do what I do not want . . . it is no longer that I do it. . . . I can will what is right, but I cannot do it. For I do not do the good I want, but the evil I do not want is what I do. Now if I do what I do not want, it is no longer I that do it . . . when I want to do right. (7:15-21)

Paul's dramatic performance aims to vividly bring "before the eyes" (Greek, *enargeia*; Latin, *demonstratio*) of those who know the law (or Jewish believers who practice the law) the internal human drama as he depicts the ongoing struggle between what is *good* (what the anguished sinner in despair wants to do; commandment/rational part) and what is *evil* (what he hates to do; sin/nonrational part).[34] This text represents somehow the dramatization of Philo's cognitive description of the push-and-pull fight in the human soul symbolized by "clean" (reason/rational part) and "unclean" (desire/nonrational part) animals.[35] Paul understands practical exercises, such as "desire" (*epithymia*), as instrumental in passions and pleasures. Thus, he appeals to human emotions through mental images (Greek, *phantasiai*; Latin, *visiones*) of the sinner in despair to prove ineffective the practice of the commandment. In ancient Greek rhetorical-poetic discourse, *phantasia* (imagination), which is a quality of *enargeia* (vividness), brings together imagination and vision to create an emotional effect on the hearers, hopefully in this case on "those who know the law" (Jewish believers).[36] Similar to Plato and Philo, Paul vividly dramatizes the struggle between desire (doing/flesh/nonrational part/sin) and the practice of the commandment

---

34. Recently, Elliott, who explores the biographical passages in Paul's letters (e.g., Rom 7:14-25; 1 Cor 9:19-23; 2 Cor 11:22–12:10; Phil 1:12-26; 3:4b-8), analyzed Rom 7:14-25 from the perspective of the first-person narrative of self-contradiction. In it, Elliott notes that the struggle represented in vv. 15-21 is between will and action. He brings close the identity of the "I" with Paul's self-character, arguing against scholars who tend to distance the character's experience (speech-in-character) rather than his own, and interprets the struggle in this text as "a literary figuration of the writing-self in the moment of writing, a refraction of the self's plight in writing," that is, the anguished struggle of Rom 7 is a good representation of the act of self-narration. S. Elliott, *Rustle of Paul*, 37-58.

35. See ch. 1.

36. Longinus, *Subl.* 15.1; Quintilian, *Inst.* 6.2.29.

(wanting/mind/rational part/Mosaic law).[37] He represents these two powers at war, pushing back and forth, with *epithymia* (desire) overpowering the commandment (food laws) and acting aggressively beyond measure in the believer. The two powers ultimately dominate and kill the human "mind" (*logos*) or reasoning part.[38]

Evidently Paul's connection between two powers, "sin" (*hamartia*) and "desire" (*epithymia*), stands alongside the same ethical spectrum of Philo of Alexandria.[39] Yet in Rom 7:8 ("But, sin, seizing the opportunity in the commandment [*tēs entolēs*], produced in me all kinds of desires [*pasan epithymian*]. Apart from the law sin lies dead"), Paul sharply diverts from Philo by linking sin exclusively with the practice of "the commandment" (*tēs entolēs*), which leads to the observance of the tenth commandment (*ouk epithymēseis*). For Paul, sin finds an opportunity in the practice of the commandment to produce "all kinds of desires" (*pasan epithymian* [Rom 7:8]). In the past, prohibitions in the food laws wherein Moses stipulated which animals were to be eaten and which were to be avoided were followed by other Jewish Hellenistic authors like Philo, 4 Maccabees, and the Letter of Aristeas. They claimed the laws were beneficial for inciting "self-control" (*enkrateia*) or "temperance" (*sōphrosunē*) and training the soul in "moderation" (*metriopatheia*). Paul indirectly refuted these. After his prophetic call, the "practice" (*askēsis*) of Moses's food laws is not in Paul's ethical agenda, for they produce "all kinds of desires" (*pasan epithymian*), "sinful passions" (*ta pathēmata tōn hamartiōn*), and "sinful beyond measure" (*kath' huperbolēn hamartōlos*), thus creating more problems rather than a solution.

The role of sin, especially in Rom 7 (also Rom 6–8), concords with Plato's assumptions, which represent passions and desires of the soul, if wrongly directed, as evil controlling "reason" (*logos*) for disastrous ends.[40]

37. I disagree with Wasserman, who claims that the warfare in Paul is between "the appetites and reason." Wasserman, *Death of the Soul*, 108.

38. Fitzmyer describes this battle between "the Egos of flesh dominated by sin and the spiritual law of God," emphasizing neither desire (or passions) nor the practice of the commandment but the human condition itself. Fitzmyer, *Romans*, 473.

39. For details, see Naveros Córdova, "Worst of the Passions."

40. Wasserman, *Death of the Soul*, 83. In a detailed analysis of the metaphor "slavery to a master," Bowden states that in Rom 6–8 Paul explains that gentiles in Rome became metaphorical slaves to sin after encountering the Jewish law (*ho nomos gramma*). Especially in 7:7, Paul provides the example of the specific law (*hē entolē*) "You shall not covet" (*ouk epithymēseis*; see also Exod 20:17 LXX; Deut 5:21 LXX). Paul mentions *epithymeō* in 7:7 because in Roman imperial texts, cognates of this lexeme were often associated

Paul's vehement and vivid expression, "I do the very thing I hate," in Rom 7:15b induces the ineffectiveness of the Mosaic prescription of the food laws, not the law itself.[41] Resembling the description of Plato's "tyrannical man" (*tyrannos*) overpowered by "irrational" (*alogos*) passions, Paul shows the power of sin indwelling the carnal body (the flesh), which enslaved to sin lives at the mercy of sinful passions and desires.[42] Consistent with the Greek technique of "speech-in-character," Paul heightens the dramatic climax of his soliloquy when the sinner cries in desolation, "Wretched man that I am!" (Rom 7:24a).[43] In this way, desire for the forbidden is stirred up and becomes an insatiable (excessive sexual) desire or " irrational desires" (*alogos epithymiai*), a force whose final outworking is death.[44] His vivid performance of the anguished sinner exposing his state of mind with ominous and graphic clarity echoes Medea's cries of despair (Seneca, *Med*. 990, and more generally, 907–919).[45] Even though the law of God is in the human mind willing to practice its commandment, the flesh serves "the law of sin"

---

with the metaphor "slavery to a master" (Rom 3–8). Because gentiles in Rom 7 have been exposed to the law, they now recognize sin in themselves (7:7–8), and because they chose to worship the creation (1:23), God gave them over to desires, disgraceful passions, and debased mind. However, the gentiles' situation changed because they came in contact with the law, which reveals their sin to them and which Paul classifies as a metaphorical master (6:12, 14). Paul tells them that they can change their situation and be freed from this master by submitting to a new ruler, that is, God (Rom 6:13). Bowden, *Desire*, 504.

41. See Rom 7:12, 13a, 14a, 16b; 7:22. As Wasserman notes, Platonist Galen (second century CE), in *On the Passions and Errors of the Soul*, dramatizes the struggle between reason and passions of the human body. He alludes to Paul's language when he writes, "I wish to stop but I cannot" and "even if he wants to" (Claudius Galenus, *Opera Omnia*, 5:29; Galen, *Hip. et Plat*. 4.2.37–4.2.39). Galen emphasizes the danger of the appetitive faculty, which overpowers the reasoning faculty. According to him, this faculty often hurls into love beyond all cure and is associated with gluttony in food, drink, and sexual pleasures. Wasserman, "Death of the Soul," 807–8. Translation is from Galen, *On the Passions* (Harkins), 47, slightly modified by Wasserman.

42. See also Rom 7:5, 8, 21. Philo explains the same idea in philosophical categories: the nonrational part overpowers and enslaves the rational part of the soul (see ch. 1).

43. Within the context of metaphorical slavery, Bowden interprets this text as the gentile's cry, which was a common expression in the Roman Empire, as he writes, "Expressing the groaning of a person who recognizes his or her slavery to a metaphorical master, but his or her inability to free themselves from this master." Bowden, *Desire*, 502. For a good treatment of v. 24a, see Elder, "Wretch I Am!"; Kümmel, *Römer 7*; Lyonnet, "Tu ne convoiteras pas"; Lambrecht, *Wretched "I"*; Grieb, *Story of Romans*, 71–75.

44. See also Gen 3:4, 13. Dunn, *Theology of Paul*, 99.

45. See also Ovid, *Metam*. 7.18; Epictetus, *Diatr*. 2.17.18. Wasserman, *Death of the Soul*, 79–80.

(Rom 7:23bc). Paul's dramatic statement in Rom 7:24a depicts the reasoning part of the soul as powerless; philosophically speaking, "reason" (*logos*) is fundamentally good and rational but becomes completely ineffectual.[46] This (Rom 7:24a) is Paul's last resort to demonstrate that the food laws (or *tēs entolēs*) are not the effective means to acquire "moderation" (*metriopatheia*) and offer a solution to the problem of "desire" (*epithymia*). Unlike Philo and 4 Maccabees, in Paul, there is a higher power that would not only free believers, both Jewish and gentile believers, from enslavement but also control the passion of desire as well as eliminate the (excessive) quantity of (sexual) desire, and thus avoid sexual immorality and vices.

Slaves to Sinful Passions Versus Slaves to Righteousness

For Paul, there is a clear problem that arises from the practice of the law, and that problem is "desire" (*epithymia*). He illumines two ethical realities regarding the law: its goodness (positive, for Jewish believers) and the limitation of its practice (negative, for gentile believers). Human nature is caught up in a continuous struggle between the power of desire and the observance of the Mosaic law. So, Paul's vivid performance of the sinner in despair is crucial to prove the limitations of the practice of the commandments of the law to those who know (practice) the law. Ultimately, it is in "the grace of God" (*charis theou* or *charis tou theou*) through Christ and the work of the Spirit (e.g., Gal 5:1—6:10; Rom 8) that Paul's positive alternative to solve the problem of desire and its sequels rest. In the grace of God, believers would become more flexible in their thinking, comfort those who are losing faith in Christ, and give hope to those who are expecting clarity in the gospel he received (1 Cor 15:3). This was the beginning of a "new religion," Christianity, as it expands toward the western gentile territories. With a Platonically oriented approach he demonstrates that the Mosaic law and the practice of the ethical commandment of the food laws are no longer relevant for a virtuous living.

In light of this approach, Paul's exhortation to the mixed community of believers in Rome emphasizes the theme of sanctification (Rom 6–8) and freedom from sin's tyranny (Rom 6). In Rom 6:12 ("Therefore, do not let sin exercise dominion in your mortal bodies, to make you obey their desires [*tais epithymiais autou*]") Paul develops a contrast between freedom (newness of life or freedom from sin) and slavery (enslavement to sin). Paul

---

46. Wasserman, "Death of the Soul," 812–13.

warns the believers against sin's lustful power to establish its reign in the "body" (*sōma*), which is the "flesh" (*sarx*).⁴⁷ Fitzmyer notes that believers might still have been in the sinful body or flesh (Rom 6:6) and might have been seduced by its cravings. If one obeys such cravings that came from sin, one allows sin itself to enter the soul and reduce one to bondage. In this way, one loses the freedom from sin achieved in Christ Jesus.⁴⁸ Paul puts himself among the Jewish believers to exhort them: we are no longer slaves to sin, for Jesus' resurrection has brought us freedom from sin (Rom 6:6–7). The "body of sin" (the flesh) denotes the state of mind in which even baptized believers might have found themselves; with such a sinful flesh they, too, could still be subject to the dominion or power of sin (Gal 3:22; Rom 3:9).⁴⁹ The result of that sinful empowerment in the flesh is obedience to its sinful or excessive desires.

In light of the ancestors' idolatrous and sinful sexual experience in the wilderness (1 Cor 10),⁵⁰ Paul also exhorts against the dangers of idolatry, when he writes, "Therefore, God gave them up in the desires [*epithymiais*] of their hearts to impurity [*akatharsia*], to the degrading of their bodies among themselves" (Rom 1:24).⁵¹ Paul believes that idolatry arouses excessive sexual desires in the hearts and bodies of the unfaithful ones, and

---

47. Räisänen, "ΕΠΙΘΥΜΙΑ und ΕΠΙΘΥΜΕΙΝ," 97.

48. Fitzmyer, *Romans*, 446. On the topic of the sinful body, see "Sinful Body," in Engberg-Pedersen, *Paul and Philosophy*, 309–29.

49. Fitzmyer states that the believers are still human beings and have in themselves the effects of Adamic sin. What Paul says of sin in this passage came to be understood as *concupiscentia* (concupiscence) or the *fomes peccati* (the tinder of sin) in the Augustinian tradition. Fitzmyer, *Romans*, 446. Scholars who have made a connection between Rom 1:18–32 and Gen 3 argue that Paul develops his argument through the effects of Adam and Eve's transgression. See, for example, Dunn, *Theology of Paul*, 82. For a similar view, see Levison, "Adam and Eve," 521; Räisänen, "ΕΠΙΘΥΜΙΑ und ΕΠΙΘΥΜΕΙΝ," 93. However, this theory is unconvincing; unlike 1 Cor 15, Rom 1 says nothing about Adam. I concur with Loader, who states that "Paul does not derive same sex relations or having same sex passions from the fall of Adam." Loader, "Reading Romans 1," 129. For discussion on this topic, see Stowers, *Rereading of Romans*, 86–87; Bowden, *Desire*, 477–78; Fitzmyer, *Romans*, 274.

50. See ch. 2.

51. In Rom 1:24, Paul speaks of desire(s) of the flesh in negative terms. This is a close reference to Ps 78:79 and Num 11:31–35. See Dunn, *Theology of Paul*, 120; Loader, "Reading Romans 1," 122. The term *akatharsia* (impurity, uncleanness) denotes sexual immorality, not *only* ritual uncleanness (see 1 Thess 4:5; Wis 2:16). In Paul, the term appears several times, and sometimes it is linked with *porneia*, e.g., 2 Cor 12:21; Gal 5:19; Eph 5:3; Col 3:5.

through the unlawful sexual behavior they (Paul's ancestors), like gentiles/Egyptians, degraded their bodies before God's eyes.[52] A life enslaved to the lower passions of the body (flesh) is the sign of God's wrath upon the gentile world. Thus, Paul constantly urges them to avoid sinful or excessive desires of the body (flesh); he commands, "Don't let sin reign in your mortal body [*sōmati*], as to obey the desires [*epithymiais*] of the body [*autou*]" (Rom 6:12). And in Gal 5:17a Paul gives a similar exhortation but this time using the term "flesh" (*sarx*) instead of "body" (*sōma*): "For what the flesh desires [*epithymei*] is opposed to the Spirit [*pneumatos*]."[53] Interestingly, in both cases, Paul connects the flesh/body with *epithymia* in its plural form. Paul reaffirms the evil nature of sin in Rom 6:12 using the metaphor of slavery; those in Christ are no longer slaves to sin (Rom 6:6) as opposed to those who are governed by passions and desires (Rom 7:7–8; 13:9). Paul's exhortation in Rom 6:12, then, allows believers to see their body's capacity for all kinds of sinful desirous actions (*pasan epithymian* [Rom 7:8]), which include actions related to sexual vices (e.g., *toiauta, tauta, kakoi*).[54]

The plural noun "desires" (*epithymiais*) in Rom 6:12 appears in a context where Paul is describing the evil consequences of the passion of *epithymia*. In the next verses, he expounds further his exhortation against desire, saying,

> No longer present your members to sin as instruments of wickedness [*adikia* (literally, unrighteousness)], but present yourselves to God as those who have been brought from death to life, and present your members to God as instruments of righteousness [*dikaiosunēs*]. For sin will have no dominion over you, since you are not under law but under grace. (Rom 6:13–14)

---

52. See also Gal 5:24; Eph 2:3; 2 Tim 3:6; Titus 3:3; 1 Pet 1:14; 4:2–3; 2 Pet 2:18.

53. See also 1 Tim 3:1. In reference to Gal 5:16–17, Bowden makes an interesting observation: the manifestations of *epithymia* and *epithymeō* are clarified in the vice list in Gal 5:19, "the works of the flesh." The author explains that Paul mentions *epithymia sarkos* (desires of the flesh) in Gal 5:16 and *hē sarx epithymeō* (the flesh desires). In each instance, this desire is spoken of generally and is contrasted with the Spirit. The vices mentioned in Gal 5:19–21 clarify some specific things this desire, which is mentioned in 5:16–17, consists of. Paul clarifies this by mentioning *ta erga tēs sarkos* (the works of the flesh) in 5:19, which parallels *epithymia sarkos* (desire of the flesh) in 5:16 and *hē sarx epithymeō* (the flesh desires) in 5:17. The list of vices, therefore, clarifies specific manifestations of *epithymia* and *epithymeō* mentioned in 5:16 and 17. Bowden, *Desire*, 466, 471.

54. See ch. 2.

Using the metaphor of military language, Paul exhorts especially Jewish believers, who defend the practice of the law, not to allow their human bodies (the flesh) to become "instruments of wickedness" (*hopla adikias*), and invites them to be servants of the Lord by offering themselves to God as people brought back to life from the dead.[55] Paul's main point is that the believers come to recognize that they are no longer instruments of sin; rather, they ought to see themselves as instruments of righteousness, for they are freed from sin, passions, and sinful desires. Paul emphatically writes, "You ... have become slaves of righteousness [*dikaiosunē*]" (Rom 6:18). They are expected to become weapons in God's service.[56] "Righteousness for sanctification" (*dikaiosunē eis hagiasmon* [Rom 6:19]) is particularly the special invitation to those defenders of the law's teachings. The Jewish believers, radical in their thinking, are exhorted to become slaves to righteousness through faith (Rom 9:30–33) and not slaves to passions and sinful desires through the practice of the commandments of the law.

Paul's goal for all believers is to gain eternal life, which is a gift of God (Rom 6:22–23). In his baptismal exhortation (Rom 6:12–23; Gal 3:27), Paul truly wants to make his point. So, when he presents his radical view of sin, passions, and desire, which can become sinful beyond measure through the law, he explains the idea of having "died to sin"—sinful passions (*ta pathēmata tōn hamartiōn*), all kinds of desires (*pasan epithymian*), sinful beyond measure (*kath' hyperbolēn hamartōlos*)—as a presupposition of the continuance (Rom 5:12–21) of the notion of sin as a power that tyrannizes the human soul.[57] As we shall see in the next chapter, with Paul, righteousness acquires, in light of the Christ-event, a new ethical nuance; just as Jesus Christ has been the supreme instrument of God's saving righteousness in the world (Rom 3:21–26), so Jesus is also the principal cause of the remedy to control the passion of "desire" (*epithymia*) and eradicate sinful or excessive (sexual) desires. Therefore, living in Jesus Christ and through baptism into Christ (1 Cor 12:12–13; Gal 3:27–28) would grant the believers all the life-giving Spirit (1 Cor 15:45) and free them from the power of sin, from the fleshy lustful condition represented by Paul as sinful passions, and desires beyond measure.

---

55. Byrne, *Romans*, 194.
56. Fitzmyer, *Romans*, 447.
57. Byrne, *Romans*, 189.

CONCLUSION

In this chapter, we explored the way Paul reevaluated the ethical role of the law and the practice of the commandment. He highlighted the problem of desire and its negative sequels: irrational, immoderate, and excessive (sexual) desire. He understood and explained the problem of desire within the Greek philosophical and Hellenistic Jewish traditions. As he presented his understanding of the evil nature of sin in close connection to the passion of desire, Paul had his mixed audience in mind (Jewish and gentile believers). He was consistently clear, emphasizing the two ethical realities of the law: its goodness but limited ability to avoid desires; and its limited ability to eliminate sinful or excessive passions along with every kind of (evil) desire. As for Philo, 4 Maccabees, Plato, and the Stoics, so it was for the Hellenistic Jewish believer and apostle: the ethical realities of the law were intrinsically connected with sexual immorality and vices. He appealed to his knowledge of Greek rhetorical techniques to demonstrate that the law leads to sin, which is a power controlling the individual's inner heart and mind. Paul provided the example of the tenth commandment to show the problem of the practice of the commandment, e.g., food laws. He told those who observe the law that sinful passions actually are aroused by the practice of the commandment. His dramatic performance in Rom 7 highlighted the intrinsic connection between sin and desire and between desire and sinful passions beyond measure and sexual immorality/vices. In other words, through the practice of a commandment, sin produces all kinds of desires, and sin becomes sinful passions and sinful beyond measure, or in philosophical terms, beyond the limits of reason (tyrannical, irrational, or immoderate). So, sin becomes an irrational and excessive desire too.

But when Paul directed his dramatic speech especially to the Jewish believers, he went even beyond his dramatic performance of the sinner in despair within the Platonic representation of the tyrannical man. His understanding of the nature of desire reflects both his Hellenistic Jewish and Greek philosophical traditions, and his identification of desire as an evil passion goes in line with the Stoic doctrine of desire. However, in his treatment of the problem of *epithymia*, Paul showed both continuity (*tradition*) and discontinuity (*experience*) with his Jewish tradition. Paul's source of the problem of desire, its negative sequels—sinful passions, all kinds of desires, and irrational/excessive (sexual) desire—challenged the remedy offered by Philo, 4 Maccabees, and Greek philosophers. Paul's Christocentric approach allowed him to reject the practice of the ethical commandments of the law, especially the food laws, a Mosaic "commandment" (*entolē*)—according to Philo—prescribed to observe the tenth commandment. It also led Paul to speak about desire and the law's limitation in terms of pagan idolatry and sexual vices, the latter being identified also as the works of the flesh and further expressed in the language of *toiauta, tauta, kakoi*. In the next chapter, Paul develops his doctrine of the solution to the problem of "desire" (*epithymia*) in conjunction with his understanding of the Spirit as the divine "enabler" and the love commandment or the law of Christ (Gal 5:2) in the grace of God.

4

The Grace of God in Love and the Spirit
The "Foundation" of the Remedy of Desire

HAVING IN MIND "THOSE who know the law," in Romans Paul presents his understanding of the solution to the problem of *epithymia* in light of the Christ-event (Rom 12:1—15:13). The analysis in previous chapters has shown that the passion of "desire" (*epithymia/orexis*) is often closely associated with excessive sexual desires and vices, in particular those vices that lead to sexual immorality (*porneia*). Especially when Paul uses either *epithymia/orexis* or *epithymeō*, he generally has in mind its connection to vices that lead to sexual immorality. As a matter of fact, with the exception of Rom 1:28–32, where the vices listed are not sexual, in Rom 13:13–14, only two of the six vices are not sexual, and in the catalog of vices in Gal 5:19–21, seven of the fifteen vices are not sexual. In his understanding of desire as a negative and deadly passion, Paul, a Hellenistic Jewish believer, is greatly influenced by the Greek philosophical and Hellenistic Jewish traditions. The analyses of texts where the terms *epithymia* and *epithymeō* appear, and especially Paul's rhetorical-poetic representation in Rom 7, have clearly demonstrated that his approach to desire and the way he represents the problem of desire and its negative sequels shows a Hellenistic believer who, like the philosophers and Hellenistic Jewish authors (discussed in this study), engaged in the discussions about *what* the proper definition of desire should be, and *what* can solve the problem of desire.

In his doctrine of the remedy of desire, however, Paul moves beyond both traditions. Against the backdrop of Philo and 4 Maccabees, Paul articulates his position in this way: the practice of the commandment (e.g., the Jewish food laws) is not the solution to the problem of desire (*ouk epithymēseis*). Paul's argument diverts from that of Philo (*Spec.* 4.79b–4.131) and 4 Maccabees (see ch. 1), whose doctrine of desire proposes the practice of the food laws as the solution to the problem of desire. It is important to point out that unlike Philo and 4 Maccabees, who propose *how* the virtue of "self-control" (*enkrateia*) or "temperance" (*sōphrosunē*) is to be achieved or mastered, Plato and the Stoic philosophers do not move further from the question of *what* (*enkrateia* or *sōphrosunē*) can moderate or extirpate (excessive) desire. In this case, Paul's solution of the passion of "desire" (*epithymia*), like Philo and 4 Maccabees, moves from the *what* to the *how* question. But, while Philo and the author of 4 Maccabees opt for the practice of the food laws (*tēs entolēs*) as the best course to *how* one can moderate desire, Paul's choice (of what is the best course to *how*) exhibits a Christocentric approach in relationship to the ethical benefits that come with the Christ-event.

In view of the Christ-event, by "the grace of God" (*charis theou* or *charis tou theou*) the believers now have free access to "righteousness" (*dikaiosunē*) in the Spirit and the love commandment. So, the practice of virtues and the avoidance of all kinds of (sexual) vices and desires come through faith in Christ and the possession of the Holy Spirit. And faithfulness and obedience to God's law come through the practice of the love commandment or the law of Christ (Gal 5:2), not through the practice of "the commandment" (*tēs entolēs*) or the food laws. It is at the point when Paul is addressing the topic of the practice of righteousness in the world (Rom 13) that Paul intends to reconcile his Jewish tradition with the new law of "love" (*agapē*) brought about by the Christ-event. Genovesi argues that for Paul the law of love comes in the grace of God and is a law that is produced by the Holy Spirit.[1] This new law in the grace of God is likewise interpreted in terms of "love our neighbor," as we shall see in this chapter.

We have seen that Paul maintains his continuity with his Jewish tradition by believing that the law is good and holy, and that the commandment is holy, good, and righteous. But his reconciliation between the law and the new law grounded in the "Spirit" (*pneuma*) is understood in terms of the virtue of "love" (*agapē*) as the fulfillment of the law (Rom 13:8–10),[2] and

---

1. Genovesi, *In Pursuit of Love*, 53.

2. Something similar is found in the Gospel tradition, especially Matthew (chs. 5–7) when Jesus as the new Moses tells the mixed Matthean community, "Do not think that

not in the subordinate virtue of self-control or the generic virtue of temperance in the Greek catalog of virtues. In Paul's catalog of virtues, love is depicted as a generic virtue, the virtue par excellence.³ In 1 Thessalonians, love is mutually expressed among the believers in the virtue of "brotherly love" (*philadelphia*). In Galatians, the letter where Paul sets up the framework of his ethical teaching for the first time,⁴ he mentions nine virtues as the "fruit" of the Spirit (*love*, joy, peace, patience, kindness, generosity, faithfulness, gentleness, and self-control).⁵ Love is the leading virtue, the *first* fruit of the Spirit (Gal 5:22), and the only Christian virtue among the other Greek virtues (Gal 5:22–23). Paul explains the fact that "love" (*agapē*) is the way faith works itself out (Gal 5:6).⁶ The fruit of the Spirit reaches its climax in the fulfillment of the Greek ideal of "self-control" (*enkrateia*), a subordinate virtue to "temperance" or "moderation" (*sōphrosunē*); this is a virtue that Paul, before his experience on the road to Damascus, knew in the stories of key Jewish figures who either possessed or lacked it.⁷ This outstanding position of self-control, as Hans Dieter Betz points out, is unique in Paul and may indicate that he quotes the entire passage from a source.⁸

In 1 Cor 13, Paul elaborates his understanding of Christian love and describes love as being "everything" (*panta*), holding everything, and enduring everything (1 Cor 13:4–7). In 2 Corinthians, the virtue of love is associated directly with God when Paul calls him "the God of love" (2 Cor 13:11–13). In Philippians, love is highly valued in the community where

---

I have come to abolish the law or the prophets; I have come not to abolish but to fulfill" (Matt 5:17). Later, the Matthean Jesus exclaims what is called "the Golden Rule" in the Christian tradition: "In everything do to others as you would have them to do to you; for this is the law and the prophets" (7:12). In the Epistle of James, the author refers to Pauline love in this way: "I by my deeds will show you my faith" (Jas 2:18). See Fitzmyer, *Romans*, 677.

3. See 1 Cor 12:31; 13:13; 2 Cor 6:6; Gal 5:22–23; Phil 4:8; Col 3:12.

4. Naveros Córdova, *Live in the Spirit*, 49.

5. Concerning the nine virtues, Betz asserts that they are not virtues in the Greek sense of the term. In fact, they do not represent qualities of personal behavior that a person can elect, cultivate, and appropriate as part of his/her character. These nine "concepts" are not good deeds in the sense of Jewish ethics; instead, the nine concepts should be taken as "benefits" that were given as or together with the Spirit. Betz, *Galatians*, 286.

6. See also Gal 5:13–14. In his analysis of *agapē* in Gal 5:6, 13–14, Andrew Bowden interprets these texts in connection with *epithymia* in Gal 5:16–17, 24. For his analysis and a good bibliography, see *Desire*, 453–71.

7. E.g., Joseph (Gen 39) and David (2 Sam 11). For a brief analysis, see appendix C.

8. Betz, *Galatians*, 288.

the believers are united in love and in one Spirit committed to live virtuously and in holiness (Phil 2). In Philemon, the virtue of love is linked with the gospel as Paul, Onesimus, Philemon and his household live out the gospel teaching "out of love." In Romans—Paul's mature presentation of his understanding of the Spirit—the virtue of love is identified as the law of the Spirit (8:2–3; see also 15:30), which in Galatians is the law of Christ (Gal 6:2). Thus, in Paul, love as a commandment in the Spirit takes a Christocentric approach; in the grace of God, love in the Spirit (of God/of Christ) is the foundation for the solution of the problem of "desire" (*epithymia*) and its negative sequels, and indeed the virtue in which the believers find unity ("*love* our neighbor") in the complexities of the larger Greco-Roman world.

PAUL'S DOCTRINE OF THE SOLUTION TO THE PROBLEM OF DESIRE AND ITS NEGATIVE SEQUELS

Paul has demonstrated in various ways that the practice of the food laws to attain moderation is not the solution to the problem of "desire" (*epithymia*). The observance of the commandment of the Mosaic law proved to be an ineffective remedy to control desire and eliminate excessive and sinful desires and (sexual) vices of the "flesh" (*sarx*). In Paul's catalog of vices, he considers the sexual vices as passions and desires of the flesh (Gal 5:19, 24), which must be avoided. In his discussion of Rom 7, Craig S. Keener states, "In Romans as in Galatians, the 'flesh' offers an inadequate response to the righteousness of God standard in the law."[9] He adds, "The law is good, but flesh is weak (Rom. 7.14)." Similarly, Keener, drawing upon N. T. Wright, points out that "'the material on which' the law 'had to work was inadequate' for generating true righteousness."[10] Thus, the law is no longer necessary for the acquisition of virtues and the avoidance of vices. Being in the law, what flows from the human heart is "sin" (*hamartia*), and when the individual gratifies the desires of the flesh, he or she becomes a slave to sin. Because God is not pleased with wrongdoers, God shows his wrath toward them (Rom 13:4). Bruce J. Malina and John J. Pilch argue that God's wrath means God is prepared to get satisfaction for actions of public dishonor, e.g., vengeance for being publicly dishonored so as to maintain his

---

9. E.g., Rom 7:5, 14, 25; 8:3–4, 7; see also 2:28; 3:20; Gal 2:16; 3:3, 5; 5:16–19; 6:12–13. Keener, *Mind of the Spirit*, 118.

10. Keener, *Mind of the Spirit*, 118, and quoting Wright, *Faithfulness of God*, 507.

honor.[11] For Paul, the wrath of God also signifies God's displeasure with the believers' moral behavior but in accord with the love commandment/ the law of Christ/the law of the Spirit and not in the observance of the ethical commandments of the Mosaic law. In Paul's solution to the problem of *epithymia*, there is no need to distinguish between "clean" and "unclean" animals for food.

Against the backdrop of Philo's theory of moderation rooted in the Mosaic prescriptions of the food laws (*Spec.* 4.79b-4.131), Paul articulates his position in this way: the practice of the commandment (e.g., the Jewish food laws) is not the solution to the problem of desire (*ouk epithymēseis*). For Paul, the "old" has come to its end as he writes, "We serve not under the old written code [*palaiotēti grammatos*] but in the new life of the Spirit [*en kainotēti pneumatos*]" (Rom 7:6cd). Now, the Jewish believers live in the newness of "the Spirit of God" (*pneuma theou*) and of the "new creation" (*kainē ktisis*).[12] As he develops his doctrine to avoid all kinds of passions, desires, and (sexual) vices, Paul trusts in a more powerful law (than the Mosaic law), that of the Spirit and of Christ, *the love commandment* (Rom 13:8-9; Gal 5:14), which is also expressed throughout his seven letters in the "love of our neighbor." The grace of God through Christ, not through the practice and observance of a commandment (food laws), brings forth two gifts: first, it frees human beings from enslavement to the passion of desire and leads the soul upwardly to God; second, it expands the understanding of the love commandment toward inclusivity. Again, through a dramatic performance centered in God and Christ (Rom 7), Paul is not only able to bring to the fore the "real" problem of *epithymia* (which involves the *what* question), but most importantly, he offers both Jewish and gentile believers a more effective and inclusive "solution" (which involves the *how* question). His Christocentric solution would liberate them from enslavement to sinful passions beyond measure, sexual vices, and all kinds of desires.

To solve the problem of "desire" (*epithymia*) and ultimately eliminate the law of sin, Paul distances himself from the value of the ethical character of the law and beyond the traditional understanding of the value of the practice of the commandments of the Mosaic law and food laws. Influenced by his Christocentric view and Christocentric monotheism (see ch. 2), Paul proposes a new ethical avenue to solve the problem of desire and its negative sequels. His solution centers in the virtue of "love" (*agapē*) and God

---

11. Malina and Pilch, *Social-Science Commentary*, 228.
12. Rom 8:18-25; 1 Cor 8:5-6; 2 Cor 5:17; Gal 6:15.

acting through Christ and in the "Spirit" (*pneuma*).[13] For Paul, it is not about *what* to observe, e.g., observe the restrictions about "clean" and "unclean" animals as Philo and the author of 4 Maccabees promote. It is about *Who*. In his dramatic performance in Rom 7 when the sinner in despair cries out, asking, "*Who* will rescue me from this body of death?" (Rom 7:24), Paul declares succinctly, "God through Jesus Christ our Lord! Christ, who has been raised from the dead" (Rom 7:4). Later in Rom 8, in Paul's exposition on the Spirit-versus-flesh contrast, he claims there is no "condemnation for those who are in Christ Jesus" (Rom 8:1). While Philo and the author of 4 Maccabees rely on a Greek virtue (*enkrateia* or *sōphrosunē*) for the remedy of desire as in the Greek ethical systems, Paul hopes that especially those who know the law (Jewish believers) would come to understand that through Jesus' salvific action (his death on a cross) by the grace of God and his faithfulness, they are freed from the law's curse (Gal 3:10–14). The Christ-event brought about freedom from "sinful passions" (*ta pathēmata tōn hamartiōn*), "every kind of desire" (*pasan epithymian*), and sins and (sexual) desires that are "excessive" (*pleonazousa*) or "beyond measure" (*kath' huperbolēn*).[14] Paul tackles the problem of desire and its evil passions, excessive desires, and excessive or sinful sexual pleasures and vices in light of God's faithfulness in terms of: (1) the intrinsic relationship between Christ and the Spirit of God in love; and (2) God's authority and reward.

The Centrality of Christ and the Spirit in Love

Paul hopes that believers (those who know the law [Rom 2:17–24; 7:1]) would understand that through the body of Christ they have died to the law of sin and death. In Rom 8:1–4, Paul explains how they have died to "the

---

13. Fitzmyer notes that the word "love" (*agapē*) "is neither *eros*, 'the love of desire,' which is aimed at the possession of the person or thing loved, not *philia*, 'love of friendship,' which rejoices in the free response of the beloved, but rather a self-sacrificing openness, an outgoing concern and respect of one person for another in concrete acts or deeds that result in the diminution of the lover's 'self' and subordinates the lover's personal ends to that of the one loved." Fitzmyer, *Romans*, 138–39. See also Rom 13:8–10.

14. Dunn explains that even believers at the present age are still caught in the yoke of sin and death, which continue working in and through their body. In this context Dunn speaks of the eschatological tension of "already" and "not yet" and takes both Rom 7:14–25 and 8:1–9 as representing the two ends of the eschatological tension (flesh versus Spirit). Dunn, *Theology of Paul*, 475–80. See also Van den Beld, "Romans 7:14–25," 496.

law of sin and death" (*tou nomou tēs hamartias kai tou thanatou* [Rom 8:2]) in baptism through Christ, and that they no longer live in the flesh but in the Spirit of God (Rom 8:5–17). Friedrich Wilhelm Horn rightly noted that Rom 8 is the zenith of Paul's thought regarding the role of the Spirit in the life of believers.[15] The Spirit is not only the Spirit of life and a law (Rom 8:2), it is a divine gift of grace through Christ leading the way to a new life (Rom 7:6d) to "bear fruit for God" (Rom 7:4d). With the advent of the Christ-event, Jewish and gentile believers have received the ethical instructions (1 Thess 4:5). Our Father's faithfulness came to those who believe in Jesus Christ and live according to the Spirit, which means according to the love commandment or the law of Christ.[16] There is no greater law that would help believers to overcome the desires of the flesh. Paul explains that in Christ believers are freed from the law of sin and death through the Spirit by faith (Gal 5:16) and the law of the Spirit of life in Christ Jesus (Rom 8:2); Paul writes, those who belong to Christ Jesus have crucified their flesh with "its passions and desires" (*tais pathēmasin kai tais epithymiais* [Gal 5:24]).

Paul's argument points out the believers' new experience, contrasting the results of two ways of life (Rom 8:5–17; Gal 5:17). These are two possible ethical attitudes that distinguish the consequences of walking "according to the flesh [*kata sarka*]" (vices/desires/passions) and "according to the Spirit [*kata pneumati*]" (virtues/love),[17] that is, "walking according to love" (*kata agapēn peripateis* [Rom 14:15]). The former (*kata sarka*) belongs to *tradition* prior to the act of God's grace, righteousness, and faithfulness in Christ and the Spirit, and the latter (*kata pneumati*) belongs to *experience*, the present situation, a life in love.[18] Correspondingly, Paul contrasts *sarx* and *pneuma* (Rom 8:4–9, 13): a human being subject to earthbound tendencies (*sarx*) and a human being open to the influence of the Spirit of God (*pneuma*).[19] According to Paul, the "flesh" (*sarx*), which produces vices and all kinds of (sexual) desires, is in opposition to the "Spirit" (*pneuma*), which produces virtues and love; and the flesh (vices) is in association with the law

---

15. Horn, "Wandel im Geist," 167; Kowalski, "Brokerage of the Spirit"; Robinson, *Metaphor, Morality*, 8; Dunn, "Spirit Speech," 82; Dunn, *Theology of Paul*, 642.

16. Gal 5:1—6:10; 1 Cor 13; Rom 6–8.

17. Rom 8:4, 5, 12, 13. See Naveros Córdova, *Live in the Spirit*, 112.

18. McFadden rightly points out that Paul speaks of a new age in salvation history, the present condition in which believers are freed from the law to serve in the newness of the Spirit. McFadden, "Fulfillment," 486.

19. Fitzmyer, *Romans*, 127.

and passions and desires (Gal 5:16–25).[20] It is important to note that Paul's treatment of *epithymia* is similar to his treatment of *sarx*; Heikki Räisänen explains this similar connection in his statement that "*epithymia* has its seat in the flesh."[21] As Paul frames his ethical discourse in Galatians (5:1—6:10), using the contrast between "flesh" (*sarx*) and "Spirit" (*pneuma*) in terms of "the works of the flesh" (*ta erga tēs sarkos*) and "the fruit of the Spirit" (*ho karpos tou pneumatos*), he lists specific Greek vices as the works of the flesh in Gal 5:19–21. Interestingly, as we have seen in chapter 2, several of these pagan vices are associated with sexual vices and desires: sexual immorality (*porneia*), sensuality (*aselgeia*), idolatry (*eidōlolatria*), drunkenness (*methai*), and carousing (*kōmoi*).[22] Paul consistently believes that "those who belong to Christ Jesus have crucified the flesh with its passions [*pathēmasin*] and desires [*epithymiais*]" (Gal 5:24).[23] Within the philosophical and Hellenistic Jewish traditions, Paul stresses the virtue of "self-control" (*enkrateia*), which correlates again with both "sexual immorality" (*porneia*) and "idolatry" (*eidōlolatria*), leading to a concluding remark on the crucifixion of the flesh with its passions and desires, which include sexual vices.[24] In Galatians, too, Paul's use of the expressions "things like these" (*homoia toutois*) and "those who do such things" (*ta toiauta* [Gal 5:21]) are allusions

---

20. As part of his discussion, Bowden examines Paul's use of *epithymia* in relation to the metaphors of "enslavement" and "freedom from enslavement" in both Galatians and Romans. In his analysis of Galatians, Bowden argues that the law constitutes the metaphorical slaveholder who enslaves people. When referring in Gal 5 to slavery and to freedom from the law, Paul links this metaphor three times with "desire" (*epithymia/epithymeō* [5:16, 17, 24]). According to Bowden, Paul teaches that having been metaphorically freed from the law of works and circumcision, gentile believers should serve the law of Christ (Gal 6:2), a law that consists of love. Therefore, believers who walk by the Spirit "no longer fulfill the desire of the flesh" (*epithymia sarkos ou mē telesēte* [Gal 5:16]). The law makes use of the desire of the flesh to enslave people. Having been freed by means of the Spirit, believers choose to serve a different master by loving others as they themselves want to be loved. Paul uses the same imagery in Rom 1:6–8 and Rom 13. Bowden, *Desire*, 433–512.

21. Räisänen, "ΕΠΙΘΥΜΙΑ und ΕΠΙΘΥΜΕΙΝ," 89.

22. The other vices are impurity, sorcery, enmities, strife, jealousy, anger, quarrels, dissensions, factions, and envy (Gal 5:19–21).

23. The noun *epithymian* appears in Rom 7:7, 8; Gal 5:16; Phil 1:23 (good desire).

24. In this case, like in Philo, Paul's connection between *enkrateia* and sexual pleasures reflects the tradition of Sextus Empiricus, *Math.* 9.153–9.154, who describes *enkrateia* as self-control regarding sexual pleasures, as opposed to "endurance" (*karteria*). See Gourinat, "*Akrasia* and *Enkrateia*," 229; Reno, "Pornographic Desire," 183.

to sexual sins or vices that lead to sexual vices.²⁵ Thus, Paul's message is: believers now live in the new era (new covenant), the "new creation" (*kainē ktisis* [Gal 6:15; 2 Cor 5:17]).

The solution to the problem of "desire" (*epithymia*) and its negative sequels is brought by the law of the Spirit of life in Christ Jesus (Rom 8:1–2) to those who are in Christ (Rom 8:5–11) and reaffirms an experience of love in the "new creation" (*kainē ktisis*).²⁶ The indwelling Spirit (Rom 8:9–10), the grace of God, and his faithfulness (Rom 9–11) become instrumental in moving the believers forward to the present experience in Christ. Along this line, Keener claims that "in contrast to the flesh's inability to achieve the ideal law, the Spirit empowers true righteousness, providing an internal rather than external law" (e.g., Rom 8:2, 4; see also Rom 7:6; Gal 3:2, 5; 5:18, 23).²⁷ The mind of the Spirit is indeed a mind led by righteousness.²⁸ It can be safely argued that the Spirit, the divine "enabler," focuses on the mind and not only on the actions; in other words, for Paul, the Spirit as the divine "enabler" empowers the believer's "mind" (*nous*) as it does his or her doings. While Paul's use of the "Spirit" (*pneuma*) language is dependent on the Stoic tradition,²⁹ Paul departs from the interpretation of the Spirit's cosmological role. Now the Spirit is the Spirit of God and the Spirit of (Jesus) Christ (Rom 8:9; Phil 1:19) or the Spirit of God's Son (Gal 4:6). This new law lived out in "faith working through love" (Gal 5:1–12) is the ethical instrument through which "all kinds of desire" (*pasan epithymian*), "excessive desires beyond measure" (*kath' huperbolēn hamartōlos*), and "sinful passions" (*ta pathēmata tōn hamartiōn*), including excessive sexual desires, are eliminated.

Elsewhere, in my analysis of Paul's ethical discourse founded on the Spirit, I identify the Spirit as the divine "enabler" and "font" to practice virtues and avoid vices.³⁰ Indeed, it is in Rom 8 that the Spirit language

---

25. See discussion in ch. 2.
26. Rom 8:18–25; 1 Cor 8:5–6; 2 Cor 5:17; Gal 6:15.
27. Keener, *Mind of the Spirit*, 118.
28. Keener speaks of the "mind of the Spirit" within the context of the understanding of "the mind of Christ" (1 Cor 2:16), thinking the way that Jesus did (Phil 2:5), and thinking according to the Spirit (Rom 8:5). Within the same framework, we can argue that Paul speaks of the law of the Spirit within the parameters of the law of God, the law of Christ, and the law of love (love commandment). Keener, *Mind of the Spirit*, 127.
29. For the Stoic understanding of the concept of *pneuma* (spirit), see Naveros Córdova, *Live in the Spirit*, 7–8.
30. Naveros Córdova, *Live in the Spirit*, 136.

becomes invasive, as Paul carries on the connection that he first established between the Spirit and ethics in Gal 5:1—6:10. Paul further develops his understanding of the virtue of "love" (*agapē*) within the understanding of the commandment "love your neighbor as yourself" (Rom 13:9; Gal 5:14). He fleshes it out as the "queen" virtue in 1 Cor 13–14, and he catalogues love as supreme when he redefines the "fulfillment of the law" in Rom 13:8-10. Therefore, his solution to solve the problem of the passion of desire and its negative sequels represents his own *experience* of his reinterpretation of the love commandment—a *tradition* he inherited from his Jewish tradition—within the context of his understanding of the history of salvation. The "grace of God" (*charis theou* or *charis tou theou*), which is a gift of the Christ-event, came in the Spirit and in love to all believers who believed in Christ. As Timo Laato rightly asserts, salvation is not only by faith alone but also by God's grace. And faith never remains alone; it is always active through love.[31]

God's Authority and Reward in Love and the Spirit: Two Blessings

One of the essential aspects in Paul's presentation of his theocentric and Christocentric approach to deal with the passion of desire and other passions and pleasures in connection with sexual vices is his emphasis on God's authority and the benefits of being obedient to God's will. In his ethical exhortation, Paul describes the faithfulness of God in close relation to the will of God (1 Thess 4:1–4); God's authority must be respected and accepted by all believers (1 Thess 4:8). To those who do so, God promises the outpouring of "his Holy Spirit" (*to pneuma autou to hagion* [1 Thess 4:8]). God is faithful and a provider for those who believe and have the Spirit for endurance against the desires of the flesh (1 Cor 6:13). Similarly, the faithfulness of God brings about his righteousness upon believers without distinction (Rom 1:11)—Jews and gentiles—if they believe and guide their lives according to God's law (Rom 7:21–25). God expects that believers become God's instruments of righteousness (Rom 6:13–16) and slaves of righteousness for sanctification (Rom 6:19). For Paul, in Christ believers have become the righteousness of God (Rom 1:16–17; 3:21–26).[32] In this

---

31. Laato, "Salvation by God's Grace," 175.

32. For discussion on the word *dikaiosunē* (righteousness or justice), see Dunn, *Theology of Paul*, 341–46.

way, sin no longer rules (Rom 6:14), and believers can remain in the grace of God and in Christ (6:14).[33]

When an individual lives according to his/her own deeds, the individual moves away from the righteousness of God and the opportunity of receiving eternal life, the reward of God's glory, honor, and peace. For Paul, it is not about being Jewish (does practice of the law) or being Greek/gentile (does not practice the law); salvation is available to all, Jews and gentiles alike (Rom 9–11). For Paul writes, "There is no distinction between Jew and Greek" (1 Cor 12:13); "the same Lord is Lord of all and is generous to all who call on him" (Rom 10:12). Salvation thus is a universal event because of the righteousness of God, the faithfulness of God, and the Christ-event. Paul is explicit in his position: God is impartial because God is faithful to his promise and because of his righteousness (Rom 11:1). If believers are faithful and obedient to God's law (the love commandment in the Spirit), then God is also faithful; God is a provider for all believers to endure passions and "desires of the flesh" (*epithymias sarkos* [1 Cor 10:13; Gal 5:16]).

Furthermore, Paul's call to righteousness represented an avenue not only to solve the problem of desire but also to break the boundaries of divisions among both Jewish and gentile believers. Certainly, Paul's view of desire and its remedy to avoid (excessive) sexual passions and desires, moves in the same direction as the general worldview of his ethics. We see more clearly that in the new law or love commandment in the Spirit, Jews and gentiles alike receive God's faithfulness and become part of God's righteousness. As Mark D. Nanos proposes, Paul's ethics—and I would add his ethics on desire and his remedy to avoid desire—are concerned not with what we might call "individual ethics," but with the effect of a separated person from the identity and purity of the group. It is the whole community that matters first and foremost in light of the whole persona.[34]

Paul explains his understanding of God's authority by focusing on his theocentric approach in his ethical teaching. Paul points out elements that reflect God's centrality in human affairs and the sacredness of the human body. For Paul, the miraculous event changing the destiny of believers is certainly Christ's resurrection through which believers living in the new era have the choice of living free from sin and in Christ (Rom 6:7). In this context Paul speaks of the resurrection of the "body" (*sōma*), putting emphasis on the idea that the human body is important and must be respected (1 Cor

33. Byrne, *Romans*, 194–95.
34. Nanos, *Mystery of Romans*, 440.

15:35–58). For example, in 1 Thess 4:4, believers are exhorted to "control" (*ktasthai*) their bodies in "holiness" (*hagiasmō*) and "honor" (*timē*), and in Rom 6:18–19 to present their bodies in a holy manner as "slaves of righteousness for sanctification" (*doula tē dikaiosunē eis hagiasmon*). This is, according to Paul, the midway path "to know God" (*eidota ton theon* [1 Thess 4:5]). As seen in chapter 2, knowledge of God is closely linked with virtue and contrasted with lack of knowledge of God, vices, and excessive desires.

Paul writes to the Corinthian church, "For just as the body is one and has many members, and all the members of the body, though many, are one body, so it is with Christ. For in the one Spirit, we were all baptized into one body—Jews or Greeks, slaves or free—and we were all made to drink of one Spirit. Indeed, the body does not consist of one member but of many" (1 Cor 12:12–14a). In this context, indeed using the language of "instrument" (*hoplon*), Paul exhorts believers to avoid being instruments of wickedness, sin, and death, but instead, choose to be "instruments of righteousness" (*hopla dikaiosunē* [Rom 6:13]). The idea that believers, both Jews and gentiles, are one, instills in the believers' heart/mind the notion that they, too, partake in God's righteousness and God's faithfulness. The language of "taking part in" refers in Paul's theological context of salvation to the believers becoming "instruments" (*hopla*) of righteousness and "slaves" (*doula*) of righteousness.

This "reversal approach," introduced by the Christ-event, is how the believer may receive "the grace of God" (*charis theou* or *charis tou theou*). The body is good (1 Cor 15), and believers must present their bodies as "slaves to righteousness for sanctification" (*doula tē dikaiosunē eis hagiasmon* [Rom 6:19]). This is the secure way to eternal salvation (Rom 6:22–23). So, Paul glosses his presentation of the dangers of idolatry and a path to sexual vices and immorality with the theme of sanctification around the themes of God's righteousness and faithfulness (Rom 6–8) to create a balance between prohibition and reward. With freedom from sin's tyranny, the believers are also freed from idolatry and sexual vices. In Paul's language (less philosophical) these vices are expressed through the language of "sinful passions" (*ta pathēmata tōn hamartiōn*), "all kinds of desires" (*pasan epithymian*), and "sinful beyond measure" (*kath' huperbolēn hamartōlos*).

Likewise, through the Christ-event and the virtue of obedience, believers, unlike gentiles, come to know God; they are able to bear fruits for God and they are prompted to practice love toward one another, the other, each other, and the neighbor, as we shall see below. Being "a servant" (*diakonos* [Rom 13:4]) of God allows believers to live out a holy life—honorably and virtuously, not in vices, passions, and desires (Rom 13:13; 1 Thess 4:7)—and receive God's grace and the abundance of his providential care for people and the world. God is a provider Father for all who believe and endure, in love and in the Spirit, the ethical challenges faced in the Greco-Roman world (1 Cor 10:13). Thus, the faithfulness of God and his righteousness are understood in one word: goodness (*agathōsunē* [Rom 15:14]). God is a life-giving God and a rewarding God, and his goodness was, is, and will be given without discrimination to all believers, for God is impartial in the new era of Christ (Gal 3:28). While for Philo and the author of 4 Maccabees, the goal is piety and immortality, for Paul the goal is God's rewarding gift: glory, honor, and peace (Rom 2:10). These are essential spiritual attributes of love and of "the kingdom of God" (*hē basileia tou theou* [Rom 14:17; 1 Cor 15:24]). The final eschatological expectation then comes when all believers attain the "kingdom of God" (*basileian theou* [1 Cor 15:50; Gal 5:21b]), for "our citizenship is in heaven" (*hēmōn gar to politeuma en ouranois* [Phil 3:20]), the kingdom of God.

In light of Paul's Christocentric approach, the renewal of humanity comes to all believers through the belief in Jesus Christ. In Rom 7, the straight answer to the sinner's question in despair—"*Who* will rescue me from this body of death?" (7:24)—is found in Paul's statement "God through Jesus Christ our Lord! Christ, who has been raised from the dead" (7:4). It is because Jesus saves all indiscriminately from sin and human corruption that the gift of the outpouring of the Holy Spirit comes into the believers' hearts. Paul explains two blessings (belief and the Holy Spirit). He exhorts believers to "walk by *faith*" (2 Cor 5:6–10) and "walk/live by the *Spirit*" (Gal 5:16–26). For example, his solution to the problem of "desire" (*epithymia*) and its negative sequels imparts divine blessings, which provide believers opportunities to live according to God's law (the love commandment or the law of Christ) in the Spirit. Then, when Paul speaks about the "new creation" (*kainē ktisis* [2 Cor 3:1—6:2; Gal 5:1—6:10]) within the context of his theology and eschatology, he embraces God's gifts—e.g., holiness, sanctification, the Holy Spirit, the kingdom of God, salvation, and eternal life in heaven—and shares these divine gifts with all believers (Gal 3:28). Paul speaks of the faithfulness of God and his righteousness; and in turn, all believers ought to respond positively to God's invitation to live according to love in the Spirit.

Sanctification and holiness come to believers from Jesus' giving himself out of love (Phil 2:6–11); the belief in this free giving brings them the Holy Spirit, which enables believers to live holy lives and maintain their bodies pure as God's temple and the temple of his Spirit. To prevent believers from excessive sexual desire, and thus redirect them to healthy sexual desire in marriage, Paul exhorts them, saying that the "body is not for sexual immorality [*porneia*]" (1 Cor 6:13) and informs them, "The one who sins sexually [*porneuōn*] sins against his own body [*sōma*]" (1 Cor 6:18).[35] With a rhetorical question, he reminds the believers, "Do you not know [*ouk oidate*] that your body [*to sōma hymōn*] is a temple [*vaos*] of the Holy Spirit [*hagiou pneumatos*] within you, which you have from God, and that you are not your own?" (1 Cor 6:19). Paul adds a powerful statement: "You were bought with a price [*timēs*]; therefore, glorify God [*doxasate ton theon*] in your body [*sōmati*]" (1 Cor 6:20). Similarly, in 1 Cor 7:23 he writes, "You have been purchased with a price [*timēs*]. Do not become slaves to human beings [*douloi anthrōpōn*]." The believers' bodies are important; they are divine, for they belong to God. Thus, human correspondence in terms of love depends on the idea that the spiritual elements of reward, eternal life, and salvation must find harmony with how believers treat their bodies (1 Cor 15:32–58). Positive attitude regarding God's ethical expectation is nonetheless what knowledge of God entails (something that gentiles do not know or lack, *agnoia*), measured by the love commandment. What is key for Paul in his doctrine is the free disposition to acknowledge the ethical value of the human body and its care in the newness of life in the Spirit of God. The greatest honor is to offer God blameless bodies as his temple.

---

35. Gil Arbiol offers a fresh argument regarding 1 Cor 16:12-20. He argues that the believers who engaged in sexual immorality with prostitutes understood the slogan "everything is lawful for me" as the answer to the end of an ethical role of "any law" (including the Jewish law) in the *ekklesia*. For the Corinthian believers, it was not necessary to obey any law because God was above all laws. To deal with the issue, Paul uses a strategy: this is not an "individual" problem, but a communal problem. In other words, Paul emphasizes the problem of the members in the community, urging them that "their bodies are members of Christ." In this way, Paul exhorts those who believe that they are free from ethical norms to see themselves not as "individuals, strong or weak" but as parts of "an all" that has a defined identity (1 Cor 6:19). Gil Arbiol, *Qué se Sabe de*, 154-57.

THE EFFECTIVENESS OF LOVE IN THE SPIRIT: "LOVE OUR NEIGHBOR" IN PAUL'S ETHICAL PERSPECTIVE

This chapter cannot be concluded without a presentation on the effectiveness of the virtue of "love" (*agapē*) and its role in the ethical journey of believers as neighbors, brothers, and sisters (Gal 6:1–10). God has been faithful, and his fidelity has been perceived in his supreme act of love by sending his only beloved Son to save humanity and the world (Gal 4:4; Phil 2:5–11). God, through Jesus' resurrection, has given believers the gift of baptism in Christ (Rom 6:3–4) and brought about participation in the body of Christ (1 Cor 12–14). In Jesus' death and resurrection as expressions of God's faithfulness, the love commandment rooted in the gospel of Christ was first established by Jesus during his earthly ministry: "Love one another as I have loved you" (John 13:34) and "In everything, do to others what you would have them do to you" (Matt 7:12; Luke 6:31). Thus, "love" (*agapē*) as a virtue that endures and surpasses everything fulfills the requirements of the Mosaic law (Rom 13:8–10).

In Paul, the gifts, or fruits of the virtue of love, are manifested by the Spirit of God in the lives of the believers.[36] Paul's proclamation of his gospel is also a manifestation of the Spirit of God and his power (1 Cor 2:4). Paul's words are related to the spiritual believers because they are taught by the Spirit (1 Cor 2:13). The Spirit's gifts are also virtues, which are also intrinsically connected with the Spirit of God.[37] The virtue of love is not only the "queen" of all the virtues but encompasses everything and endures everything (1 Cor 13:1–13). In 1 Cor 13:4–7 Paul emphasizes a special relationship between love and the other virtues and disassociates love from vices and sexual vices (Gal 5:22). Therefore, there is no longer the absence of "the grace of God" (*charis tou theou*); as a matter of fact, Christ and the Spirit of God/of Christ abides in the hearts of believers who have faith in Christ. Paul tells believers that in Jesus' gospel they can endure everything (1 Cor 9:12) and live a life pleasing to God (1 Cor 1:21; 7:32; 10:5, 33). This lifestyle, rooted in the power of the gospel of Christ, leads them to "be saved in the power of God" (1 Cor 1:18; 15:1–2) and in the power of the Spirit (1 Cor 2:13–14).

---

36. 1 Cor 3:13; 12:1–11; 14:2, 25.

37. 1 Cor 7:34; 14:3–6; see also 1 Cor 6:17.

For Paul, the virtue of *agapē* as a grace of God in the Spirit is to govern the believers' ethical life, for love is the most excellent way (1 Cor 12:31b) and the greatest virtue (1 Cor 13:13). What is paramount for our purpose is that in light of the Christ-event the commandments of the Mosaic law and/or Decalogue are summed up in one single commandment of God: "Love your neighbor as yourself" (Rom 13:9).[38] Paul ascribes to love super qualities, which are generally ascribed to God in the Stoic language of *panta*: "Love covers all things, believes all things, hopes all things, and endures all things" (1 Cor 13:7). Significantly, the expression "love covers all things" is a reference analogous to the Stoic notion of the role of *logos* (reason) and *pneuma* (spirit) in creation: the *logos/pneuma* permeates everything in the *kosmos* (world, universe). Therefore, in Paul's thought, love surpasses the letter (the commandments of the Mosaic law). The following examples are meant to show how the effectiveness of love in the Spirit is represented in Paul's inclusive understanding of the expression "love our neighbor," expressed in the horizontal axis and beyond the practice of the commandments of the law.

The Ethical Commandments of the Decalogue

To reinforce his teaching on "love" (*agapē*), Paul brings to the fore the list of the Decalogue from his Jewish tradition. He writes in Romans,

> Owe no one anything except to love one another [*ei mē to allēlous agapan*]; for the one who loves another [*ho gar agapōn ton heteron*] has fulfilled the law [*nomon peplērōken*]. The commandments, "You shall not commit adultery; you shall not murder; You shall not steal; You shall not covet [literally, desire]"; and any other commandment [*hetera entolē*] are summed up in this word, "Love your neighbor as yourself [*agapēseis ton plēsion sou ōs seauton*]." Love [*hē agapē*] does no wrong to a neighbor [*tō plēsion kakon ouk ergazetai*]; therefore, love [*hē agapē*] is the fulfilling of the law [*nomou*]. (Rom 13:8–10)[39]

This is a crucial passage because, as Fitzmyer says, Paul mentions Catholic commandments sixth, fifth, seventh, and a combination of both the ninth and tenth commandments from the Decalogue of Deut 5:17, 18, 19, and

---

38. Matt 7:12; Luke 6:31.

39. In 4 Maccabees, "reason" (*logismos*) is said to sum up all: "You shall not covet [literally, desire] your neighbor's wife, or anything that belongs to your neighbor" (2:5–6).

21 in the order of the LXX.⁴⁰ There are two important points to highlight. First, Paul is faithful to his Jewish tradition (*continuity*), for he reconfigures his thought within the Jewish understanding of the law. Paul follows on the footsteps of other Jewish Hellenistic thinkers (e.g., Philo and the author of 4 Maccabees), the tradition of Deuteronomy (Deut 6:4–5) and Leviticus (Lev 19:18) of the LXX, and the rabbis. This last group summed up the 613 commands and prohibitions of the Torah and their developments.⁴¹ The Christ-event inspired Paul to reconfigure his new law centered in love (the commandment of love) and the Spirit in such a way that it reflects the teachings of other Jewish authors. But unlike them, Paul's new law (*experience*) also creates a bridge between the "we" and the "others," the "us" and "them."

Paul launches a shocking statement to his audience, placing himself as one among them: we all are baptized into Christ and were clothed with Christ, thus "there is no longer Jew or Greek, there is no longer slave or free, there is no longer male and female, for all of you are one in Christ Jesus" (Gal 3:27–28; also Rom 10:12; 1 Cor 12:13).⁴² In the context in which the apostle writes this statement, there is no doubt that his "ideal" of eradicating religious and social *distinctions* between Jews and Greeks, slaves and freemen, men and women, had not only strong social and religious implications then but also political ones.⁴³ As Betz notes regarding the phrase "there is neither Jew nor Greek," a variation of the well-known Hellenistic political slogan "Greeks and barbarians" from Rom 10:12, "We may conclude that Paul has in mind the removal of the distinctions which customarily separates the Jew and the non-Jew."⁴⁴ Mona West and Robert E. Shore-Goss argue that Paul's adoption of this slogan of unity envisions some sort of ideal non-diversity, where "oneness" involves assimilation into

---

40. The order to the first two differs from that of the Hebrew in Exod 20:13–17 and Deut 5:17–21; it is reflected in the LXX ms. B and certain other witnesses. In his analysis of the metaphor "slavery to a master" because of desire in Rom 13:9, Bowden points out that Paul focuses on specific laws with the general *nomos*. Bowden, *Desire*, 507. See also Byrne, *Romans*, 396. For discussion, see Fitzmyer, *Romans*, 678–79.

41. Fitzmyer, *Romans*, 679.

42. For the various arguments regarding Paul's words "no male and female" in Gal 3:28, see Martin, *Sex and Single Savior*, 77–90.

43. Betz, *Galatians*, 190.

44. Betz, *Galatians*, 190–91. According to Rom 3:1–20; 9:3–5, this eradication pertains to the religious prerogatives claimed by the Jews and symbolized by the observance of circumcision (Rom 2:25–29; 4:9–12; 1 Cor 7:19; Gal 5:6; 6:15; Phil 3:3).

the body of Christ and erases the diversity existing in the communities.⁴⁵ Paul intends to establish a healthy relationship between Jews and gentiles.

This ideal leads to the second important point. While Paul reevaluates the ethical value of the Mosaic law and the Decalogue, his *experience* allows him to establish a new law in love and the Spirit that is inclusive in nature and/or universal. A good example is the "neighbor" (*ho plēsion*) language employed in his argument of "love" (*agapē*). In Rom 13:8, he explicitly uses the pronoun "one another" (*allēlous*), which at first glance is horizontal and restricted to fellow Jewish believers: love one another. However, it also indirectly alludes to another group: gentiles. Hence, Jewish believers, too, are exhorted to expand their love to gentile believers. But Paul also uses the general term of "another" or "somebody else" (*ton heteron*): one who loves another or somebody else has also fulfilled the law. The expression of love toward *ton heteron* points to Paul's openness to include gentiles into the Jewish believers' communion of love. Now, in the next verse (Rom 13:9) the term "another" (*ton heteron*) becomes "your neighbor" (*ton plēsion sou*): love your neighbor as yourself (*agapēseis ton plēsion sou hōs seauton*). Similarly, in 1 Cor 16:14, Paul exhorts, "Let everything that you do be done in love [*panta humōn en agapē ginesthō*]." According to his understanding of love and, interestingly, in continuity with his Jewish tradition of "the neighbor" (*ho plēsion*) language, Paul employs the terms *allēlōn* and *ho heteros* (literally, the other, another) like he does in other Pauline texts—1 Cor 6:1 (*ton heteron*); 10:24 (*tou heterou*), 29 (*tou heterou*); 14:17 (*ho heteros*); and Gal 6:4 (*ton heteron*)—as the equivalent of *ho plēsion* (neighbor), the word that occurs in the OT citations in Rom 13:9.⁴⁶ This leads us to suggest that Paul is expanding further and methodically his understanding of Christian love, envisioning the horizontal expression of "love our neighbor" that has now reached a wider Jewish and gentile audience alike.⁴⁷

The Exhortation of the Real Circumcision

When dealing with the topic of "circumcision" (*peritomē/katatomē*), Paul demonstrates his harshness toward those who wrongly seek to please God in the practice of a commandment and his gentleness toward those who are called unrighteous by "those who know the law." In early Jewish

---

45. West and Shore-Goss, *Queer Bible Commentary*, 652.
46. Fitzmyer, *Romans*, 678; Bowden, *Desire*, 507.
47. Col 3:14; 1 Tim 1:5; 1 John 4:11.

Christianity, the observance of circumcision was a law that must be practiced; there was no room for arguing whether a Jew should or should not be circumcised. Obedience to the practice of physical circumcision was also expected among early Jewish believers. Even for new Jewish believers who became members of the church of God, circumcision was an important identifier, especially in the Jerusalem community where the "circumcision party," according to Paul, was strong (Gal 2). But the arguments about the practice of circumcision in the new movement created tensions and divisions between two parties among believers: the "circumcision party" (*peritomē*) and the "uncircumcision party" (*akrobustias* [Gal 2:7]). Paul's letters, especially in Galatians, evince the tension in the communities mostly formed by gentile believers throughout Asia Minor (e.g., Galatian territory). In the letter, where Paul argues against the practice of the physical circumcision in the community at Antioch, the hostility and feelings of extreme hatred toward one another or "the neighbor" (*ho plēsion*) become apparent. This is particularly true on the part of the circumcision party (the Jerusalem church) toward the uncircumcision party (Paul, his coworkers, and their followers).[48]

Surprisingly, in his dealing with circumcision Paul is generally on the side of the "rejecters"! In a letter, he shows his radical position on this topic. He shamelessly shows his opposition to the circumcision party when he writes, "I wish those who unsettle you would castrate themselves!" (Gal 5:12). For him, his approach is an either-or situation, not both-and. Thus, in the eyes or opinion of those so-called "righteous," Jewish believers, Paul and the other believers in Antioch are disobeying God's commandment and putting in great danger a divine and ancient Jewish tradition (Gen 17:10–14; Gal 3:1–14). There is a progression in Paul from ambivalence to spiritual circumcision. To appease both groups, Paul expresses the irrelevance of the practice of the physical circumcision.[49] With the Christ-event the practice of circumcision prescribed by the law of Moses is no longer necessary, and he gives priority to the metaphorical or spiritual circumcision, which is an inner circumcision. In 1 Corinthians, Paul shows his ambivalence toward its practice when he states, "Circumcision means nothing, and uncircumcision means nothing; what matters is keeping God's commandments" (7:19; also Gal 6:15). In Romans, true circumcision is a matter of the heart in the Spirit

---

48. See Gal 2–6.

49. Rom 2:28–29; 3:1, 30; 4:9–12; 15:8; 1 Cor 7:19; Gal 2:7–9, 12; 5:6, 11; 6:15; Phil 3:2–5.

and in faith (Rom 2:25–29). Like his position about *eidōlothyton* in 1 Corinthians (8:8; 10:30), Paul puts himself on the side of "defenders" to express the value of "circumcision" (*peritomē*) only when the ones who are circumcised also "observe the law" (Rom 2:25; Gal 6:12–13). Paul explains to believers that a circumcised heart is that of a transformed individual who in obedience (Rom 6:17) and faith (Rom 10:8–10) lives out love, a life experienced in the Spirit, virtue, and holiness. In light of his *experience*, he challenges those who are defenders of the law, saying that a real Jew is not one who bears a physical mark but the one who participates in Christ's life by living out the law of Christ or the love commandment in the Spirit (Gal 5:6; 6:1–10; Phil 3:2–3).[50] Similar to Philo, who spiritualizes the observance of circumcision,[51] Paul internalizes the practice of circumcision by completely rejecting the letter, for the commandment kills (2 Cor 3:4–6), and highly emphasizes the virtue of love. For with baptism in Christ, circumcision comes to an end (1 Cor 7:17–20; Gal 5:2–6).[52]

For Paul, it is crucial that his divided audience understands that crucifixion with Christ replaces the role of circumcision.[53] Therefore, in this case, unlike his position on the food laws (see below), he crystallizes his radical stand that it is an either-or situation, not both-and (Gal 5:11). Paul understands the new covenant in Christ as the appropriate path for believers, thus he reaffirms his position with a bold statement: "Those who belong to Christ have crucified the flesh together with its passions [*pathemasin*] and desires [*epithymiais*]" (Gal 5:24). This is the same ideal Philo has in his argument of pro-spiritual circumcision: the ethical circumcision helps with "the excision of excessive pleasure" and all passions of the soul (*QG* 3.48) and helps the individual moderate the appetites of the passions and vices (*Spec.* 1.305).[54] Paul challenges the defenders of the observance

---

50. In his analysis of Phil 3:2–3, Nanos discusses Paul's statement "we are the circumcision" (v. 3) in reference to the "mutilation" (*katatomēn*) language. He proposes that Paul sets out circumcision as a "metonym for Christ-following identity in contrast to Jewish identity or in contrast to other Christ-following groups." Nanos also finds a connection between Paul's statement in v. 3 and the Maccabean slogan "we are the circumcised" in 1 Macc 1:15, 48, 60–61; 2:44–46; 2 Macc 6:10. Nanos, "Out-Howling the Cynics," 197–99.

51. In *Spec.* 1.305, Philo says that true circumcision is of the "heart." See also *Spec.* 1.6–1.11; *Congr.* 52; *Migr.* 18; *Mut.* 189; *Praem.* 44; *QE* 1.21, 2.2, 2.43; *QG* 3.48, 3.61. While Philo spiritualizes the practice of circumcision, he also continues defending the value of the physical circumcision in *Migr.* 86–93 (Gen 12:2); *QG* 47–48.

52. Rom 6:3; 13:14; Gal 3:2–3, 27–29.

53. Gal 5:11, 24; 6:13–14.

54. For studies on Philo's view of circumcision, see Borgen, *Philo, John, and Paul,*

of physical circumcision; it is not circumcision that liberates "you" from passions and desires (Gal 5:19–24; 6:13–14). Therefore, the viewpoint held by (some) Jewish believers is wrong! For Paul, righteousness comes from the new law, the love commandment in the Spirit (Gal 5:14; 6:2) lived out in/by Christ's faith.

In the context of Paul's treatment of circumcision, I suggest that the love commandment refers to love lived out dynamically by both groups, Jewish and gentile believers. In love, Paul is able to internalize the law of circumcision (it is of the heart, that is, an internal positive disposition to love the neighbor above the law); as a result, he eliminates the boundary between Jews and gentiles (Rom 10:12; 1 Cor 10:32; 12:13; Gal 3:27–29).[55] Since "real" circumcision is now internal and of the heart, then the ethical value of circumcision stems from the baptismal ritual. Remarkably, Paul finds a strategic course to redefine the tradition he inherited from his forefathers (*tradition*). We wonder about the extent of his argument against physical circumcision and how the three pillars (James, Peter, and John) of the Jerusalem church, for example, and the other apostles felt about Paul and his novel approach to holiness and salvation. According to Galatians (2:1–10, 15–21), Paul's redefinition of the practice of physical circumcision was too much to bear for the three pillars, the members of the Jerusalem church, and even some followers of Paul. As he writes, "Even Barnabas was led astray by their hypocrisy" (Gal 2:13; see Acts 15:36).[56] Nevertheless,

---

61–71, 233–54; Borgen, "Observations"; Hecht, "Exegetical Contexts"; Barclay, "Paul and Philo"; Tolbert, "Philo and Paul," 400–402.

55. See McEleney, "Conversion, Circumcision"; Nolland, "Uncircumcised Proselytes?"

56. One of the cruxes of Paul's argument in Galatians is the topic(s) in discussion: circumcision and/or table fellowship or the observance of the food laws. Apparently, Paul brings up the problem of circumcision, which was already resolved at the Jerusalem Council (Acts 15:6–35; Gal 2:1–10), in the church at Antioch. At that event in Jerusalem, Paul and Barnabas, coworkers in agreement with the leaders of the Jerusalem church, went to the gentiles (or uncircumcised) to preach the gospel. However, in Gal 2:11–14 Paul discusses another problem that apparently was not resolved at the Jerusalem Council, that is, table fellowship (eating with gentiles [v. 12]) or food laws. As Paul addresses this problem, stirred by those who came from James, then the leader of the Jerusalem church, Barnabas, his coworker and friend, leaves Paul and opts to follow Cephas and the circumcision party (v. 13). In Paul's argument in Gal 2:15–21, it seems that Paul goes back to the first topic introduced in discussion in Galatians: circumcision. However, the way he develops his argument in 2:15–21 shows his position in relation to gentile believers. But it is not clear whether his reference to the "works of the law," used three times in v. 16, and to the term *nomos*, used six times in vv. 16 (3x), 19 (2x), and 21, are also

Paul's innovative vision offers to his mixed audience a window to edify the neighbor and the path to inclusivity.

Eating Meat Sacrificed to Idols

Paul spends a good deal of time giving his personal evaluation about eating meat sacrificed to idols (*eidōlothytōn*), bought at the marketplace, and eaten at the temple precinct, especially in 1 Cor 8:1–13 and 10:18–33.[57] The Corinthian believers asked Paul for his advice and viewpoint on this topic. He introduces the topic concerning the "food sacrificed to idols [*tōn eidōlothytōn*]" in 8:1 or the "eating of food sacrificed to idols [*tēs brōseōs tōn eidōlothytōn*]" in 8:4. Paul has Corinthian believers in mind; so, out of "love" (*he agapē*), which "edifies" (*oikodomei*) the Corinthian community composed of Jewish and gentile believers (8:1b), he announces the consequences for believers (probably gentile believers) who partake in idolatrous sacrifices and the eating of food/meat offered to idols. In *continuity* with the tradition of Jewish monotheism, he shows his radical position about idols by restating his Christocentric monotheism: there is no god except one, for gentile believers there is also one God who is Father and Creator, and there is one Lord Jesus Christ through whom all things came into existence (8:4, 6). Although Paul expresses some ambivalence in 8:8 ("Food will not bring us close to God. We are no worse off if we do not eat, and no better off if we do"), he exhorts them not to use their liberty and become a stumbling block to "anyone" or "others" (*tis*) in the community who are "weak" or have a weak "conscience" (*suneidēsis* [8:9]). Malina and Pilch's interpretation of

---

references to eating with gentile believers, food laws (table fellowship), or circumcision only. I suggest that in Gal 2:1–21 Paul has in mind both issues, circumcision and food laws. Thus, when Paul says, "I died to the law" (v. 19a), it is also a reference to the food laws (he died to the observance of the food laws) and not only to circumcision.

57. The literal translation of *eidōlothytōn* (1 Cor 8:7; 10:19) is "that which has been offered before images." The meaning of the Greek *eidōlon* (idol) is obscure. According to Malina and Pilch, during Paul's time *eidōlon* was a neutral term referring to an image. Images were to be found in Greek and Roman temples as well as in households (e.g., busts, statues, and death masks). In households, images of ancestors were venerated and taken to burial places for periodic funerary celebrations involving eating and drinking as a show of respect for ancestors. Therefore, it is not clear whether Paul refers to the original eating of food presented before statues of deities or food presented to household ancestors at funerary celebrations. Malina and Pilch, *Social-Science Commentary*, 92. For various arguments on the meaning of *eidōlothytōn*, see also Theissen, *Social Setting*, 126–27; Fee, *First Epistle to Corinthians*, 357.

the ambivalence of Paul may depict what he might have had in mind. They state, "Paul agrees but argues that it is not what one eats but with whom one eats that fills what one eats with meaning" (1 Cor 8:8–10).[58]

However, Paul is clear in his argument rooted in love and the Spirit. If believers see a (gentile) believer "in an idol temple reclining and eating [*in eidōleiō katakeimenon*]," Paul poses a rhetorical question: "Might they not, since their conscience is weak, be encouraged to the point of eating food sacrificed to idols [*ta eidōlothyta esthiein*]?" (8:10).[59] Christ died also for the weak "brother" (*ho adelphos*), whether Jew or gentile. Thus, the one who participates in eating food sacrificed to idols sins against the brothers and sisters in the community and Christ (8:12). To stress his point of view, Paul places himself as one of them and says what he would want his brothers and sisters to do: "If food [*brōma*] causes my brother and sister to stumble [*skandalizei ton adelphon mou*], I should never eat meat [*ou mē phagō krea eis ton aiōna*], so that I may not cause him or her to stumble [*hina mē ton adelphon mou skandalisō*]" (8:13). In other words, for the sake of love and the edification of one another, brothers and sisters—believers—should never participate in eating and drinking in an idol worship service (1 Cor 8:1–13).[60] In this case, we observe in Paul's response to the Corinthian believers the initial reflection of his orientation towards the benefits of love. His priority now is primarily their edification in the love of God, and certainly his sincere and loving concern of the weak ones (gentile believers), and he invites all believers to do the same.

It is again in his discussion about partaking in idolatrous worship and feasting with idolaters in 1 Cor 10:18–33 that Paul openly expresses his personal reflection about "eating food sacrificed to idols" (*eidōlothyton*)

---

58. Malina and Pilch, *Social-Science Commentary*, 94.

59. This text is a good example to see how Paul viewed the gentile believers at Corinth. They were "weak" and had a weak conscience. Paul saw them as infants and fed them with milk, not solid food, for they were not yet ready for solid food. In Paul's eyes, these brothers and sisters were still of the flesh (1 Cor 3:2).

60. Cousar, *Letters of Paul*, 71. While early believers were not to attend festivals at the pagan cults, the eating of meat previously offered to idols became a matter of indifference. Some scholars argue that in 1 Cor 8 and 10:1–22 Paul has in mind eating in the temple precinct (which he forbids), and that in 10:23–30 Paul is thinking of food sold in the marketplace or eaten at a private residence. While others state that Paul is opposing the eating of all sacrificial meat on the basis of the halakah of Torah, whether in a temple dining hall or anywhere else, others argue that Paul is prohibiting participation in *eidōlolatreia*, actions that are construable as worship of the idols. For a good summary, see Willis, "1 Corinthians 8–10."

and eaten in the temple precincts. On this occasion, however, he is more explicit as he presents the issue, *eidōlothyton*, and exposes his reflection in light of his new understanding of love. He starts off with a rhetorical question directed, this time, to gentile believers restating what he had previously questioned: "Are not those who eat the sacrifices partners in the altar? What do I imply then? That food sacrificed to idols [*eidōlothyton*] is anything or that an idol [*eidōlon*] is anything?" (1 Cor 10:18-19). Within the pagan context, he provides his rationale: "The things that they [pagans] sacrifice" [*ha thuousin*], they sacrifice to "demons [*daimoniois*], and not to God [*ou theō*]." Then, out of love toward his Corinthian brothers and sisters, he expresses his wish: "I don't want you to become sharers of the demons [*humas koinōnous tōn daimoniōn ginesthai*]" (10:20). Then, he seriously exhorts them not "to drink" (*pinein*) and not "to take part of" (*metexein*) *eidōlothyton* by creating two contrasts between "the cup of the Lord [*potērion kyriou*]" and "the cup of demons [*potērion daimoniōn*]" and between "the Lord's table [*trapezēs kyriou*]" and "a table of demons [*trapezēs daimoniōn*]" (10:21). It is at this point that, in light of his Christocentric monotheism (10:22) and out of his understanding of love in the Spirit, Paul presents a sublime reflection of the value of others: what is "a good thing" (*sumpherei*) for and what "edifies" (*oikodomei*) others. Indeed, he exhorts believers with an imperative: "Seek [*zeteitō*] not your own advantage but that of others [*tou heterou*]" (10:24).

In 1 Cor 10:25-28, Paul speaks again on behalf of the good of "others" (*heteroi*), which refers to gentiles. In it, he proposes to the Corinthians believers three points of consideration about eating idol meat from the market: (1) out of consideration "for the other" (*tou heterou*) and for the sake of his "conscience" (*suneidēsin*), "eat [*esthiete*] everything that is sold in the meat market [*pan to en makellō pōloumenon*]" (1 Cor 10:25), for the idols do not exist, thus the meat itself belongs to the Lord, not to the idols (1 Cor 10:26); (2) if "any unbeliever (gentile) invites you and you want to go," out of consideration of "conscience" (*suneidēsin*), "eat [*esthiete*] everything that is set before you without raising questions" (1 Cor 10:27); and (3) if "anyone" or "someone" (*tis*) informs you that "this [meat] has been offered in sacrifice [*touto hierothyton*]" for the sake of his "conscience [*suneidēsin*]," "do not eat [*mē esthiete*]" (1 Cor 10:28).[61] Paul again worries that believers might use their liberty wrongly (1 Cor 8:1-13, especially v. 9) and clarifies what he means in light of love practiced also toward nonbelievers: it

---

61. See also Luke 10:8; 10:1-12. Bailey, *Paul Through Mediterranean Eyes*, 289-92.

is not about your own conscience but "the other's" (*tēn tou heterou*) and/ or "another's conscience" (*allēs syneidēseōs*) (1 Cor 10:29). Paul concludes his personal reflection and exhortation with powerful words that edify the Corinthian community of believers (Jews and gentiles) in love, strengthens their social relations with pagans or nonbelievers at Corinth, and strengthens their deeper relationship with God: "So whether you eat or drink [*eite oun esthiete eite pinete*], or whatever you do, do everything for the glory of God [*panta eis doxa theou paiete*]. Avoid giving offence [*aproskopoi*], whether to Jews or Greeks [*kai Ioudaiois kai Hellēsin*] or the church of God [*kai tē ekklēsia tou theou*], just as I try to please everyone [*pasin*] in every way, not seeking my own edification [*symphoron*] but that of the many [*to tōn pollōn*], that they may be saved [*hena sōthōsin*]" (1 Cor 10:30–33; also Rom 15:2; Phil 2:4). We envision a Paul who intends to edify three relationships: (1) believers and other believers; (2) believers and nonbelievers; and (3) believers and God.

The Expectation of Food Laws

Another example where "love" (*agapē*) in the Spirit is reflected is found in Paul's treatment of the food laws. In Rom 14:1—15:3, Paul's approach is reoriented towards building community and inclusivity. Paul embraces diversity by showing both sensitivity and tolerance among believers, especially the "weak,"[62] or gentiles. Particularly in Romans, there are statements rooted in the virtue of love where Paul uses the example of the practice of the food laws to challenge all believers and himself to help them come to good terms with a "brother or sister" (*adelphos*), with "another" (*allotrios*), and with "the neighbor" (*ho plēsion*) in the following:

> One [*hos*] believes in eating anything [*phagein panta*], while the weak [*asthenōn*] eats [*esthiei*] only vegetables [*lachana*]. The one eating [*ho esthiōn*] must not despise the one who abstains [*ton mē esthionta*], and the one who abstains [*ho mē esthiōn*] must not pass judgment on the who eats [*ton esthionta*]; for God has welcomed them. Who are you to pass judgement on servants of another [*allotrion*]? (Rom 14:2–4a)

---

62. For discussion on Paul's language of "weak" and "strong," see Barclay, "Faith and Self-Detachment," 196–97, 200–205.

> The one who observes the day, observe it in honor of the Lord. Also the one who eats [*ho esthiōn*], eats [*esthiei*] in honor of the Lord, since he gives thanks to God; while the one who abstains [*ho mē esthiōn*], abstains [*ouk esthiei*] in honor of the Lord and gives thanks to God. (Rom 14:6)
>
> Why do you pass judgment om your brother or sister [*adelphon*]? Or you, why do you despise your brother or sister [*adelphon*]? For we will all stand before the judgment seat of God. (Rom 14:10)
>
> Let us therefore no longer pass judgment on one another [*allēlous*], but resolve instead never to put a stumbling-block [*proskomma*] or hindrance [*skandalon*] in the way of the brother or sister [*tō adelphō*]. (Rom 14:13)
>
> Nothing is unclean [*ouden koinon*] in itself, but it is unclean [*koinon*] for that person [*ekeinō*] who thinks it unclean [*koinon*]. (Rom 14:14b)
>
> If your brother or sister [*adelphos*] is being injured by what you eat [*brōma*], you are no longer walking in love [*ouketi kata agapēn*]. Do not let what you eat [*brōmati*] cause the ruin of one [*ekeinon*] for whom Christ died. (Rom 14:15)
>
> The kingdom of God is not food [*brōsis*] and drink [*posis*] but righteousness [*dikaiosunē*] and peace [*eirēnē*] and joy [*chara*] in the Holy Spirit [*en pneumatic hagiō*]. (Rom 14:17)
>
> Do not, for the sake of food [*brōmatos*], destroy the work of God. Everything is indeed clean [*panta men kathara*], but it is wrong for you to make the person [*anthrōpō*] fall [*proskommatos*] by what you eat [*esthionti*]. (Rom 14:20)
>
> It is good not to eat meat [*kalon to mē phagein krea*] or drink wine [*mēde piein oinon*] or do anything that makes your brother or sister [*adelphos*] stumble [*proskoptei*]. The faith [*pistin*] that you have, have as your own conviction before God. (Rom 14:21–22)

Paul then concludes his exhortation about food laws restating in a summary form the main topic in discussion, "love our neighbor," in this way:

> We who are strong [*dunatoi*] ought to put up with the failings of the weak [*asthenēmata*], and not to please ourselves. Each of us

must please our neighbor [*hemōn tō plēsion*] for the good purpose of edifying the neighbor [*oikodomēn*]. For Christ did not please himself; but, as it is written, "The insults of those who insult you have fallen on me." (Rom 15:1–3)

Similar to the topic of the practice of the Mosaic law in love, the observance of the food laws (or table fellowship) is another topic on which early believers agreed and/or disagreed among themselves. Paul addressed the issue before, at least once, when he confronted the church's authority (Gal 2).[63] Now, more mature in his theological and ethical thinking, he introduces himself to the Roman believers[64] and lays out his position regarding the food laws, keeping in mind his experience with both Jewish and gentile believers: defenders of the observance of the food laws as well as rejecters of the food law and the law as a whole.

There are important points throughout Rom 14:1—15:3 that are worth highlighting. As the chosen texts above show, there is a real problem in the early Christian communities: the ethical value of the practice of the Jewish food laws. It shows that some believers are practicing this commandment, but most gentile believers are not; both groups are also engaged in a negative criticism toward one another. Paul and his coworkers hope for a change, a change that would edify "the neighbor" (*ho plēsion*) so that brothers and sisters could be one and in the same Spirit (*experience*). The Jewish believers (defenders), who see themselves as righteous before God, are "judging" (*krinōn*) and despising the gentile believers (rejecters) who are not following the observance of the food laws (Rom 14:1–4, 10, 20). According to the Jewish believers, gentile believers are not only eating and drinking "unclean" (*koinon*) food/drink (Rom 14:6, 14), they are behaving like pagans, who are considered impure and unholy, are known for being idol worshipers, and are known for engaging in sexual vices. In other words, they live a life that is repugnant to the holy commandments of the law.[65] These Jewish believers are viciously attacking the gentile believers for morally embarrassing their fellow brothers and sisters in Christ. That group, those who knew the law (Rom 7:1), are telling those who do

---

63. For an exploration on the conflicts and comparisons between Galatians and Acts, see Matera, *Galatians*, 105–10.

64. Gaventa explores the problem Paul faces and the conflicting groups among his audience and offers a specific plan and practical response. Gaventa, "Reading for the Subject."

65. Josephus, *A.J.* 12.2.14; 13.1.1.

not practice the law what is lawful and unlawful, that is, what is lawful to eat and drink and what is unlawful to eat and drink (Rom 14:6). Within the Jewish tradition, these Jewish believers are directly commanding the gentile believers to eat/drink "clean" (*kathara*) food (Rom 14:10, 20), as Moses the lawgiver prescribed to their ancestors. They see themselves as the "defenders" of Moses's prescriptions.

In Paul's view, the defenders are looking at the gentile believers with contempt, literally treating them unkindly and without love (Rom 14:2–4a, 20).[66] Those who practice the commandment of the food laws, eating and drinking according to what is permissible, wrongly consider the "others" (rejecters) "weak," that is powerless, physically and morally without strength, indeed, "weak" in faith (Rom 14:1).[67] But, Paul reassures that both groups of Jewish and gentile believers are actually those who are "weak" (Rom 15:1), and Paul and those who follow him are actually the "strong" believers (Rom 15:1). Thus, with the rhetorical questions in Rom 14:10 ("Why do you pass judgment on your brother or sister? Or you, why do you despise your brother or sister?"), Paul invites both groups to become like him and practice tolerance with one another, with each other, and with their "neighbor" (*plēsion*). He enters the picture to solve the problem of disunity and eliminate the negative criticism existing in the early Christian communities. He emphasizes his understanding of love in the Spirit and God's stand in this matter.

First, Paul elucidates that righteousness does not depend on what one eats/drinks (defenders) or what one does not eat/drink (rejecters).[68] His mind operates in this way: even those who do not eat or drink (unclean food) could lack righteousness if they cause their brothers and sisters stumble by not eating or drinking for the sake of them (Rom 14:21). Similar to his reflection concerning eating food sacrificed to idols (1 Cor 8:1–13, 10:18–33), Paul manifests the truth of his teaching that the kingdom of God is about living "according to love" (*kata agapēn*),[69] that is, according to the love commandment, and possessing virtues of "righteousness" (*dikaiosynē*), "peace" (*eirēnē*), and "joy" (*chara*) in the "Holy Spirit" (*pneumamati hagiō*),

---

66. Other Pauline passages where the word "despise" (*echoutheneitō*) appears are Rom 14:10; 1 Cor 1:28; 16:11; 2 Cor 10:10; Gal 4:14; 1 Thess 5:20.

67. "Being weak" (*asthenōn*) is a favorite word for Paul; see Rom 4:19; 8:3; 14:2; 1 Cor 8:11, 12; 2 Cor 11:21, 29; 12:10; 13:3, 4, 9.

68. Rom 14:14b.

69. Rom 14:15. See also Rom 5:5, 8; 8:35, 39; 12:9; 13:10; 14:15; 15:30; 1 Cor 4:21; 8:1; 13:1, 2, 3, 4.

not in the commandment of the food laws (Rom 14:17). This is for Paul the ethical course that all believers, too, must follow. Indeed, Paul and his co-workers intend to edify "the neighbor" (*ho plēsion*) walking in "love" (*agapē* [Rom 14:15]). Therefore, whether they eat/drink "clean" food/drink or not, Jewish and gentile believers could "give thanks to God" (*eucharistei theō* [14:6]);[70] it is the "faith" (*pistis*) they possess in unison that puts them in good terms with their "neighbor" (*ho plēsion*) and before God (Rom 14:22).

Second, Paul assures both Jewish believers and gentile believers that rather than edifying "one another" (*oikodomēs tēs eis allēlous* [Rom 14:19]), brothers and sisters (the community in Christ), they are destroying the unity of the Christian community (Rom 14:20) with their negative attitudes toward "one another," "another," and "neighbor." In 1 Cor 3:9, Paul reminds the believers that they are "God's fellow workers," "God's farming," and "God's building" (*theou oikodomē este*). For Paul, his gospel creates, as N. T. Wight states, "Not a bunch of individual Christians, but *a community*" (emphasis added).[71] Therefore, Paul launches a direct exhortation to both groups: "Let us therefore no longer pass judgment on one another [*allēlous*]," and "Never put a stumbling-block [*proskommatos*]" to your brother and sister (*anthrōpō* [Rom 14:13, 20]).[72] Then he exhorts them, saying, "Do not, for the sake of food [*brōmatos*], destroy the work of God" (Rom 14:20). Paul explains that passing judgment about what your brother or sister eats and drinks occasions another to act against his/her conscience. Once more, Paul relies on his rhetorical skills as his weapon to persuade them and to become like him, as he himself was persuaded by the Lord (Rom 14:14). In 1 Corinthians, Paul writes one of his favorite statements: "I appeal to you, be imitators of me" (1 Cor 4:16), and "Be imitators of me, as I am of the Christ" (1 Cor 11:1). He hopes that Jewish and gentile believers have the same confidence as he has (1 Cor 4:17) to listen to him, to obey the Lord, and to put their trust in him as in the Lord. Out of love in the Spirit, Paul wants them to believe in his words and care for the neighbor, brothers, and sisters.

Third, Paul skillfully poses challenging rhetorical questions to Jewish believers of the observance of the commandments of the law: "Why do you pass judgment [*krineis*] on your brother or sister [*ton adelphon*]? Or you,

---

70. Giving thanks to God is Paul's favorite word, e.g., Rom 1:8, 21; 16:4; 1 Cor 1:4; 10:30; 11:24; 14:17, 18; 2 Cor 1:11.

71. Wright, *Saint Paul Really Said*, 157.

72. See also Rom 9:32–33; 16:17; 1 Cor 1:23; 8:9; Gal 5:11.

why do you despise [*exoutheneis*] your brother or sister [*ton adelphon*]?" (Rom 14:10). In other words, Paul tells them, "Your behavior is making your brother and sister stumble in the same way gentile believers make you stumble when they refuse to practice the food laws (Rom 14:21); and the faith you have, have it as your own conviction before God (Rom 14:22).

In Rom 15:1-3, Paul continues exhorting the believers in love and the Spirit. In verse 1, he invites them to practice love toward each other; he urges those who share the same point of view, like him, to be strong with those who are weak to please God (Rom 15:1a). The ethical message to the strong ones, "us," is that for the sake of "love" (*agapē* [Rom 14:15]), "each of us [*ekastos hemōn*] ought to be kind toward our neighbors [*hemōn tō plēsion*]"—Jews and gentiles—"for the good purpose of edifying the neighbor [*oikodomēn*]" (Rom 15:1b-2).[73] To reaffirm his ethical position grounded on the ethical statement "walking in love" (*kata agapēn peripateis*), Paul focuses in verse 2 on "our neighbor" (*hemōn tō plēsion*) language once more,[74] but this time to exhort the "weak": "Each of us must please our neighbor" (*ekastos hemōn tō plēsion*), who are gentile believers, those who do not practice the food laws. Likewise, in verse 3, Paul's exhortation is directed to the "strong" and "weak," where the language of "our neighbor" (*hemōn tō plēsion*) also refers to Jewish believers who observe the food laws (*tradition*). If it is for "the good" (*to agathon*) of the community (Rom 14:6, 21; see also 13:10), it is permissible not to eat (unclean) food or drink (Rom 14:21); it is permitted to practice the food laws. This is "good" (*agathon*); indeed, it is virtuous to think of your neighbor first and for the sake of love do what is good for your neighbor. Paul intends to edify both the neighbor and the community by addressing Jews and gentiles in love and the Spirit (Rom 15:2).[75] Paul reaffirms once more that Christ is the example of love, for he did not please himself but his Father God (Rom 15:3).

The Ethical "Fruits" in Love and the Spirit Toward "Our Neighbor"

Returning to Paul's use of the language of "the other" or "one another" (*heteros* or *allēlōn*), "brother" or "sister" (*ho adelphos*), "anyone" (*tis*), and "the neighbor" (*ho plēsion*) within the context of the two groups (Jewish and

73. Rom 15:2; 1 Cor 3:9; 14:3, 5, 12, 26; 2 Cor 5:1; 10:8; 12:19; 13:10.
74. Rom 13:8-10; 15:2; Gal 5:14.
75. Rom 14:1, 19; 1 Cor 9:19; 10:24, 33.

gentiles) and in connection to love and the Spirit, I argue that Paul's use of these indefinite pronouns is intentional. "The one [*ho*] who loves another [*agapōn ton heteron*] has fulfilled the law [*nomon peplērōken*]" (Rom 13:8) not only needs the prescriptions of the law, as Fitzmyer and others have argued,[76] but it also needs to treat the other, one another, anyone, brother, or sister ultimately as "our neighbor" (*hemōn to plēsion*). Paul's new reinterpretation of the love commandment—"You shall love your neighbor as yourself" (*Agapēseis ton plēsion sou hōs seauton* [Rom 13:9])—intends to edify an inclusive and dynamic community of believers. Paul wants believers to see *others* as *my* neighbors.

In Paul's new law of love in the Spirit, the language of inclusivity is transformed into a true understanding of the neighbor language of the commandment (*entolē*), which eliminates offenses to one another and the dividing boundaries, among not only Jewish believers but also gentile believers. In other words, in Paul the language of "the neighbor" (*ho plēsion*) receives a new ethical nuance in which the Jewish understanding of it has failed to reach the demands of "love" (*agapē*) and to acquire the "fruits" of love necessary to edify the church of God. In Paul's Christian view, the meaning of *ho plēsion* extends to any fellow human being with whom believers live or whom they encounter in their complex pagan world (*experience*). In the new interpretation of the language of *ho plēsion* Paul brings about the virtue of love to a higher dimension of an ethic that is founded in the love commandment; for Paul, love to *ho plēsion* extends beyond any legal system or Roman and Jewish laws. Thus, his statement in Gal 3:28 (see also Eph 2:11–22) *then* represented the epitome of love to the Jewish and gentile believers.

Moreover, Paul's redefinition of the neighbor language understood through the lens of love in the Spirit brings forth the "fruits" of love, which are virtues. He depicts "love" (*agapē*) as the most important virtue. It is a virtue superior to knowledge (1 Cor 8:1; 14:26), the sublime way (1 Cor 12:31), and the greatest virtue (1 Cor 13:13). In his exposition of the virtue of love (1 Cor 13–14), he writes, "Now remains these three [virtues] faith, hope, and love [*agapē*]; and the greatest of these is love [*agapē*]" (1 Cor 13:13).[77] Paul claims that if he has no love, he is nothing (1 Cor 13:2),

76. Fitzmyer, *Romans*, 678–79.

77. Fitzmyer notes that *agapē* (love) is superior to the virtues of *pistis* (faith) and *elpis* (hope) not only because *agapē* plays an important role in the ethical life of the Corinthian believers, but "especially because it perdures even into 'the age to come.'... It is eschatological, has eternal value, and is the reason why the Christian will 'know' fully'

suggesting that if he has love he has everything, including the other virtues.⁷⁸ This is clearly observed in his description about the nature of love in 1 Cor 13:1-13. He writes in his introduction, "If I do not have love, I am a sounding brass or clanging cymbal. . . . I am nothing. . . . I have gained nothing" (13:1-3). Paul then presents love's virtuous attributes (the ethical fruits) that need to be reflected toward "the neighbor" (*ho plēsion*):

> Love is patient, love is kind, [love is] not jealousy, [love does] not brag, [love] is not puffed up, [love] does not behave dishonorably, [love] does not seek for itself, [love] is not hot tempered, [love] does not put down to one's account of evil, [love] does not rejoice over injustice, but rejoices in the truth. [Love] covers all things [*panta stegei*], believes all things [*panta pisteuei*], hopes all things [*panta elpizei*], and endures all things [*panta hypomenei*]. (1 Cor 13:4-7)

Paul mentions the special relationship of love with other virtues and its disassociation from vices. This connection further expands the close relationship that Paul has established between the Spirit and love (love is the first fruit of the Spirit [Gal 5:22]). First, Paul depicts the supremacy of the virtue of love by accentuating the intrinsic connection between love and virtues in relation to *ho plēsion* language. Second, he identifies love as the source of all virtues like the Spirit in Galatians (Gal 5:22-23). Paul understands both the Spirit and the virtue of love as sharing the same (divine) nature and attributes; both have their source in God himself, and both have the power to produce virtues. For Paul, the virtue of love cannot coexist or be expressed without the Spirit of God, and the Spirit cannot function as the divine "enabler" or be expressed without the love of God.

The statement "[love] covers all things [*panta stegei*], believes all things [*panta pisteuei*], hopes all things [*panta elpizei*], and endures all things [*panta hupomenei*]" in 1 Cor 13:7 embodies three essential virtues (faith, hope, and endurance) that must operate within love. To possess God's Spirit, according to Paul, requires "faith" (*pistis*); to attain the goal of life requires "hope" (*elpis*); and to do all things in love, according to the gospel of Christ, requires "endurance" (*hupomenō*). In 1 Cor 13:1-11, we

---

and be 'fully known', i.e., by God." Fitzmyer, *First Corinthians*, 502. See also Ciampa and Rosner, *First Letter to Corinthians*, 665.

78. Paul's treatment of *agapē* is in a way analogous to the Platonic, Stoic, and Aristotelian view of the virtue of "prudence" or "practical wisdom" (*phronēsis*), which is the main virtue in their ethical systems. For details, see Naveros Córdova, *Live in the Spirit*, 67-69.

find Paul's illustration of three important ways that love is meant to be lived out: love to God, love to Christ, and love to the neighbor, which includes the "unrighteous" or gentile (1 Cor 13:5–6). Within this threefold dynamic of love, together with the twofold relationship in love—Jewish believers and gentile believers—stands the most essential component for the edification of the believers. Thus, the phrase "love does no wrong to a neighbor" (*tō plēsion kakon ouk ergazetai*) in Rom 13:10a means, for Paul, that believers live out, according to the demands of love, embracing differences in reciprocity and respecting the neighbor without distinction.

"Faith" (*pistis*) is a virtue closely associated with "love" (*agapē*). Paul says that love is "the working out of faith" (Gal 5:6; see 1 Cor 13:4–6) and that faith working through love pursues all that is good in life, the "fruits" of love. True faith involves an inclusive love or the twofold expression of love that pursues all that is good for "the neighbor" (*ho plēsion*) who is also "our" brother or sister. As Paul writes, the love of God has been poured into their hearts through the Holy Spirit given to us (Rom 5:5). Therefore, the expression "for love [*hē agapē*] is the fulfillment of the law [*plērōma nomou*]" in Rom 13:10b reaffirms Paul's basic principle of "you shall love your neighbor as yourself" (*agapēseis ton plēsion sou hōs seauton*), now lived out in love in the Spirit. If Christ is the end of the law (Rom 10:4; Gal 3:19–25)—the goal toward which the history of salvation is aimed—then love not only motivates soteriological activity (Rom 8:34–36) but love is also the fulfillment of the law itself.

As a result, Paul's love commandment does not reject the law completely. Rather, the law is revised and reinterpreted according to the believers' real situation in the pagan world (*experience*). Indeed, he asserts, "The faith [*pistis*] that works itself out through love [*di' agapēs*]" (Gal 5:6) actually "upholds the law [*nomon*]" (Rom 3:31).[79] It is important to note that Paul's exposition of his new love through real examples of everyday life—ethical commandments of the law, circumcision, eating food sacrificed to idols, and food laws—is presented within the eschatological framework. In other words, everything Paul teaches has salvation as its object. According to Paul, the end is near. Hence, believers must wake up and walk/live in love, for salvation is coming! (Rom 13:11). His ethical doctrine of edifying the neighbor in the community requires a single commandment—"Love your neighbor as yourself"—yet it is meant to be understood inclusively, where the understanding of *agapē* and *ho plēsion* reaches out to those whom the

---

79. Fitzmyer, *Romans*, 679.

practice or observance of the commandments of the Mosaic law excludes. Significantly, the Christ-event, as understood by Paul's own *experience*, redefines the meaning of love. In turn, love becomes the foundation of goodness from which the "fruits" of love flow forth to form noble character and/or positive behavior toward the neighbor, as well as holiness in the midst of unholiness in the pagan world.

CONCLUSION

This chapter explored Paul's solution to the problem of desire and its negative sequels. His doctrine centered in love and the Spirit of God given to all the believers who believe in Jesus and in his Spirit. In Paul's doctrine of "desire" (*epithymia*), as well as in his remedy to avoid desire, which intends to eliminate sinful desires, all kinds of passions, irrational desires, or excessive desire and sexual vices, the believers find neither the virtue of self-control and the practice of the food laws as in Philo and philosophers nor reason and the practice of the food laws as in 4 Maccabees. Instead, they find Jesus Christ, who comes to them by the grace of God and becomes active in the virtue of love, and the divine "enabler," who is the reasoning Spirit, the *font* of Paul's ethical teaching. Within his Hellenistic Jewish tradition, Paul reconciled the law and the love commandment, love your neighbor as yourself. He moved apart from his Jewish tradition, yet not completely, and reinterpreted the love commandment within the parameters of his Christocentric view and Christocentric monotheism (the law of Christ). In love, lived out in Christ and the Spirit, he offered the remedy to avoid vices, all kinds of desires, and eradicate excessive desires, sinful passions beyond measure, and sexual vices.

With the effective practice of the love commandment, Paul put into perspective the inclusion of Jewish and gentile believers in the early Christian communities. Using four examples from his Jewish tradition—the ethical commandments of the Mosaic law, food laws, eating food sacrificed to idols, and circumcision—Paul showed how his new understanding of love in the Spirit should work in the community of believers. Like his inclusive interpretation of monotheism as Christocentric monotheism, he also viewed the virtue of love with the same outlook. Love is inclusive, exhorts unity, and fosters empathy toward the "other," "another," and "neighbor." Through the dynamic love, the "other" becomes "our neighbor," and the gifts and fruits of the Spirit, which are virtues, are also possessed by the "other," "another," and "neighbor" alike. God's faithfulness, his righteousness, and his grace are effective in all believers who walk/live in love and in the Spirit, and sanctification and salvation are given to those who believe in Christ and obey the will of God. For Paul, by "living by the Spirit" (virtues), the fruits of love/of the Spirit are practiced and vices avoided; through love in the Spirit the language of neighbor becomes supreme, for God is love. Therefore, Paul's reconfiguration of the understanding of the love commandment (or the law of Christ) in the Spirit, the divine "enabler," represents the universalization of the virtue of love in salvation and in his ethics.

5

Conclusion

In this book, we analyzed Paul's larger Greco-Roman context and his own Hellenistic Jewish perspective of "desire" (*epithymia*), its connection with sexual vices, and the remedy to avoid this deadly passion and its negative sequels. In his understanding of the passion of desire, and the way he treats this passion and provides his solution of the problem of desire and its negative sequels, Paul was not only influenced by the Hellenistic Jewish and Greek philosophical traditions of interpretations but he was also navigating like a *philosophos* within the larger and complex Greco-Roman world where discussions about desire as an evil and deadly passion were taking place. The complexity of the understanding of the relationship between *epithymia* and *pleonazousa* was certainly debated among philosophers, and Paul's writings reflect that discussion. What he had clear, like philosophers and Hellenistic Jewish authors, was the notion that the passion of "desire" (*epithymia*) had a close connection with sexual immorality and vices, and desire without control or moderation could become "irrational" (*alogos*) and tyrannical.

In chapter 1, we explored Paul's Greek philosophical and Hellenistic Jewish traditions in the writings of Plato, the Stoics, Philo of Alexandria, and 4 Maccabees. The authors shared important similarities in the way they depict the passion of desire; it is a deadly passion, so it should be either moderated or eradicated. The Hellenistic Jewish thinkers, Philo, and the author of 4 Maccabees followed the philosophical tradition in that they described the sinful attributes of desire in close connection with the understanding of gluttony, idolatry, and sexual immorality, Greek vices commonly associated in the Greek ethical systems. An important feature was the threefold relationship—desire-belly-tongue—which is reflected in Plato, Philo, and 4 Maccabees. Desire with the "help" of this threefold relationship becomes irrational, immoderate, or tyrannical desire. Thus, to control or moderate desire and eliminate the excessive quantity of desire, philosophers, Philo, and the author of 4 Maccabees proposed the practice of self-control or temperance, one of the four cardinal or generic virtues in the ethical systems of Plato and the Stoics.

The "mind" (*nous*) and "reason" (*logos*) played a vital role in their doctrine of the remedy to avoid desire. In fact, these authors dramatically depicted the internal struggle between two powers: on one side, (irrational) desire; and on the other (rational), reason (desire versus reason). These powers were also metaphorically identified as the lover of pleasure (desire) versus self-control (reason), the former fighting with the help of desire and the latter counterattacking with the support of reason. Both Hellenistic Jewish authors went beyond self-control, the remedy of desire; they offered advice on how an individual could acquire self-control. Within the parameters of Jewish tradition and its laws, they relied on the practice of the food laws as prescribed by Moses, the lawgiver. The antidote to solve the problem of desire and its negative sequels—irrational, excessive, immoderate desire, passions, and sexual appetites—was the food laws, and it was also reason in 4 Maccabees. They presented their solution in light of their Jewish tradition, their understanding of the tenth commandment (you shall not covet), but using Stoic and platonic language and ideas about desire. The authors also explained why the problem of desire must be resolved, that is, both Hellenistic Jews spoke of piety and immortality as the goal of self-control and the practice of the food laws.

In chapter 2, we explored Paul's view of desire in close connection with idolatry, the source of vices, and sexual immorality and vices common in the pagan world. Jewish and gentile believers lived in the midst of pagan idolatry, sexual desires, and vices. Within the Greek philosophical and Hellenistic Jewish traditions, Paul developed his argument about desire's dangers threatening the ethical life of the believers. He was a Hellenistic Jewish believer, and as such, he showed the complexities of his understanding of sinful passions, all kinds of passions, and sinful desires beyond measure or excessive/irrational/immoderate (sexual) desires, using his knowledge of

CONCLUSION

Jewish monotheism and the law. In the light of Judaism and the covenantal formula "you are my people, and I am your God" (Exod 6:7; Ezek 36:28; Jer 7:23; 30:22),[1] Paul showed how excessive sexual desires and sexual immorality and vices are in opposition to God's covenant and obedience to God. In the context of his Jewish *tradition*, Paul showed his dramatic transformation in his religious belief and convictions toward Jewish laws and Christ. But his *experience* (the Christ-event) led him to reevaluate his Jewish monotheism in a way that his belief in one God became a Christocentric monotheism, which allowed him to speak to Jewish and gentile believers. Certainly Paul knew how to navigate within Jewish monotheism and pagan deities; through his Christocentric monotheism he was able to reconcile Jewish and gentile believers. Furthermore, Paul skillfully fleshed out his understanding of sexual desires and the dangers of excess, all kinds of passions, and the lack of knowledge of God, bringing into his presentation pagan practices of idolatry or idol worship, Greek vices related to pagan sexual immorality and vices, and the Jewish negative experience in the wilderness (*tradition*). Paul's reflection on the dangers of idolatry as the source of pagan sexual vices and immorality was meant to send a positive ethical message to believers: be aware of the dangers of desire, flee from idolatry, flee from sexual immorality, and believe in Christ. Indeed, sexual immorality is a sin "against the body itself" (1 Cor 6:18).

In chapter 3, we further analyzed Paul's reevaluation of the practice of the law in terms of the intrinsic relationship between desire and sin, using Greek rhetorical techniques of persuasion. Paul's treatment of the tenth commandment in connection with a commandment interpreted as the food laws was presented within the context of his understanding of the passion of desire. Paul tackled the problem of desire using the practice of the commandment (food laws) as an example in order to philosophically observe the tenth commandment and its dangerous sequels. Like Philo (see ch. 1), his understanding of desire was described Stoically and his view of the dangers of desire was exposed Platonically. Paul's urgency to deal with the problem of "desire" (*epithymia*) fits into the Stoic doctrine of desire, which is that the remedy is really the avoidance of desire for it is an evil and deadly passion. However, when Paul gave his advice about marriage (1 Cor 7), he clearly did not condemn sexual desire, but the problem was identified as inappropriate, excessive, or misdirected sexual desire—what he called

---

1. See also Gen 17:7; Ezek 34:24; Jer 31:33.

in Romans "corrupted passions," "sinful passions," and "sinful [passions] beyond measure."

Paul's advice intended to help the Corinthian believers to handle sexual passion/desire. Consistent with the Platonic tradition of the reasoning faculty of the soul, Paul transformed the believers' understanding of sin, divine grace, God's righteousness through faith, God's faithfulness, and the ethical nature of the Mosaic law. He presented to the believers a detailed persuasive argumentation against desire and the practice of the commandments of the law. Equally important, Paul presented Christ (the law of Christ) as the fulfillment of the Mosaic law and, together with the grace of God and his faithfulness, the fulfillment of the purpose of the food laws. Viewed in light of Rom 10:4, Paul showed once again that the goal of the Mosaic law is the law of Christ, or Christ is the goal of the Mosaic law.[2] Paul's presentation of the contrast between the flesh and the Spirit in terms of "the works of the flesh" versus "the works of the Spirit" exhorted the idea that human beings are no longer slaves of desire but slaves of God and of righteousness (Rom 6:18, 22), free to practice virtues and avoid vices and passions. In other words, Paul contrasted passional slavery, servitude to excessive or irrational desire, with divine servitude, or slavery to God who purchased our bodies.[3] He exhorted the believers to become instruments of righteousness and to present their bodies as slaves of righteousness through faith. He emphasized God's righteousness and faithfulness in terms of instruments of righteousness versus instruments of wickedness. Paul gave his rationale of the remedy of desire in the light of his Christocentric monotheism; even though Paul spoke of the goodness of the law (it has divine origin), he acknowledged its limitation to control desire and eliminate the excessive quantity of passions and desires. In terms of sexual desire, Paul followed the Jewish and philosophical traditions of Philo, 4 Maccabees, Plato, and the Stoic Chrysippus and later Stoics who viewed sexual desire as problematic only when it was driven by intemperance and excess.

In chapter 4, Paul as a Hellenistic Jewish believer provided a further exposition of his understanding of love in the Spirit, the remedy to avoid desire and its negative sequels. We have seen that in the ethics of Philo and 4 Maccabees, the central virtue is "piety" (*eusebeia*), and in Paul's ethical exhortation it is the Christian virtue of "love" (*agapē*), the queen virtue. Based on his *experience* of Christ (discontinuity), Paul developed a suitable

2. Tobin, "Romans 10:4."
3. Reno, "Pornographic Desire," 185.

"law" (the love commandment or the law of Christ) inspired by his understanding of the grace of God, the virtue of love, and the Spirit, the divine "enabler." His solution to the problem of desire was neither grounded in Jewish Scripture alone, nor in Greek philosophical ethical systems; indeed, he went beyond them. Within the understanding of his Christocentric monotheism, he offered a solution to the problem of desire and its negative sequels. For him, his doctrine is brought about by God's faithfulness/righteousness through faith and the Christ-event. So, Paul's approach to eliminate irrational sexual desire, sinful passions, and desires beyond measure was likewise founded in Christ and love in the Spirit. Paul moved beyond a simple "practical" Mosaic approach—law/practice/self-control. His solution exhibited a "psychological," mental character that dynamically combined the work of God's grace/Christ/Spirit/faith founded in the virtue of love (the love commandment/the law of Christ). His soliloquy in Rom 7 intellectually and emotionally transformed the Christian believers' minds and disposition to believe in the Spirit. The believers' heart, reason, and mind—love's three attributes—are moved by faith and the Spirit of God. The Spirit is the divine "enabler" who acts in the believers to practice virtues and avoid vices (the works of the flesh). His approach makes sense when we place Paul within the boundaries of Judaism. He glossed his Jewish understanding of sexual desire in marriage—it is good and God's gift—and advised the control of excessive sexual desire, influenced by his interpretation of Christ's role and the Christ-event. Within his Christocentric monotheism, Paul was able to develop his own interpretation of the remedy of the passion of desire and to give a new ethical nuance to his understanding of love and neighbor.

Paul's new approach to the love commandment (or the law of Christ) allowed Paul to exhort Jewish and gentile believers to a reflection on the theme "love our neighbor," focusing on Jewish examples: the ethical commandments, food laws, eating food sacrificed to idols, and circumcision. Following his *tradition* in the virtue of love, Paul planted the seed as the starting point for a healthy living among the believers to encounter a transformative experience in their views of "love our neighbor." Paul urged the Jewish and gentile believers to be imitators of him as he was of the Lord Jesus Christ, for in imitating him they are imitating Jesus' teaching on love: "Love your neighbor as yourself." Love is founded in the centrality of Jesus, that is, in Jesus' reinterpretation of the Jewish Shema (Deut 6:4–6; Matt 22:34–40; Mark 12: 28–31). The first part—"You shall love the Lord your

God with all your heart, with all your soul, and with all your mind"—is clearly *theocentric* (*tradition*); the second part—"You shall love your neighbor as yourself"—touches the heart of Paul's *new understanding of love* (*experience*). In the law of love (or the law of Christ), the virtue of love's attributes goes beyond piety's attributes found in Hellenistic Jewish ethics, e.g., Philo and 4 Maccabees.

The fruit(s) of love/Spirit were in close connection with Paul's understanding of the imperatives "walk by love" and "walk/live by the Spirit" and his sublime and inclusive understanding of the "neighbor" language—viewing the other, one another, and another as "our neighbor." Love centered in the intrinsic relationship between Christ and the Spirit and God's authority allowed all believers to live lives pleasing to God and according to the will of God's law, understood by Paul as the love commandment or the law of Christ. The Christian virtue of love must be the divine power ruling the human "mind" (*nous*) and "reason" (*logos*) with the help of the Spirit, the divine "enabler." Therefore, for Paul, the understanding of the language of instrument of righteousness through faith and the two blessings—faith and the Holy Spirit—fulfilled Paul's theocentric approach of salvation and eternal life in love. In God's faithfulness and his goodness, all believers become citizens of heaven. For Paul, in the "new creation" believers freely could say within both his theocentric and Christocentric approach: we turned to God from indifference and dissensions "to serve a living and true God, and to wait for [Jesus] his Son from heaven" (1 Thess 1:9–10).

Appendix A
Shocking Examples of Sexual Desire and Immorality in Paul's Jewish Tradition

THE FIRST QUESTION TO address is: What biblical knowledge might Paul have known about sexual behavior and sexual immorality before his prophetic call?[1] The biblical quotes in this section come from the LXX, the Jewish Scripture that Paul knew. When we explore the story of the destruction of Sodom in Gen 19:1–29 (from the Yahwist source), inhospitality and sexual perversion are the sins for which the city is condemned. As we read the story of Lot and his two daughters, we encounter a shocking event: Lot attempts to placate the two strange men's sexual drives by offering to give them his two virgin daughters to satisfy their uncontrollable sexual desires and appetites. Today, it is inconceivable to think that a father would do such a thing with his young daughter! For the ancient audience, such paternal behavior was not viewed as a horrifying act; indeed, they would have seen in Lot's response a virtuous act, a "noble attempt, even if extreme, to fulfill the demands of hospitality."[2] What is at stake in the story is hospitality, which is a virtue, and in ancient times it was regarded as greater than a woman's virginity or a woman's sexual rights.

While some scholars regard this story as a violation of hospitality only, there is more than the theme of hospitality and sexual perversion in this story and, in particular, the hospitality that must be shown to male individuals only. Along this line, Gareth Moore argued that instead of welcoming the visitors—"two angels" (Gen 19:1a NETS) who are fed and offered

---

1. Scholars have reassessed traditional interpretations of sexual immorality in Scripture. See, e.g., Wright Knust, *Unprotected Texts*; Martin, *Corinthian Body*.
2. Bergant and Karris, *Collegeville Bible Commentary*, 58.

shelter by Lot—the men of Sodom (Sodomites), both young and old (Gen 19:4), want to "rape them."[3] While Sodomite men threaten Lot's hospitality (19:2–7), Lot tries to protect the two strangers or visitors and also his grand hospitality, no matter the cost of it (19:8).[4]

Particularly at first glance, Gen 19:5–8 leads us to see the Lord's rejection of homosexual activity. The author writes,

> They called Lot, "Where are the men who came to you tonight? Bring them out to us, so that we may have relations with them." And Lot went out to the doorway to them, but he shut the door after him. And he said to them, "By no means, brothers, *do not act wickedly*. Now I have two daughters who have not known a man. I shall bring them out to you, and *use them as it may please you*; only do not do anything unjust to these men, inasmuch as they have come in under the shelter of my beams." (NETS)[5]

While this passage sounds quite shocking to modern readers, Lot's behavior reveals two important points: first, the high place of the virtue of hospitality; and second, the place of women in the ancient biblical world. The phrase "have relations with them" in verse 5c followed by Lot's moral exhortation, "do not act wickedly," indicate the young and old Sodomites' immoderate sexual desire to engage aggressively in an unapproved homosexual act with these two men (visitors). This interpretation is strengthened by Lot's shocking offer: "I have two daughters who have not known a man" and "use them as it may please you" (19:8ab NETS). Later, the prophet Ezekiel not only echoes this horrendous behavior in Sodom but also connects it with a social justice theme as he writes, "As I live, says the Lord God, your sister Sodom and her daughters have not done as you and your daughters have done. This was the guilt of your sister Sodom: she and her daughters had pride, excess of food, and prosperous ease, but did not aid the poor and needy" (Ezek 16:48–49). What is clear is that Gen 19:1–8 suggests the prohibition of homosexual behavior explicitly and the rejection of forbidden sexual desire implicitly. Most importantly, the real ethical issue in Gen 19

---

3. Moore, *Body in Context*, 188–89.

4. The rape of a single woman in the Deuteronomistic tradition (Deut 22:28–29) is treated differently; there is no penalty against the woman because it does not involve the breach of any marriage relationship. This, though, ignores the single woman's trauma resulting from a rape; it will not be any less severe than that of a married woman. The law attempts to protect the raped woman's rights, but not in a way our culture finds acceptable. See Bergant and Karris, *Collegeville Bible Commentary*, 220.

5. Emphasis mine.

is also that of *nonconsensual* sexual activity between men. Thus, the gravity of the homosexual behavior is not only the consensual or approved sexual desire to engage in a sexual act; the sinfulness is also in the Sodomite men's excessive or impulsive desire to engage in homosexual activity *without the two men's previous approval or consent* (Gen 19:9–26).

Thus, this interpretation leads to the following argument: Gen 19 condemns homosexual behavior, even more when it is *nonconsensual*. This passage emphasizes two important values in ancient Israel. First, it is the "preservation of offspring," which forces women, for example, Tamar (Gen 38:1–30), to have sexual relations with her husband's brothers without her consent or request. Second, nonconsensual intercourse between a man and a woman is approved, and ethically speaking, it is accepted; indeed it is encouraged above consensual or nonconsensual homosexual acts, which were considered sinful and abominations.

Moreover, a similar story in Judg 19:22–30 not only resembles Gen 19 but also shows a nuance in terms of the homosexual act and its relation to women. The story has a shocking outcome! A Levite is offered hospitality (Judg 19:1–21), and the men of the city show excessive desire for homosexual acts (Judg 19:22–26). Explicitly, the language of "ravish" (*wəʾanû* [Judg 19:24b]) denotes rape! This text, as West and Shore-Goss have noted, has been interpreted as "a perverse homosexual attack upon vulnerable guests in a city" where the Levite's status was taken into consideration. In other words, the threatened rape of the Levite was understood as a direct attack upon his ability to maintain his status.[6] In the Jewish tradition, consensual or nonconsensual homosexual intercourse was considered a wicked act (Judg 19:22–23). What is surprisingly astounding is the fact that raping a woman was not considered sinful against God's commandment, and that it was an option or a permissible act to avoid consensual or nonconsensual homosexual intercourse! The ethical rationale is this: the raping of a woman and virgin is acceptable if it avoids homosexual acts! The master of the house states, "Here are my virgin daughter and his concubine; let me bring them out now. Ravish them and do whatever you want to them; but against this man do not do such a vile thing" (Judg 19:24).[7] Then, the narrator vividly describes the horrendous sexual act in Judg 19:25b–26:

---

6. West and Shore-Goss, *Queer Bible Commentary*, 151.

7. In the versions A and B in the LXX, the word is "humiliate" instead of "ravish," but the message is the same. For an interpretation of this text in the context of honor-shame society, see West and Shore-Goss, *Queer Bible Commentary*, 153–57.

"They wantonly raped her, and abused her all through the night until the morning. And as the dawn began to break, they let her go."[8] This chilling and graphic scene proves once more that in ancient Israel women were literally sexual objects at the men's disposition to placate their excessive and uncontrollable sexual desires and satisfy their aberrant sexual impulses and cravings (Gen 19:27–29). And what is surprising is that this kind of behavior was a common practice in Jewish biblical times.

Nevertheless, explicit condemnation of homosexual intercourse in the Jewish tradition is found in Lev 18:1–30, a narrative about the sanctity of sex. In Lev 18:6–17, there is a disorderly list of incest prohibitions with a list of other "out-of-order" sexual relations. Then, in Lev 18:18, the law commands, "You shall not take a woman as a rival in addition to her sister, to uncover her shame in addition to her while she is still alive" (NETS). This text serves as a bridge to all the other sexual disorders and immoral relations prohibited in Lev 18:19–23. The sexual disorder applied in Lev 18:18a results because a man who is already united to a woman violates the covenant arrangement by marrying his sister-in-law, thus creating a polygamous relationship. This sexual disorder, according to the law in Leviticus, relates to incest and affects the community in which all, including the sister, should love the same holy life.[9]

The incest of father and daughter is included in Lev 18:6 (NETS) as God's commandment: "Person by person shall not approach any of the household of his flesh to uncover shame; I am the Lord." It is important to note that in Paul's Jewish culture the language of "uncover" had a sexual connotation.[10] Furthermore, in Lev 18:22 the author calls sexual disorder "an abomination" (NETS) when speaking against homosexual relation: "And you shall not sleep with a male as in a bed of a woman, for it is an abomination." The Hebrew word *tôʿēbâh* (abomination) expresses a strong ethical sense of an abominable act or a detestable thing, which later is reflected in Paul's letters (e.g., Rom 1) when he speaks of pagan sexual vices in connection with the dangers of idolatry. Anyone committing such a horrendous sexual immorality "shall be put to death" (Lev 20:13b). As Gareth Moore writes, "Sexual relationships between men are forbidden in

---

8. In the LXX, it reads, "The man seized his concubine and led her out to them outside, and they knew her and were sporting with her all through the night until the early morning" (A and B Judg 19:25b–26 NETS).

9. Bergant and Karris, *Collegeville Bible Commentary*, 133.

10. For an interpretation of Lev 18:6–7, see West and Shore-Goss, *Queer Bible Commentary*, 77–80.

Lev 18:23; here however there is no mention of women lying together."[11] In Lev 20:13, God through Moses, the lawgiver, speaks to the people of Israel about the penalties for violating God's commandment on sexual matters: "He who lies with a man in a bed for a woman, both have committed an abomination; by death let them be put to death; they are liable" (NETS). Both Jewish texts in Leviticus, from the Holiness Code, explicitly contradict the covenantal union between a man and a woman in sexual union (Gen 1:28; 2:24), and both texts also speak of men only.[12]

---

11. Moore, *Body in Context*, 36.
12. Salzman and Lawler, *Sexual Person*, 24.

Appendix B
Paul's Biblical Background on Desire and Sexual Immorality

THE TENTH COMMANDMENT OF the Decalogue explicitly forbids one to desire or covet the goods of other neighbors, and that includes their wives. The text in Exod 20:17 states, "You shall not covet your neighbor's wife; you shall not covet your neighbor's house or his field or his male slave or his female slave or his ox or his draft animal or any animal of his or whatever belongs to your neighbor" (NETS).[1] It is paramount to note that in ancient times and during the time of Jesus (first century CE), women, like things (e.g., houses, oxen, donkeys, slaves), were considered property of either their fathers or husbands, or if there was none of these, of their brothers. According to Michael Coogan,[2] the tenth commandment, which was directed to adult and male Israelites only, originally prohibited longing for a neighbor's house, which is "his house and all that it entails,"[3] which also included women. Clearly the understanding of human dignity in connection to women (and children) was foreign to ancient people. In an honor-shame society, when a woman had none of these protectors, her social situation was pitiful and very difficult to navigate acquiescent to the demands of a patriarchal society.[4] So this commandment, where the term "desire" appears in its verbal future indicative form (*epithymēseis*), forbids

---

1. See also Deut 5:21.

2. Coogan, *Ten Commandments*, 90–93.

3. Coogan, *Ten Commandments*, 90. In ancient Israel, women and children were considered either the father's or husband's property. Thus, it makes sense why the tenth commandment is addressed only to the fathers and husbands in Israelite society.

4. Dunn, *Theology of Paul*, 706. For a good analysis of the honor and shame topic, see Westfall, *Paul and Gender*, 18–20.

the desire of things or personal properties, including wives. Jews must obey God's commandments, and there was no excuse for disobeying it. They had to renounce the experience of natural and legitimate desires; the desire for sexual satisfaction outside marriage was especially and harshly prohibited. This kind of physical desire for sexual satisfaction in all its forms was simply sinful according to Jewish law. It was not only the forbidden sexual behavior that was called sin but also the internal urges of sexual desire outside marriage.

In one way or another, the passion of "desire" (*epithymia*) was viewed as an offense against God, who demands radical faithfulness to the covenant. According to the Jewish Shema, the creed or confession of Jewish monotheism, Jews ought to give God full obedience and show their genuine love for God from the whole heart. Deuteronomy 6:5–6 states, "You shall love the Lord your God with the whole of your mind and with the whole of your soul and with the whole of your power. And these words that I command you today shall be in your heart and in your soul" (NETS). The love envisioned is a deep loyalty and affection that Israel, God's beloved people, owes to the supreme God. In Paul's Jewish tradition, love is virtually synonymous with obedience; the love that Israel owed to God is all-encompassing. Thus, Israel is exhorted to always keep the commandments in heart and mind and under all circumstances. This fidelity and love to God are based on God's liberation of Israel from slavery (Exodus); the Lord brought the Hebrews out of the land of Egypt, out of the house of slavery (Deut 6:12–14).

Paul, who before his "prophetic call" was a Pharisee, a strict observer and defender of the Mosaic law, was certainly familiar with the LXX version of Gen 1:28 and Gen 19:1–29. In the first creation story in Gen 1:26–27, from the Priestly traditions (550 BCE, written in Babylonia), God creates humanity (Hebrew, *ādām*; Greek, *anthrōpos*) according to his "image" (Hebrew, *ṣelem*; Greek, *eikōn*) and according to God's "likeness" (Hebrew, *dəmût*; Greek, *homoiōsis*). Immediately in Gen 1:28a, "God blessed them," and then, God said to them, "Increase and multiply, and fill the earth" (Gen 1:28b NETS). According to the Jewish interpretation of this passage, "Humanity is not created as some kind of androgynous being, but rather humanity consists of the male and female. Together man and woman constitute humanity."[5] In this powerful text, we not only learn that human beings were created in God's own image and his likeness (Gen 1:28a), but also,

---

5. Bergant and Karris, *Collegeville Bible Commentary*, 40.

APPENDIX B

we find the "first" commandment that God gave to the first humans (Gen 1:28b). In other words, the first thing that God orders them (humanity as male and female) is to "have sex" and "have many babies." In other words, sex in marriage was viewed as good and God's gift. The text in Gen 1:28b shows that not only fertility but also sexual intercourse is blessed. Clearly, before the fall (Gen 3), sex/sexuality was viewed as good, and God in his infinite providence gave to humanity the wonderful gift of sex, and thus the intimate sexual relations between two individuals are part of God's gift. In Gen 2:24 ("a man will leave his father and mother and will be joined to his wife, and the two will become one flesh" [NETS]), when God, creation, and humanity were in perfect harmony, the sexual union between a man and a woman was expressed in terms of a "covenant union."[6]

However, God's command prohibits adultery because it involves a breach of the marriage relationship; thus, the penalty is severe. In Lev 20:10 the author writes, "A person who commits adultery with the wife of a man or who commits adultery with the wife of his neighbor—let both the adulterer and the adulteress by death be put to death" (NETS). Later, in Deut 22:13–29, where the laws concerning marriage and sexual relations are exposed, the author states the punishment of adultery: "Now if a man is found lying with a woman married to a man, you will kill both of them, the man who lay with the woman and the woman. And you shall remove the evil one from Israel" (Deut 22:22 NETS).[7] The betrothed woman is treated the same as a married woman, since both are committed to an exclusive relationship with a man.[8] The same is true for sexual relations before marriage in the Deuteronomistic tradition: "If there is a girl, a virgin engaged to a man, and a man finding her in the city should lie with her, bring both of them to the gate of their city, and they shall be stoned with stones, and they shall die—the young woman, because she did not cry out in the city, and the man, because he humbled his neighbor's woman. And you shall remove the evil one from yourselves" (Deut 22:23–24 NETS). In light of this OT tradition, we briefly recall the story in John 8:1–11 where the Jews want to stone the woman caught in adultery. But contrary to the Jewish law, Jesus saves her out of love. The same experience is found in Matthew's story of Mary and Joseph. When Mary is found to be with child, Joseph, being a righteous man and unwilling to expose Mary to public disgrace,

---

6. Salzman and Lawler, *Sexual Person*, 24.
7. West and Shore-Goss, *Queer Bible Commentary*, 103–6.
8. Bergant and Karris, *Collegeville Bible Commentary*, 220.

plans to dismiss her quietly. But through an angelic intervention Joseph is prevented from doing that (Matt 1:18–25).

In the Deuteronomistic tradition there is a law that in case of rape the man is punished to death and the woman is saved. Deut 22:25–26 states, "But if a man finds the engaged girl in the field and, having forced her, should lie with her, you shall kill only the man who lay with her. And you shall do nothing to the young woman; the woman has not committed an offense punishable by death, because it is as if some man would rise up against his neighbor and murder his soul; so is this deed" (NETS). Likewise, the passage in Deut 22:13–30 also reveals the place of women in society, particularly in terms of the woman's virginity and the concern of the rights for women in view of her husband's false accusations.[9] The author understands the powerful force of human sexuality and sexual urges and desire, especially for men; in Jewish tradition, sexual behavior between adult men and women including unwanted or forbidden sexual acts can have important consequences for the entire community, a tradition that is especially reflected in Paul's Letter to the Corinthians (chs. 5–7).

---

9. Bergant and Karris, *Collegeville Bible Commentary*, 219.

Appendix C
Jewish Figures Facing Sexual Desire in Paul's Jewish Tradition

A GOOD EXAMPLE IS Gen 39:1–23,[1] a story that describes the rise and fall of Joseph, the second youngest son of Jacob. The Yahwist narrative opens the story with the scene for the attempted seduction of Joseph by Potiphar's wife (Gen 39:1–6). The narrator describes young Joseph as "handsome in physique and very pleasing in appearance" (Gen 39:6 NETS). When Joseph was living in Potiphar's palace (Joseph's master), Potiphar's wife "cast her eyes upon Joseph and said, 'Lie with me'. But he would not" (Gen 39:7 NETS). Joseph refused her sexual advances and her illicit sexual desire because the act of adultery would be a sin, not only against his master's trust but most importantly an "evil matter and sin against God" (Gen 39:9 NETS). Joseph's character shows his virtues of self-control, faithfulness, and steadfastness to God by not consenting to lie beside her or to have sexual relations with her, even though "she would speak to Joseph day after day" (Gen 39:10 NETS). As a result of Joseph's virtuous continence, after the woman "drew him by his garments, saying, 'Lie with me!'" (Gen 39:12), she became outraged with Joseph and falsely accused him of trying to seduce her, saying, "See, he [her husband] has brought among us a Hebrew servant to mock us! He came into me, saying, 'Lie with me', and I cried out with a loud voice. And as soon as he heard that I raised my voice and cried out, he fled and went outside, leaving his garments behind with me" (Gen 39:14b–15 NETS).

Joseph knew that the punishment for the sin of adultery was death. So, Joseph faced a symbolic life-and-death experience similar to what we find

---

1. This story comes from the Yahwist source ("J") written around 950 BCE in Jerusalem, the Southern Kingdom.

in Gen 37 where, instead of being put to death, he was sold into slavery by his own brothers.² Similarly, in Gen 39, instead of being put to death Joseph was sent to prison (Gen 39:19–20). Interestingly, in both cases where Joseph experiences humiliation, a symbolic death, or near-death experience, he is innocent.³ However, the Jewish God and Father knew Joseph's pure heart and virtuous character, especially that of self-control and continence.⁴ In response to Joseph's obedience, God gave him the virtue of steadfast love and favor in the sight of the chief jailer. The story tells us that God was with him; and whatever Joseph did, God made it prosper (Gen 39:21–23). In this story, we see how God responds to those who are faithful to and suffer for the sake of his commandments. The important point in Paul's biblical Jewish tradition is that forbidden or excessive sexual appetites or desires were wrong and sinful for both men and women, and what was required for faithfulness and obedience to God's commandment was self-discipline, self-control, and continence in matters of sexual behavior. Indeed, even a brief or hurried sexual desire was wrong, and for the pious or righteous Jew it was a duty to control such forbidden desires.

In 2 Sam 11:2 and Job 31:1, we encounter examples where forbidden sexual activity is clearly represented as disobedience to God's commandment. In the story of David, the "anointed one" (*messiah*) and greatest king of Israel, the sins of desire for sexual satisfaction and adultery are pictured in their best expression. David sexually lusts for Bathsheba, a woman married to David's army officer Uriah (2 Sam 11:1–16). The author writes key phrases that show how David and Bathsheba disobeyed God's commandment. As David walks on the roof of the king's house, he sees the beautiful Bathsheba bathing and sends for her (2 Sam 11:2–3). The language of "sending for her" alludes to the idea that she came to David and had a sexual encounter with him. In other words, they did engage in sexual intercourse, thus committing the sin of adultery. In 2 Sam 11:5, Bathsheba also "sends" when she informs David that she is pregnant! The text reads this way: "The woman conceived; and she sent and told David, 'I am pregnant.'" Guilty of his sin of adultery

---

2. Bergant and Karris, *Collegeville Bible Commentary*, 73.

3. On symbolic-death experiences of key figures in Jewish tradition, see Levenson, *Death and Resurrection*.

4. In *On the Life of Joseph*, Philo describes Joseph's self-control and virtuous character as an expression of his true piety (*Ios.* 163–170).

David tries to create an elaborate intrigue to cover his paternity, and later in the story he plans Uriah's death in a battle.[5]

In the story of Job, as he rests his case in his own defense before God (Job 29:1—31:37), there is a moment when Job makes an important sexual moral statement: "I have made a covenant with my eyes, and I will not take note of a virgin" (Job 31:1 NETS). Clearly Job makes two significant revelations in his claim "I am innocent!": (1) the practice of the virtue chastity of the eyes, or self-control, was viewed as a covenant, which goes in line with the holy and formal agreement between God and the people of Israel; and (2) looking at a virgin with desire or lust was held as a lack of self-control and a shameful sexual behavior before God.[6] As the example of David in 2 Samuel, there was a high expectation for appropriate sexual behavior for God's sake and obedience to his commandments. The demands for sexual renunciation required regular ascetic practices, such as fasting, faithfully keeping the Sabbath, and the observance of the food laws. These practices become constituent elements in Jewish piety, especially in the Jewish diaspora, but also in sexual ascetic behavior. In Paul's biblical tradition, the consciousness of sexual sin becomes more profound, and greater emphasis is put on the impulsive, passionate desire, which withstands renunciation and obedience for the sake of God and his commandments. There is evidence in Paul's Jewish tradition where the passion of desire was not only associated with an "evil heart" (4 Esd 3:20–27) but also viewed as the chief of all sins.[7]

---

5. Bergant and Karris, *Collegeville Bible Commentary*, 287.
6. Bergant and Karris, *Collegeville Bible Commentary*, 692.
7. Büchsel, *TDNT* 3:169.

Bibliography

Aelius Theon. *Progymnasmata*. Edited by Michel Patillon with Giancarlo Bolognesi. Paris: Belles Lettres, 1997.
Annas, Julia. "Aristotle on Pleasure and Goodness." In *Essays on Aristotle's Ethics*, edited by Oksenberg Rorty, 285–99. Berkeley: University of California Press, 1980.
Aphtonius Sophista. *Aphthonii Sophistae Progymnasmata*. Edited by Rodolpho Agricolâ and Ioanne Catanaeo. Caen: Cavelier, 1666.
Aristotle. *The Complete Works of Aristotle: The Revised Oxford Translation*. Edited by Jonathan Barnes. 2 vols. Bollingen 71. Princeton, NJ: Princeton University Press, 1995.
Arnim, Hans von, ed. *Stoicorum Veterum Fragmenta*. 4 vols. Leipzig: Teubner, 1903–24.
Aune, David Charles. "Mastery of the Passions: Philo, 4 Maccabees and Earliest Christianity." In *Hellenization Revisited: Shaping a Christian Response Within the Greco-Roman World*, edited by Wendy E. Helleman, 125–58. Lanham, MD: University Press of America, 1994.
———. "Passions in the Pauline Epistles: The Current State of Research." In *Passions and Moral Progress in Greco-Roman Thought*, edited by John T. Fitzgerald, 221–37. Routledge Monographs in Classical Studies. London: Abingdon, 2008.
Bailey, Kenneth E. *Paul Through Mediterranean Eyes: Cultural Studies in 1 Corinthians*. Downers Grove, IL: IVP, 2011.
Banister, Jamie A. "Ὁμοίως and the Use of Parallelism in Romans 1:26–27." *JBL* 3 (2009) 569–90.
Barclay, John M. G. "Faith and Self-Detachment from Cultural Norms: A Study in Romans 14–15." *ZNW* 104 (2013) 192–208.
———. *Jews in the Mediterranean Diaspora: From Alexander to Trajan (323 BCE—117 CE)*. Berkeley: University of California Press, 1996.
———. "Paul and Philo on Circumcision: Romans 2:25–9 in Social and Cultural Context." *NTS* 44 (1998) 536–56.
Bauernfeind, Otto. "ἀσέλγεια." *TDNT* 1:490.
Bergant, Dianne, and Robert J. Karris, eds. *The Collegeville Bible Commentary: Based on the New American Bible with Revised New Testament*. Collegeville, MN: Liturgical, 1988.
Betz, Hans Dieter. *Galatians: A Commentary on Paul's Letter to the Churches in Galatia*. Hermeneia. Edited by Helmut Koester. Minneapolis: Fortress, 1988.
Bible Hub. https://biblehub.com.

Bobonich, Christopher, and Pierre Destrée, eds. *Akrasia in Greek Philosophy: From Socrates to Plotinus*. PhA 106. Leiden: Brill, 2007.

Bock, Darrell L., and Mikel Del Rosario. "The Table Briefing: Sexuality and Paul's Transcultural Message in Romans 1:18–32." *BSac* 172 (2015) 222–28.

Bonhöffer, Adolf Friedrich. *The Ethics of the Stoic Epictetus: An English Translation*. Translated by William O. Stephens. New York: Lang, 1996.

Borgen, Peder. "Observations on the Theme 'Paul and Philo': Paul's Preaching of Circumcision in Galatia (Gal 5:11) and Debates on Circumcision in Philo." *Paulinische Literatur und Theologie* (1980) 80–102.

———. *Philo, John, and Paul: New Perspectives on Judaism and Early Christianity*. BJS 131. Atlanta: Scholars, 1987.

Borgen, Peder, et al. *The Philo Index: A Complete Greek Word Index to the Writings of Philo of Alexandria*. Grand Rapids: Eerdmans, 2000.

Bornkamm, Günther. *Studien zum Neuen Testament*. Munich: Kaiser, 1985.

Bowden, Andrew. *Desire in Paul's Undisputed Epistles: Semantic Observations on the Use of Epithymeō, Ho Epithymētēs, and Epithymía in Roman Imperial Texts*. WUNT, 2nd ser., 539. Tübingen: Mohr Siebeck, 2021.

———. "A Semantic Investigation of Desire in 4 Maccabees and Its Bearing on Romans 7:7." In *XV Congress of the International Organization for Septuagint and Cognate Studies: Munich, 2013*, edited by Wolfgang Kraus et al., 409–24. SCS. Atlanta: SBL, 2016.

———. "Sklaverei, Gesetz und Erkenntnis der Sünde: Die Rolle der Begierde in Röm 7,7–8." In *Perspektiven auf Römer*, edited by Stefan Krauter, 17–48. Biblisch-Theologische Studien 159. Neukirchen-Vluyn, Germ.: Neukirchen, 2016.

Breytenbach, Cilliers. *Versöhnung: Eine Studie zur paulinischen Soteriologie*. WMANT 60. Neukirchen-Vluyn, Germ.: Neukirchen, 1989.

Bromiley, Geoffrey W. *Theological Dictionary of the New Testament: Abridged in One Volume*. Edited by Gerhard Kittel and Gerhard Friedrich. Grand Rapids: Eerdmans, 1985.

Brown, Raymond E., et al., eds. *The New Jerome Biblical Commentary*. Englewood Cliffs, NJ: Prentice Hall, 1990.

Büchsel, Friedrich. "ἐπιθυμία, ἐπιθυμέω." *TDNT* 3:168–72.

Bultmann, Rudolf. *Existence and Faith: Shorter Writings of Rudolf Bultmann*. Edited by Schubert M. Ogden. London: Hodder, 1960.

———. *Der Stil der paulinischen Predigt und die kynisch-stoische Diatribe*. FRLANT 13. Göttingen: Vandenhoeck und Ruprecht, 1910.

Burns, J. Patout, Jr. *Romans: Interpreted by Early Christian Commentators*. Grand Rapids: Eerdmans, 2012.

Butts, James M. "The *Progymnasmata* of Theon: A New Text with Translation and Commentary." PhD diss., Claremont Graduate School, 1987.

Byrne, Brendan. *Romans*. SP 6. Edited by Daniel J. Harrington. Collegeville, MN: Liturgical, 1996.

Ciampa, Roy E., and Brian S. Rosner. *The First Letter to the Corinthians*. Pillar New Testament Commentary. Grand Rapids: Eerdmans, 2010.

Cicero. *Tusculan Disputations*. Translated by J. E. King. LCL 141. Cambridge, MA: Harvard University Press, 1927.

Claudius Galenus. *Claudii Galeni Opera Omnia*. Edited by Karl Gottlob Kühn. 20 vols. Cambridge Library Collection—Classics. Cambridge: Cambridge University Press, 2011.

Coffey, David M. "Natural Knowledge of God: Reflections on Romans 1:18–32." *TS* 31 (1970) 674–91.
Collins, John J. "Artapanus (Third to Second Century B.C.)." *OTP* 2:889–903.
———. *Between Athens and Jerusalem: Jewish Identity in the Hellenistic Diaspora*. Grand Rapids: Eerdmans, 2000.
———. "Sibylline Oracles (Second Century B.C.—Seventh Century A.D.)." *OTP* 1:317–472.
Coogan, Michael. *The Ten Commandments: A Short History of an Ancient Text*. New Haven, CT: Yale University Press, 2014.
Cousar, Charles B. *The Letters of Paul*. Nashville: Abingdon, 1996.
Cox, Ronald. *By the Same Word: Creation and Salvation in Hellenistic Judaism and Early Christianity*. BZNW 145. Berlin: de Gruyter, 2007.
Daniélou, Jean. *Philon d'Alexandrie*. Paris: Fayard, 1958.
Danker, Frederick William, and Kathryn Krug. *The Concise Greek-English Lexicon of the New Testament*. Chicago: University of Chicago, 2009.
Deming, Will. *Paul on Marriage and Celibacy: The Hellenistic Background of 1 Corinthians 7*. SNTSMS. Cambridge: Cambridge University Press, 1995.
DeSilva, David A. *4 Maccabees*. Guides to the Apocrypha and Pseudepigrapha. Sheffield: Sheffield Academic, 1998.
———. *4 Maccabees: Introduction and Commentary on the Greek Text in Codex Sinaiticus*. Edited by Stanley E. Porter et al. Septuagint Commentary. Leiden: Brill, 2006.
Despland, Michel. *The Education of Desire: Plato and the Philosophy of Religion*. Toronto: University of Toronto Press, 1985.
Dillon, John M. *Middle Platonists: 80 B.C. to A.D. 220*. Ithaca: Cornell University Press, 1996.
———. "The Pleasures and Perils of Soul-Gardening." *SPhiloA* 9 (1997) 190–97.
Dio Chrysostom. *Discourses*. Translated by James Wilfred Cohoon and H. Lamar Crosby. 5 vols. LCL. Cambridge, MA: Harvard University Press, 1932–51.
Diogenes Laertius. *Lives of Eminent Philosophers*. Translated by R. D. Hicks. 2 vols. LCL. Cambridge, MA: Harvard University Press, 1925.
Dionysius of Halicarnassus. *Roman Antiquities*. Translated by Earnest Cary. 7 vols. LCL. Cambridge, MA: Harvard University Press, 1937.
Dodson, Joseph R. "The Convivial Background of Romans 1:26–27." *LTQ* 47 (2017) 105–21.
———. *The "Powers" of Personification: Rhetorical Purpose in the Book of Wisdom and the Letter to the Romans*. Berlin: de Gruyter, 2008.
Donfried, Karl P. "The Cults of Thessalonica and the Thessalonian Correspondence." *NTS* 31 (1985) 336–56.
Dorion, Louis-André. "Plato and *Enkrateia*." In *Akrasia in Greek Philosophy: From Socrates to Plotinus*, edited by Christopher Bobonich and Pierre Destrée, 119–38. PhA 106. Leiden: Brill, 2007.
Dunn, James D. G. *Beginning from Jerusalem: Christianity in the Making*. 2 vols. Grand Rapids: Eerdmans, 2009.
———. "The Spirit Speech: Reflections on Romans 8:12–27." In *Romans and the People of God: Essays in Honor of Gordon D. Fee on the Occasion of His 65th Birthday*, edited by Sven K. Soderlund and N. T. Wright, 82–91. Grand Rapids: Eerdmans, 1999.
———. *The Theology of Paul the Apostle*. Grand Rapids: Eerdmans, 1998.
Dunning, Benjamin H. "Same-Sex Relations." In *The Oxford Handbook of New Testament, Gender, and Sexuality*, edited by Benjamin H. Dunning, 573–91. Oxford Handbooks. Oxford: Oxford University Press, 2019.

Elder, Nicholas. "'Wretch I Am!' Eve's Tragic Speech-in-Character in Romans 7:7–25." *JBL* 137 (2018) 743–63.
Elliott, Neil. "The Question of Politics: Paul as a Diaspora Jew Under Roman Rule." In *Paul Within Judaism: Restoring the First-Century Context to the Apostle*, edited by Mark D. Nanos and Magnus Zetterholm, 203–44. Minneapolis: Fortress, 2015.
Elliott, Neil, and Mark Reasoner, eds. *Documents and Images for the Study of Paul*. Minneapolis: Fortress, 2011.
Elliott, Scott S. *The Rustle of Paul: Autobiographical Narrative in Romans, Corinthians, and Philippians*. T&T Clark Biblical Studies. London: T&T Clark, 2021.
Ellis, J. Edward. *Paul and Ancient Views of Sexual Desire: Paul's Sexual Ethics in 1 Thessalonians 4, 1 Corinthians 7 and Romans 1*. LNTS 354. London: T&T Clark, 2007.
Engberg-Pedersen, Troels. *Paul and Philosophy*. WUNT, 1st ser., 509. Tübingen: Mohr Siebeck, 2023.
———. *Paul in His Hellenistic Context*. Minneapolis: Fortress, 1995.
Epictetus. *Discourses*. Translated by W. A. Oldfather. 2 vols. LCL. Cambridge, MA: Harvard University Press, 1925.
Fairweather, William. *Jesus and the Greeks, or, Early Christianity in the Tideway of Hellenism*. Edinburgh: T&T Clark, 1924.
Fee, Gordon D. *The First Epistle to the Corinthians*. NICNT. Grand Rapids: Eerdmans, 1987.
———. *Pauline Christology: An Exegetical-Theological Study*. Peabody, MA: Hendrickson, 2007.
Fitzgerald, John T. *Friendship, Flattery, and Frankness of Speech: Studies on Friendship in the New Testament World*. NovTSup 82. Leiden: Brill, 1996.
Fitzmyer, Joseph A. *First Corinthians: A New Translation with Introduction and Commentary*. AB 32. New Haven, CT: Yale University Press, 2008.
———. *Romans: A New Translation with Introduction and Commentary*. AB 33. New York: Doubleday, 1993.
Fredriksen, Paula. *Paul: The Pagan's Apostle*. New Haven, CT: Yale University Press, 2017.
Fredrickson, David Earl. *Eros and the Christ: Longing and Envy in Paul's Christology*. Minneapolis: Fortress, 2013.
———. "Natural and Unnatural Use in Romans 1:24–27: Paul and the Philosophic Critique of Eros." In *Homosexuality, Science, and the "Plain Sense" of Scripture*, edited by David L. Balch, 197–222. Grand Rapids: Eerdmans, 2000.
———. "Passionless Sex in 1 Thessalonians 4:4–5." *WW* 23 (2003) 23–30.
Frey, Jörg. "Paul's Jewish Identity." In *Jewish Identity in the Greco-Roman World: Judische Identität in der griechisch-römischen Welt*, edited by Jörg Frey et al., 283–321. Ancient Judaism and Early Christianity 71. Leiden: Brill, 2007.
Gaca, Kathy L. "Early Stoic Eros: The Sexual Ethics of Zeno and Chrysippus and Their Evaluation of the Erotic Tradition." *Apeiron* 33 (2000) 207–38.
———. *The Making of Fornication: Eros, Ethics, and Political Reform in Greek Philosophy and Early Christianity*. Berkeley: University of California Press, 2013.
———. "The Pentateuch or Plato: Two Competing Paradigms of Christian Sexual Morality." In *A Feminist Companion to the Patristic Literature*, edited by Amy-Jill Levine with Maria Mayo Robbins, 125–37. Feminist Companion to the New Testament and Early Christian Writings 12. London: T&T Clark, 2008.
Galen. *On the Passions and Errors of the Soul*. Translated by Paul W. Harkins. Columbus: Ohio State University Press, 1963.

Gaventa, Beverly Roberts. "Reading for the Subject: The Paradox of Power in Romans 14:1—15:6." *JTI* 5 (2011) 1–12.
Gemünden, Petra von. "Der Affekt der ἐπιθυμία und der νομός: Affektkontrolle und soziale Identitätsbildung im 4. Makkabäerbuch mit einem Ausblick auf den Römerbrief." In *Das Gesetz im frühen Judentum und im Neuen Testament: Festschrift für Christoph Burchard zum 75. Geburtstag*, edited by Dieter Sänger and Matthias Konradt, 53–74. NTOA 57. Göttingen: Vandenhoeck und Ruprecht, 2006.
Genovesi, Vincent J. *In Pursuit of Love: Catholic Morality and Humanity*. 2nd ed. Collegeville, MN: Liturgical, 1996.
Gil Arbiol, Carlos. *Qué se Sabe de . . . : Pablo en el Naciente Cristianismo*. Pamplona: EVD, 2015.
Gourinat, Jean-Baptiste. "*Akrasia* and *Enkrateia* in Ancient Stoicism: Minor Vice and Minor Virtue?" In *Akrasia in Greek Philosophy: From Socrates to Plotinus*, edited by Christopher Bobonich and Pierre Destrée, 215–48. PhA 106. Leiden: Brill, 2007.
Greenberg, D. F. *The Construction of Homosexuality*. Chicago: University of Chicago, 1988.
Grieb, A. Katherine. *The Story of Romans: A Narrative Defense of God's Righteousness*. Louisville: Westminster, 2002.
Gundry, Robert H. "The Moral Frustration of Paul Before His Conversion: Sexual Lust in Romans 7:7–25." In *Pauline Studies Presented to F. F. Bruce*, edited by D. A. Hagner and M. J. Harris, 228–45. Exeter: Paternoster, 1980.
Haacker, Klaus. "Paul's Life." In *The Cambridge Companion to St Paul*, edited by James D. G. Dunn, 19–33. Cambridge Companions to Religion. Cambridge: Cambridge University Press, 2003.
Hadas, Moses, ed. and trans. *Aristeas to Philocrates (Letter of Aristeas)*. New York: Harper & Brothers, 1951.
———. *The Third and Fourth Books of Maccabees*. New York: Harper & Row, 1953.
Harrington, Daniel J. "Paul." In *The Eerdmans Dictionary of Early Judaism*, edited by John J. Collins and Daniel C. Harlow, 1034–38. Grand Rapids: Eerdmans, 2010.
———. "Pseudo-Philo (First Century A.D.)." *OTP* 2:297–377.
Hatch, Edwin, and Henry A. Redpath. *A Concordance to the Septuagint and the Other Greek Versions of the Old Testament (Including the Apocryphal Books)*. 2 vols. Graz: Akademisch, 1954.
Häusser, Detlef. *Der Brief des Paulus an die Philipper*. Historisch Theologische Auslegung. Witten, Germ.: SCM, 2018.
Hecht, Richard D. "The Exegetical Contexts of Philo's Interpretation of Circumcision." In *Nourished with Peace: Studies in Hellenistic Judaism in Memory of Samuel Sandmel*, edited by Frederick E. Greenspan et al., 51–79. Chico, CA: Scholars, 1984.
Heidland, H. W. "ὀρέγομαι, ὄρεξις." *TDNT* 5:447–48.
Hengel, Martin. "The Pre-Christian Paul." In *The Jews Among Pagans and Christians in the Roman Empire*, edited by Judith Lieu et al., 29–52. London: Routledge, 1988.
Horn, Friedrich Wilhelm. *Das Angeld des Geistes: Studien zur paulinischen Pneumatologie*. FRLANT 154. Göttingen: Vandenhoeck und Ruprecht, 1992.
———. "Wandel im Geist: Zur pneumatologischen Begründung der Ethik bei Paulus." *KD* 38 (1992) 149–70.
Horsley, Richard. "The Law of Nature in Philo and Cicero." *HTR* 71 (1978) 35–59.
Inwood, Brad. *Ethics and Human Action in Early Stoicism*. Oxford: Oxford University Press, 1985.

———. "Rules and Reasoning in Stoic Ethics." In *Topics in Stoic Philosophy*, edited by Katerine Ierodiakonou, 95–127. Oxford: Clarendon, 1999.
Irwin, Terence. *From Socrates to the Reformation*. Vol. 1 of *The Development of Ethics*. Oxford: Oxford University Press, 2007.
———. *Plato's Ethics*. Oxford: Oxford University Press, 1995.
Isaacs, Marie E. *The Concept of Spirit: A Study of Pneuma in Hellenistic Judaism and Its Bearing on the New Testament*. London: Heythrop College Press, 1970.
Janzen, J. Gerald. "Sin and Deception of Devout Desire: Paul and the Commandment in Romans 7." *Enc* 70 (2007) 29–61.
Jedan, Christoph. *Stoic Virtues: Chrysippus and the Religious Character of Stoic Ethics*. Continuum Studies in Ancient Philosophy 15. London: T&T Clark, 2012.
Josephus. *The Works of Josephus: Complete and Unabridged*. Translated by William Whiston. Rev. ed. Peabody, MA: Hendrickson, 1987.
Kalin, Everett R. "Romans 1:26–27 and Homosexuality." *CurTM* 30 (2003) 423–32.
Käsemann, Ernst. *Commentary on Romans*. Edited and translated by Geoffrey W. Bromiley. Grand Rapids: Eerdmans, 1980.
Kee, Howard C. "Testament of the Twelve Patriarchs: A New Translation and Introduction." *OTP* 1:775–828.
Keener, Craig S. *The Mind of the Spirit: Paul's Approach to Transformed Thinking*. Grand Rapids: Baker Academic, 2016.
Kennedy, George A. *Classical Rhetoric and Its Christian and Secular Tradition from Ancient to Modern Times*. 2nd ed. Chapel Hill: University of North Carolina Press, 1999.
Kim, Seyoon. "Paul's Common Paraenesis (1 Thess. 4–5; Phil. 2–4; and Rom. 12–13): The Correspondence Between Romans 1:18–32 and 12:1–2, and the Unity of Romans 12–13." *TynBul* 62 (2011) 109–39.
Klauck, Hans-Josef. "Die Heilige Stadt: Jerusalem bei Philo and Lukas." *Kairos* 28 (1986) 129–51.
Koch, Dietrich-Alex. *Die Schrift als Zeuge des Evangeliums: Untersuchungen zur Verwendung und zum Verständnis der Schrift bei Paulus*. BHT 69. Tübingen: Mohr Siebeck, 1989.
Koester, Helmut. *History, Culture, and Religion of the Hellenistic Age*. Vol. 1 of *Introduction to the New Testament*. 2nd ed. New York: de Gruyter, 1995.
———. "ΝΟΜΟΣ ΦΥΣΕΩΣ: The Concept of Natural Law in Greek Thought." In *Religions in Antiquity: Essays in Memory of Erwin Ramsdell Goodenough*, edited by Jacob Neusner, 521–41. SHR 14. Leiden: Brill, 1968.
Konradt, Matthias. *Gericht und Gemeinde: Eine Studie zur Bedeutung und Funktion von Gerichtsaussagen im rahmen der paulinischen Ekklesiologie und Ethik im 1 Thess und 1 Kor*. BZNW 117. Berlin: de Gruyter, 2003.
Kowalski, Marcin. "The Brokerage of the Spirit in Romans 8." *CBQ* 80 (2018) 636–54.
Krauter, Stefan, ed. *Perspektiven auf Römer 7*. Biblisch-Theologische Studien 159. Neukirchen-Vluyn, Germ.: Neukirchen, 2016.
Kreitzer, Larry. "R. L. Stevenson's Stranger Case of Dr. Jekyll and Mr. Hyde and Romans 7:14–25: Images of the Moral Duality of Human Nature." *JLT* 6 (1992) 125–44.
Kuhn, Karl A. "Natural and Unnatural Relations Between Text and Context: A Canonical Reading of Romans 1:26–27." *CurTM* 33 (2006) 313–29.
Kümmel, Werner Georg. *Römer 7 und das Bild des Menschen im Neuen Testament*. Zwei Studien. TB 53. Munich: Kaiser, 1974.
———. *Römer 7 und die Bekehrung des Paulus*. UNT. Leipzing: Hinrichs, 1929.

Laato, Timo. "Salvation by God's Grace, Judgment According to Our Works: Taking a Look at Matthew and Paul." *CTQ* 82 (2018) 163–78.

Lambrecht, Jan. *The Wretched "I" and Its Liberation: Paul in Romans 7 and 8.* Louvain Theological and Pastoral Monographs 14. Louvain: Peeters, 1992.

Lanci, John R. "The Stones Don't Speak and the Texts Tell Lies: Sacred Sex at Corinth." In *Urban Religion in Roman Corinth: Interdisciplinary Approaches*, edited by Daniel N. Schowalter and Steven J. Friesen, 205–20. HTS. Cambridge, MA: Harvard University Press, 2005.

Langlands, Rebecca. *Sexual Morality in Ancient Rome.* New York: Cambridge University Press, 2006.

Léon-Dufour, Xavier. *Dictionary of the New Testament: Translated from the Second (Revised) French Edition.* Translated by Terrence Prendergast. San Francisco: Harper & Row, 1980.

Levenson, Jon D. *The Death and Resurrection of the Beloved Son: The Transformation of Child Sacrifice in Judaism and Christianity.* New Haven, CT: Yale University Press, 1995.

Levison, John R. "Adam and Eve in Romans 1.18–25 and the Greek *Life of Adam and Eve*." *NTS* 50 (2004) 519–34.

Lévy, Calos. "Philo of Alexandria." *Stanford Encyclopedia of Philosophy*, Feb. 5, 2018; last updated Aug. 16, 2022. Edited by Edward N. Zalta and Uri Nodelman. Fall 2022 ed. https://plato.stanford.edu/entries/philo/.

Lichtenberger, Hermann. *Das Ich Adams und das Ich der Menschheit: Studien zum Menschenbild in Römer 7.* WUNT, 1st ser., 164. Tübingen: Mohr Siebeck, 2004.

Loader, William. *The New Testament on Sexuality: Attitudes Towards Sexuality in Judaism and Christianity in the Hellenistic-Greco-Roman Era.* Grand Rapids: Eerdmans, 2012.

———. *The Pseudepigrapha on Sexuality: Attitudes Towards Sexuality in Apocalypses, Testaments, Legends, Wisdom, and Related Literature.* Grand Rapids: Eerdmans, 2011.

———. "Reading Romans 1 on Homosexuality in the Light of Biblical/Jewish and Greco-Roman Perspectives of its Time." *ZNW* 108 (2017) 119–49.

Long, A. A. *Hellenistic Philosophy.* 2nd ed. London: Duckworth, 1986.

Long, A. A., and D. N. Sedley. *The Hellenistic Philosophers.* 2 vols. Cambridge: Cambridge University Press, 2012.

Longinus. *On the Sublime.* Translated by Stephen Halliwell et al. LCL 199. Cambridge, MA: Harvard University Press, 1995.

López, René A. "Paul's Vice List in Galatians 5:19–21." *BSac* 169 (2012) 48–67.

———. "A Study of Pauline Passages with Vice Lists." *BSac* 168 (2011) 301–16.

Lorenz, Hendrik. *The Brute Within: Appetitive Desire in Plato and Aristotle.* Oxford: Clarendon, 2009.

Lucas, Alec J. *Evocations of the Calf? Romans 1:18—2:11 and the Substructure of Psalm 106 (105).* BZNW 201. Boston: de Gruyter, 2015.

Lucian. *The Passing of Peregrinus. The Runaways. Toxaris or Friendship. The Dance. Lexiphanes. The Eunuch. Astrology. The Mistaken Critic. The Parliament of the Gods. The Tyrannicide. Disowned.* Translated by A. M. Harmon. LCL 302. Cambridge, MA: Harvard University Press, 1936.

Ludwig, Paul W. *Eros and Polis: Desire and Community in Greek Political Theory.* Cambridge: Cambridge University Press, 2002.

Lutz, Cora E. "Musonius Rufus: The Roman Socrates." *Yale Classical Studies* 10 (1947) 3–147.

Lyonnet, Stanislas. "L'histoire de salut selon le chapitre VII de l'Épître aux Romains." *Bib* 43 (1962) 117–51.

———. "Tu ne convoiteras pas' (Rom. Vii 7)." In *Neotestamentica et Patristica: Eine Freundsgabe, Herrn Professor Dr. Oscar Cullmann zu seinem 60. Geburtstag überreicht*, edited by W. C. van Unnik, 157–65. NovTSup 6. Leiden: Brill, 1962.

Malherbe, A. J. *Paul and the Popular Philosophers*. Minneapolis: Fortress, 1989.

Malina, Bruce J., and John J. Pilch. *Social-Science Commentary on the Letters of Paul*. Minneapolis: Fortress, 2006.

Manoly, Roberto. *L'histoire du salut: L'Épître aux Romains*. La Parole Éternelle, Bleu ser., 1. Lenexa, KS: Foi et Sainteté, 2013.

Martin, Dale B. *The Corinthian Body*. New Haven, CT: Yale University Press, 1995.

———. "Heterosexism and the Interpretation of Romans 1:18–32." *BibInt* 3 (1995) 332–55.

———. *Sex and the Single Savior: Gender and Sexuality in Biblical Interpretation*. Louisville: Westminster, 2006.

Matera, Frank J. *Galatians*. SP 9. Collegeville, MN: Liturgical, 2007.

———. *Romans*. Paideia: Commentary on the New Testament. Grand Rapids: Baker Academic, 2010.

McEleney, Neil J. "Conversion, Circumcision, and the Law." *NTS* 20 (1974) 328–29.

McFadden, Kevin W. "The Fulfillment of the Law's *Dikaiōma*: Another Look at Romans 8:1–4." *JETS* 52 (2009) 483–97.

McNamara, Derek. "Share the Incestuous Man: 1 Corinthians 5." *Neot* 44 (2010) 307–26.

Metzger, Bruce M. *A Textual Commentary on the Greek New Testament*. London: United Bible Societies, 1975.

Moo, Douglas J. *Epistle of the Romans*. NICNT. Grand Rapids: Eerdmans, 1996.

Moore, Gareth. *The Body in Context: Sex and Catholicism*. London: Continuum, 2001.

Motta Rios, Cesar. "Philo of Alexandria: An Introduction to the Jewish Exegete and His Intercultural Condition." *Scriptura* 114 (2015) 1–13.

Murphy-O'Connor, Jerome. *Paul: A Critical Life*. New York: Oxford University Press, 1996.

———. *St. Paul's Corinth: Texts and Archaeology*. 3rd ed. Collegeville, MN: Liturgical, 2002.

Musonius Rufus. "Lectures and Fragments." *A Stoic Breviary: Classical Wisdom in Daily Practice*, 1947. Translated by Cora E. Lutz. https://stoicbreviary.blogspot.com/p/musonius-rufus.html.

Myers, Jason A. *Paul, the Apostle of Obedience: Reading Obedience in Romans*. LNTS. London: T&T Clark, 2022.

Nanos, Mark D. *The Mystery of Romans: The Jewish Context of Paul's Letter*. Minneapolis: Fortress, 1996.

———. "Out-Howling the Cynics: Reconceptualizing the Concerns of Paul's Audience from His Polemics in Philippians 3." In *The People Beside Paul: The Philippian Assembly and History from Below*, edited by Joseph A. Marchal, 183–221. ECL 17. Atlanta: SBL, 2015.

Naveros Córdova, Nélida. "1 Corinthians 10:1–4: The Rhetorical-Poetic Effect of Vividness and Emotions in Paul's Exhortation to Monotheism in the Context of 10:1–22." *RJ* 38 (2020) 237–55.

———. *God's Presence in Creation: A Conversation with Philo, Paul, and Luke*. London: Austin Macauley, 2023.

———. *Philo of Alexandria: A Sourcebook*. Lanham, MD: Lexington, 2023.

———. *Philo of Alexandria's Ethical Discourse: Living in the Power of Piety*. Lanham, MD: Lexington, 2018.

———. *To Live in the Spirit: Paul and the Spirit of God*. Lanham, MD: Lexington, 2018.

———. "'The Worst of the Passions': Desire in Philo of Alexandria." *BR* 68 (2023) 42–57.

Niehoff, Maren. *Philo on Jewish Identity and Culture*. TSAJ 86. Tübingen: Mohr Siebeck, 2001.

Nolland, J. "Uncircumcised Proselytes?" *JSJ* 12 (1981) 173–94.

Nussbaum, Martha C. *The Theory of Desire: Theory and Practice in Hellenistic Ethics*. Princeton, NJ: Princeton University Press, 1994.

Olson, Jon C. "Idol Food, Same-Sex Intercourse, and Tolerable Diversity Within the Church." *AThR* 95 (2013) 627–47.

Onkelos. https://www.sefaria.org/texts/Tanakh/Targum/Onkelos.

Ovid. *Metamorphoses*. Translated by Frank Justus Miller. Revised by G. P. Goold. 2 vols. LCL. Cambridge, MA: Harvard University Press, 1916.

Parsons, Mikeal C., and Michael Wade Martin. *Ancient Rhetoric and the New Testament: The Influence of Elementary Greek Composition*. Waco: Baylor University Press, 2018.

Philo. *On the Embassy to Gaius. General Indexes*. Translated by F. H. Colson. LCL 379. Cambridge, MA: Harvard University Press, 1962.

———. *Philo*. Translated by F. H. Colson and G. H. Whitaker. 12 vols. LCL. Cambridge, MA: Harvard University Press, 1929.

Pieper, Josef. *Love and Inspiration: A Study of Plato's "Phaedrus."* Translated by Richard and Clara Winston. London: Faber and Faber, 1964.

Pietersma, Albert, and Benjamin G. Wright, eds. *A New English Translation of the Septuagint*. New York: Oxford University Press, 2007.

Pitre, Brant, et al. *Paul, a New Covenantal Jew: Rethinking Pauline Theology*. Grand Rapids: Eerdmans, 2019.

Plato. *The Collected Dialogues: Including the Letters; With Introduction and Prefatory Notes*. Edited by Edith Hamilton and Huntington Cairns. Bollingen 71. Princeton, NJ: Princeton University Press, 1989.

Plutarch. *Moralia*. Translated by Frank Cole Babbitt et al. 16 vols. LCL. Cambridge, MA: Harvard University Press, 1927–1976.

Preisker, Herbert. "μέθη, μεθύω, μέθυσος, μεθύσκομαι." *TDNT* 4:545–48.

Quintilian. *The Orator's Education*. Edited and translated by Donald A. Russell. 5 vols. LCL. Cambridge, MA: Harvard University Press, 2002.

Rabens, Volker. *The Holy Spirit and Ethics in Paul: Transformation and Empowering for Religious-Ethical Life*. 2nd ed. WUNT, 2nd ser., 283. Tübingen: Mohr Siebeck, 2013.

Räisänen, Heikki. "Zum Gebrauch von ΕΠΙΘΥΜΙΑ und ΕΠΙΘΥΜΕΙΝ bei Paulus." *ST* 33 (1979) 85–99.

Redditt, Paul L. "The Concept of Nomos in Fourth Maccabees." *CBQ* 45 (1983) 250–54.

Reno, Joshua M. "Pornographic Desire in the Pauline Corpus." *JBL* 140 (2021) 163–85.

Rist, John M., ed. *The Stoics*. Berkeley: University of California Press, 1978.

Robinson, William E. W. *Metaphor, Morality, and the Spirit in Roman 8:1–17*. ECL 20. Atlanta: SBL, 2016.

Rogers, Trent A. "God and the Idols: Representation of God in 1 Corinthians 8–10." PhD diss., Loyola University Chicago, 2015.

Rorty, Amélie Oksenberg., ed. *Essays on Aristotle's Ethics*. Berkeley: University of California Press, 1980.

Royse, James R. "The Works of Philo." In *The Cambridge Companion to Philo*, edited by Adam Kamesar, 32–64. Cambridge: Cambridge University Press, 2009.

Runia, David T. *Philo in Early Christian Literature: A Survey.* CRINT 3. Minneapolis: Fortress, 1993.

———. *Philo of Alexandria and the "Timaeus" of Plato.* PhA 44. Leiden: Brill, 1986.

Salzman, Todd A., and Michael G. Lawler. *The Sexual Person: Toward a Renewed Catholic Anthropology.* Washington, DC: Georgetown University Press, 2008.

Sandbach, F. H. *The Stoics.* 2nd ed. Indianapolis: Hackett, 1994.

Sanders, E. P. *Paul and Palestinian Judaism.* Philadelphia: Fortress, 1977.

———. "Paul Between Judaism and Hellenism." In *St. Paul Among the Philosophers*, edited by John D. Caputo and Linda M. Alcoff, 74–90. Bloomington: Indiana University Press, 2009.

———. *Paul, the Law, and the Jewish People.* Philadelphia: Fortress, 1983.

Sandmel, Samuel. *Philo of Alexandria: An Introduction.* New York: Oxford University Press, 1974.

Schlatter, Adolf. *Romans: The Righteousness of God.* Translated by Siegried S. Schatzmann. Peabody, MA: Hendrickson, 1995.

Schmeller, Thomas. *Paulus und die "Diatribe": Eine Vergleichende Stilinterpretation.* NTAbh, new ser., 19. Münster: Aschendorff, 1987.

Schnelle, Udo. *Apostle Paul: His Life and Theology.* Grand Rapids: Baker Academy, 2003.

———. *The Letter to the Romans.* BETL 226. Louvain: Peeters, 2009.

Scroggs, Robin. *The New Testament and Homosexuality.* Philadelphia: Fortress, 1983.

Seifrid, Mark A. "The Subject of Rom 7:14–25." *NovT* 34 (1992) 313–33.

Selby, Gary S. *Not with Wisdom of Words: Nonrational Persuasion in the New Testament.* Grand Rapids: Eerdmans, 2016.

Seneca. *Epistles.* Translated by Richard M. Gummere. 3 vols. LCL. Cambridge, MA: Harvard University Press, 1917.

———. *Moral Essays.* Translated by John W. Basore. 3 vols. LCL. Cambridge, MA: Harvard University Press, 1928.

Skinner, Marilyn B. *Sexuality in Greek and Roman Culture.* Ancient Culture. Oxford: Blackwell, 2005.

Sloan, Paul T. "Paul's Jewish Addressee in Romans 2–4: Revisiting Recent Conversations." *JTS* 74 (2023) 516–66.

Smith, Mark D. "Ancient Bisexuality and the Interpretation of Romans 1:26–27." *JAAR* 64 (1996) 223–56.

Sprinkle, Preston. "Paul and Homosexual Behavior: A Critical Evaluation of the Excessive-Lust Interpretation of Romans 1:26–27." *BBR* 25 (2015) 497–517.

Stegman, Thomas. "Reading Saint Paul on Homosexuality, Using the Two 'Hands' of Exegesis." Outreach: An LGBTQ Catholic Ministry, Oct. 16, 2022. https://outreach.faith/2022/10/thomas-stegman-s-j-reading-saint-paul-on-homosexuality-using-the-two-hands-of-exegesis/.

Sterling, Gregory E. "Prepositional Metaphysics in Jewish Wisdom Speculation and Early Christological Liturgical Texts." *SPhiloA* 9 (1997) 219–38.

———. "'The Queen of the Virtues': Piety in Philo of Alexandria." *SPhiloA* 18 (2006) 103–23.

———. "Universalizing the Particular: Natural Law in Second Temple Jewish Ethics." *SPhiloA* 15 (2003) 64–80.

Stobaeus, Ioannes. *Anthologii libri duo priores.* Edited by Curt Wachsmuth. 2 vols. Berlin: Weidmann, 1884.

Stowers, Stanley K. *The Diatribe and Paul's Letter to the Romans.* SBLDS 57. Chico, CA: Scholars, 1981.

———. "Does Pauline Christianity Resemble a Hellenistic Philosophy?" In *Paul Beyond the Judaism/Hellenism Divide*, edited by Troels Engberg-Pedersen, 81–102. Louisville: Westminster, 2001.

———. "Paul and Self-Mastery." In *Paul in the Greco-Roman World: A Handbook*, edited by Paul Sampley, 524–50. Harrisburg, PA: Trinity, 2003.

———. *A Rereading of Romans: Justice, Jews, and Gentiles.* New Haven, CT: Yale University Pres, 1994.

Svebakken, Hans. "Exegetical Traditions in Alexandria: Philo's Reworking of the *Letter of Aristeas* 145–149 as a Case Study." In *From Judaism to Christianity: Tradition and Transition; A Festschrift for Thomas H. Tobin, S.J., on the Occasion of His Sixty-Fifth Birthday*, edited by Patricia Walters, 93–112. NovTSup 136. Leiden: Brill, 2010.

———. *Philo of Alexandria's Exposition of the Tenth Commandment.* SPhiloM 6. Atlanta: SBL, 2012.

Swancutt, Diana. "Sexy Stoics and the Rereading of Romans 1:18—2:16." In *The Bible, Gender, and Sexuality: Critical Readings*, edited by Rhiannon Graybill and Lynn R. Huber, 205–33. Critical Readings in Biblical Studies. London: T&T Clark, 2021.

Tan, Jean Page. "The Denial of *Eros* in Lysias' Speech: Discourse and Desire in Plato's *Phaedrus.*" *Bhudi* 2 (1998) 197–218.

Termini, Cristina. "Dal Sinai alla creazione il rapport tra legge naturale e legge rivelata in Filone di Alessandria." In *La rivelazione in Filone di Alessandria: Natura, legge, storia; Atti del VII convegno di studi del Gruppo Italiano di Ricerca su Origene e la Traditioine Alessandrina (Bologna 29–30 settembre 2003)*, edited by Angela M. Mazzanti and Francesca Calabi, 159–91. Biblioteca di Adamantius 2. Villa Veruchio: Pazzini, 2004.

Theiler, Willy. *Die Vorbereitung des Neuplatonismus.* 2nd ed. Berlin: Weidmann, 1964.

Theissen, Gerd. *The Social Setting of Pauline Christianity: Essays on Corinth.* Edited and translated by John Howard Schütz. London: T&T Clark, 1982.

Thompson, James W. *Moral Formation According to Paul: The Context and Coherence of Pauline Ethics.* Grand Rapids: Baker Academic, 2011.

Tobin, Thomas H. "The Beginning of Philo's *Legum Allegoriae.*" SPhiloA 12 (2000) 29–43.

———. *Paul's Rhetoric in Its Contexts: The Argument of Romans.* Peabody, MA: Hendrickson, 2004.

———. "The Prologue of John and Hellenistic Jewish Speculation." *CBQ* 52 (1990) 252–69.

———. "Romans 10:4: Christ the Goal of the Law." SPhiloA 3 (1991) 272–82.

———. *The Spirituality of Paul.* Eugene, OR: Wipf & Stock, 1973.

Tolbert, Mary A. "Philo and Paul: The Circumcision Debates in Early Judaism." In *Dem Tod nicht glauben: Sozialgeschichte der Bibel; Festschrift für Luise Schottroff zum 70. Geburtstag*, edited by Frank Crüsemann et al., 394–407. Gütersloh: Gütersloh, 2004.

Unnik, Willem C. van. *Tarsus or Jerusalem: The City of Paul's Youth.* Translated by George Ogg. London: Epworth, 1962.

Van den Beld, A. "Romans 7:14–25 and the Problem of Akrasia." *RelS* 21 (1985) 495–515. https://www.jstor.org/stable/20006224.

Van der Horst, P. W. "Pseudo-Phocylides (First Century B.C.—First Century A.D.)." *OTP* 1:565–82.

Vander Waerdt, Paul A. "The Original Theory of Natural Law." SPhiloA 15 (2003) 17–34.

Vernon, Mark. "Plato, Thomas and the Daring Ethics of Friendship." *ThS* 12 (2006) 203–16.

Ward, Roy Bowen. "Why Unnatural? The Tradition Behind Romans 1:26–27." *HTR* 90 (1997) 263–84.

Wasserman, Emma. "The Death of the Soul in Romans 7: Revisiting Paul's Anthropology in Light of Hellenistic Moral Psychology." *JBL* 126 (2007) 793–816.

———. *The Death of the Soul in Romans 7: Sin, Death, and the Law in Light of Hellenistic Moral Psychology*. WUNT, 2nd ser., 256. Tübingen: Mohr Siebeck, 2008.

Webb, Ruth. "The *Progymnasmata* as Practice." In *Education in Greek and Roman Antiquity*, edited by Yun Lee Too, 289–316. Leiden: Brill, 2001.

Weima, Jeffrey A. D. *1–2 Thessalonians*. BECNT. Grand Rapids: Baker Academic, 2014.

Weisser, Sharon. "The Perils of Philosophical Persuasion: Philo on the Origin of Moral Evils." In *The Evil Inclination in Early Judaism and Christianity*, edited by James Aitken et al., 95–114. Cambridge: Cambridge University Press, 2021.

West, Mona, and Robert E. Shore-Goss, eds. *Queer Bible Commentary*. 2nd ed. London: SCM, 2022.

Westfall, Cynthia Long. *Paul and Gender: Reclaiming the Apostle's Vision for Men and Women in Christ*. Grand Rapids: Baker Academic, 2016.

Wheeler-Reed, David, et al. "Can a Man Commit πορνεία with His Wife?" *JBL* 137 (2018) 383–98.

Willis, Wendell. "1 Corinthians 8–10: A Retrospective After Twenty-Five Years." *ResQ* 49 (2007) 103–12.

Wilpert, Paul. "Begierde." *Reallexikon für Antike und Christentum: Sachwörterbuch zur Auseinandersetzung des Christentums mit der antiken Welt*, edited by Franze Joseph Dölger and Theodor Klauser, 2:62–78. Stuttgart: Dassmann, 1954.

Winston, David. "Judaism and Hellenism: Hidden Tensions in Philo's Thought." SPhiloA 2 (1990) 1–19.

Witherington, Ben, III, and Jason A. Myers. *New Testament Rhetoric: An Introductory Guide to the Art of Persuasion in and of the New Testament*. 2nd ed. Eugene, OR: Cascade, 2022.

Wolfson, Harry Austryn. *Philo: Foundations of Religious Philosophy in Judaism, Christianity, and Islam*. 2 vols. Cambridge, MA: Harvard University Press, 1948.

Wright, N. T. *Paul and His Recent Interpreters: Some Contemporary Debates*. Minneapolis: Fortress, 2013.

———. *Paul and the Faithfulness of God*. Minneapolis: Fortress, 2013.

———. *Paul: In Fresh Perspective*. Minneapolis: Fortress, 2005.

———. *What Saint Paul Really Said: Was Paul of Tarsus the Real Founder of Christianity?* Grand Rapids: Eerdmans, 1997.

Wright Knust, Jennifer. *Abandoned to Lust: Sexual Slander and Ancient Christianity*. Gender, Theory, and Religion. New York: Columbia University Press, 2005.

———. *Unprotected Texts: The Bible's Surprising Contradictions About Sex and Desire*. San Francisco: HarperOne, 2012.

Ziesler, J. A. "The Role of the Tenth Commandment in Romans 7." *JSNT* 33 (1988) 41–56.

Index

Note: Page numbers followed by "n" denote footnotes.

akatharsia (impurity, uncleanness), 76, 109, 109n51
  See also sexual immorality *(porneia)*
apatheia, 28, 36n92, 103, 103n28
appetite, 18n16, 27
Arbiol, G., 127n35
Aristotle, 103n28
  appetite, 18n16
  epithymia, 16n4
  pleasure, 19n18
Aune, D. C., 2n4, 11, 12, 43n124, 46, 64n46, 64n47

Barber, M. P., 9
Betz, H. D., 116, 130
Bock, D. L., 98
bodily pleasure, 17, 19, 19n18
body *(sōma)*, 124–25
  God's temple, 127
  polluting agents, 2, 3
Bowden, A., 4–5, 4n12, 6n21, 43, 44, 46, 48, 49, 53, 64n47–65, 66, 67n52, 69n61, 71, 72n76, 73, 73n80, 77, 77n97, 77n100, 86, 86n135, 87n139, 96n10, 107n43, 110n53, 121n20
brotherly love *(philadelphia)*, 11, 116

celibacy, 77–79

Christ-event, 13–14, 13n46, 54–90, 92, 95, 100, 115, 120, 125, 130, 153
Christocentric monotheism, 55–59, 82, 87, 135, 137, 151, 153
Chrysippus, 29–31, 31n74
Cicero, 29
circumcision, 133n50, 134n56
  Paul's opposition to, 132
  Philo's view of, 133, 133n51
  physical, 131–32
  true, 132–35
Coffey, D. M., 72, 72n75
The Corinthian Body (Martin), 2
Cynicism, 21n29–22, 41n115

The Death of the Soul in Romans 7 (Wasserman), 3, 3n7
Decalogue, 59, 129–31
Del Rosario, M., 98
DeSilva, D. A., 43, 47
desire-belly-tongue, 37, 39, 150
Dodson, J. R., 71n69
drunkenness *(methais)*, 61–62, 61n32–62, 85
Dunn, J. D. G., 74, 76, 119n14

eating food/meat sacrificed to idols, 82, 85–86, 86n135, 135–38, 135n57, 136n60
eating for food, 41

179

INDEX

Elliott, N., 85n133
Elliott, S. S., 105n34
Ellis, J. E., 78
epithymeō, 2, 4–6, 18, 49, 110n53
eternal life (in heaven), 111, 124, 126, 127
excessive impulse, 28–31, 34, 104
excessive sexual desire, 22, 103
    human mind, 27
    idolatry and, 76–82, 109
    love, 23–25
    reason, 26–28
    See also gluttony

faith *(pistis)*, 142
    love and, 144–46, 144n77
Fitzmyer, J. A., 58n17, 59n22–60, 74, 82n121, 97n14, 106n38, 109, 109n49, 119n13, 129, 144, 144n77
flesh *(sarx)*, 59, 59n22, 60, 81, 117
    epithymia vs. *epithymeō*, 110n53
    and *pneuma*, 120–21
    sinful, 109
food laws, 38–40, 38n102, 43n122, 44–46, 150
    ineffectiveness of, 102, 107
    "love our neighbor," 138–43
    practice of, 99, 100, 102, 115, 117
    prohibitions in, 106
Fredrickson, D. E., 12, 12n44, 12n45
freedom, 119
    from law, 96, 97
    from sin, 108–9

Gaca, K. L., 103n29
Gaventa, B. R., 140n64
gender stereotyping, 3
Genovesi, V. J., 92, 115
gluttony
    idolatry, 83–84
    passions and, 44–46
    Philo, 37–38
    Plato, 20–26
God
    authority, 123, 124
    faithfulness, 54, 54n5, 123–26, 152
    goodness, 126
    grace of, 101, 101n26, 101n27–102, 108, 115, 118, 123, 125
    kingdom, 80, 126, 141
    lack of knowledge, 72–75, 80, 125
    reward, 124–27
    righteousness, 87, 87n139, 111, 115, 123–26, 141, 152
    wrath of, 117–18
golden calf (idolatry), 83–85, 83n124
Gourinat, J.-B., 30n70
grace of God, 101, 101n26, 101n27–102, 108, 115, 118, 123, 125
Grieb, A. K., 69n61

Harrington, D. J., 15n1
holiness *(hagiasmos)*, 76, 76n92, 127
homosexual (same-sex) relations, 62n34, 65
    idolatry and, 68–72, 75
Horn, F. W., 120

idolatry *(eidōlolatria)*, 25, 53, 82–83, 121, 125, 150–51
    excessive sexual desire, 76–82, 109
    gluttony, 83–84
    golden calf, 83–85, 83n124
    homosexual practices, 68–72, 75
    lack of knowledge of God, 72–75, 80, 125
    male prostitution, 80, 80n112, 81
    and monotheism, 68, 75, 82
    sexual vices, 68–75, 77, 80–82
idol *(eidōlon)*, 135n57
illicit sex *(koitais)*, 62
imagination *(phantasia)*, 105
immortality, piety and, 41–42, 50, 126, 150
impulse *(hormē)*, 28–31, 28n54
integrity, 21, 22
intemperance *(akolasia/akrasia)*, 69, 69n62–70, 78, 79, 84
    Philo, 36
    Plato, 23n32, 26
    Stoics, 30, 30n70, 31
Inwood, B., 30
irrational desire, 18n16, 19, 24, 28, 34–35, 38, 47–50, 104, 107

INDEX

Isaacs, M. E., 60

Jewish identity, 8–10, 92
John J. P., 135, 135n57
Judaism, 7, 7n23, 8, 39, 92, 96
judgment, 24, 142

Keener, C. S., 117, 122, 122n28
Kincaid, J. A., 9
Konradt, M., 67n51

Laato, T., 123
Laertius, D., 22n31, 28
Laws (Plato), 19, 27
licentiousness *(aselgeiais)*, 62–63, 62n36
Loader, W., 17n9, 36, 48, 48n150, 48n153, 62n34, 68, 71, 74, 79, 95, 99, 103
López, R. A., 63
Lorenz, H., 19
love *(agapē)*, 118, 119n13, 144n77, 152
    centrality of Christ and Spirit in, 119–23
    and faith, 144–46, 144n77
    Paul's treatment of, 144–47, 145n78
    Spirit and, 145
    virtue of, 115–17, 123, 128–29
love *(erōs)*, 23–25, 23n37, 27n51, 79
"love our neighbor," 118, 123, 153–54
    circumcision, 131–35
    eating food sacrificed to idols, 135–38
    ethical commandments, 129–31
    food laws, 138–43
    language of inclusivity, 118, 144
    Paul's treatment of *agapē*, 144–47, 145n78
Lucas, A. A., 74
Lyonnet, S., 98n15

4 Maccabees, 42–50, 149–50
    irrational desire, 47–50
    piety, 45, 50
    practice of food laws, 43n122, 44–46
    reason, 43–46, 43n122, 129n39
    self-control, 45–46
    temperance, 45–46, 115

Malina, B. J., 83, 117, 135, 135n57
Manoly, R., 68n58, 101n27–102
marriage, 77–79, 77n99, 103n29, 151
Martin, D. B., 2–3, 74, 80n112
Matera, F. J., 59n22, 74
McFadden, K. W., 120n18
Meno (Plato), 20
mind *(nous)*, 26–28, 34, 35, 122, 122n28, 150
moderation *(metriopatheia)*, 25, 25n42
    apatheia vs., 103, 103n28
    Philo, 34, 36, 39, 118
    Plato, 27
monotheism, 58n17, 85n133
    Christocentric, 55–59, 82, 87, 135, 137, 151, 153
    and idolatry, 68, 75
    Jewish, 55, 56, 59, 151
Mosaic law, 8, 39, 45, 59, 64, 92
    freedom from, 96, 97
    ineffectiveness of, 117
    practice *(askēsis)*, 95–102, 97n14, 104
    purpose of, 97
Motta Rios, C., 39, 39n106
Myers, J., 54n5

Nanos, M. D., 124, 133n50
new creation *(kainē ktisis)*, 118, 122, 126

oneness, 130–31
On the Passions and Errors of the Soul (Galen), 107n41
orexis, 2, 11, 11n36, 74

passions *(pathos)*, 43, 64n46
    corrupted, 99
    and gluttony, 44–46
    sexual vices, 64, 64n46
    of soul, 16, 17, 19, 33, 44, 102
Paul, a New Covenantal Jew: Rethinking Pauline Theology (Pitre, Barber, and Kincaid), 9
Paul and Gender (Westfall), 3, 3n6
Pentateuch, 32, 33n83
Phaedrus (Plato), 24, 25
Philebus (Plato), 20

Philo, 17, 104n33, 105, 149–50
　circumcision, 133, 133n51
　On the Decalogue, 33
　epithymia, 32–34
　gluttony, 37–38
　On the Migration of Abraham, 37
　moderation, 34, 36, 39, 118
　piety, 41–42, 49–50
　reason, 35, 40–42
　self-control, 36–37, 38n100, 39–42, 115
　temperance, 42, 115
　tenth commandment, 33, 33n85, 35, 47
　thumos, 18n11
Pieper, J., 27n51
piety *(eusebeia)*, 18n10, 126, 150
　4 Maccabees, 45, 50
　Philo, 41–42, 49–50
Pilch, J. J., 83, 117
Pitre, B., 9
Plato, 3, 13, 149–50
　epithymia, 16, 18–19, 18n16, 21
　gluttony, 20–26
　love, 23–25, 23n37, 27n51
　moderation, 27
　reason, 26–28
　self-control, 21–22, 22n32–23, 27
　tyrannical man, 104, 107
pleasure *(hēdonē)*, 20. *See also* bodily pleasure
Plutarch, 104
practical wisdom *(phronēsis)*, 45, 145n78
prepositional metaphysics, 57n16
progymnasmata, 9
prophetic call, 7–8, 54
prostitution, 127n35
　in Corinth, 77n98
　male, 80, 80n112, 81

Rabens, V., 1n1
Räisänen, H., 121
Reasoner, M., 85n133
reason *(logos)*, 87n143, 99, 108, 129, 150
　4 Maccabees, 43–46, 43n122, 129n39
　Philo, 35, 40–42
　Plato, 26–28

Stoics, 29–31
Redditt, Paul L., 44n132
Reno, J. M., 61, 79
replenishment, 20–21
Republic (Plato), 20, 25, 27
resurrection, 109, 124, 128
revelry *(kōmois)*, 61–62, 85
righteousness *(dikaiosunē)*, 111, 115, 122, 123–26, 141, 152
Rist, J. M., 16
Rodgers, T., 70
"The Role of the Tenth Commandment in Romans 7" (Ziesler), 3

salvation, 54–55, 124–27
sanctification, 96, 108, 125, 127
Satan, 11n39, 12
Selby, G. S., 103n31
self-control *(enkrateia)*, 30n70, 78, 106, 115–16, 121, 150
　definition, 22n31
　4 Maccabees, 45–46
　Philo, 36–37, 38n100, 39–42, 115
　Plato, 21–22, 22n32–23, 27
　and sexual pleasures, 121n24
　See also intemperance *(akolasia/akrasia)*
self-love, 38n29
"A Semantic Investigation of Desire in 4 Maccabees and Its Bearing on Romans 7:7" (Bowden), 4
sexual desire, 3, 38
　Chrysippus's view, 31, 31n75–32
　control of, 77–79
　erōs, 23–25
　polluting agent, 2, 3
　See also excessive sexual desire
sexual immorality *(porneia)*, 25, 25n44, 26, 59–67, 61n30, 73n77, 81, 95, 121, 127n35
　and *akrasia*, 79
　and idolatry, 67–75
Shore-Goss, R. E., 130
sinful beyond measure, 104–8
sinful individuals, 73, 80
sinful passions, 53, 59, 66, 72, 88, 90, 99, 108–11, 119, 125

sin *(hamartia)*, 94, 94n6, 100, 103–4, 106, 109n49, 117
sinner in despair, 103, 103n31, 105, 108, 119
slaves, 117, 152
    metaphorical, 106n40–107, 107n43, 110, 121n20
    sinful passions *vs.* righteousness, 108–11
sodomites *(arsenokoitai)*, 80n112
soul, 21, 26
    enslavement, 40
    passions of, 16, 17, 19, 33, 44, 102
    Philo's doctrine of, 40–41, 41n114
    tripartite, 38n100
speech-in-character *(prosōpopoiia)*, 94, 98, 101, 101n23, 107
Spirit *(pneuma)*, 16n3, 115, 119
    as divine enabler, 122, 153
    and ethics, 1, 1n1
    love in *see under* "love our neighbor"
    mind of, 122, 122n28
    role of, 120
    sarx and, 120–21
Stegman, T., 69, 72
Sterling, G. E., 57n16
Stobaeus, I., 25n42, 30n70
Stoic doctrine of desire, 28–31
Stowers, S. K., 70n65
Svebakken, H., 33n85
Symposium (Plato), 23

temperance *(sōphrosunē)*, 116
    4 Maccabees, 45–46, 115
    Philo, 42, 115
    Plato, 22, 22n32–23, 27
    Stoics, 30

tenth commandment *(ouk epithymēseis)*, 3, 93, 94, 99–100, 106
    4 Maccabees, 47–48
    Philo, 33, 33n85, 35
thirst, 20, 47
thumos, 18, 18n11, 43
Timaeus (Plato), 26
Tobin, T. H., 29, 41n114
tyrannical desire, 30, 34–35, 38, 79
tyrannical man, 104, 107

Vernon, M., 38n29
virtue(s), 20, 116n5
    as knowledge, 75
    Socrates, 21n28, 25n42
    See also love *(agapē)*; self-control *(enkrateia)*; temperance *(sōphrosunē)*
vox media, 18, 94n5

Wasserman, E., 3, 3n7
Weima, J. A. D., 67n52
West, M., 130
Westfall, C. L., 3, 3n6, 60n23, 60n26, 77n98, 77n99
wisdom *(sophia)*, 87, 87n143
Wright, N. T., 10n32, 55, 117, 142
Wright Knust, J., 63, 67n52, 77n97

Zeno of Citium, 28
Ziesler, J. A., 3–4

www.ingramcontent.com/pod-product-compliance
Lightning Source LLC
Chambersburg PA
CBHW031429150426
43191CB00006B/460